Deaf Pla
Major League

Deaf Players in Major League Baseball

A History, 1883 to the Present

R. A. R. Edwards

McFarland & Company, Inc., Publishers

Jefferson, North Carolina

This book has undergone peer review.

ISBN (print) 978-1-4766-7017-1
ISBN (ebook) 978-1-4766-4000-6

LIBRARY OF CONGRESS AND BRITISH LIBRARY
CATALOGUING DATA ARE AVAILABLE

Library of Congress Control Number 2020027674

Front cover: Illustration of William Ellsworth "Dummy"
Hoy of the Washington Nationals, 1888 (Detroit Public Library)

Printed in the United States of America

*McFarland & Company, Inc., Publishers
Box 611, Jefferson, North Carolina 28640
www.mcfarlandpub.com*

Table of Contents

Preface

I come to this topic largely because I teach at the Rochester Institute of Technology (RIT) in Rochester, New York. RIT is home to the National Technical Institute for the Deaf (NTID), which was established in 1965 to serve as a kind of counterpoint to Gallaudet University in Washington, D.C. Whereas Gallaudet provides a liberal arts education to deaf students, NTID's mission is to offer a technical education to deaf students. By agreeing to serve as the host university for NTID, both RIT and Rochester were transformed. Rochester, on a per capita basis, has the highest population of deaf citizens in the nation. RIT's student body is roughly 10 percent deaf. Sign language use is very common here. My classrooms are regularly filled with a combination of deaf and hearing students.

I am fortunate to teach courses about the history of baseball. Because this is Rochester, my deaf students frequently ask if I knew of "Dummy" Hoy, to which I always said yes. "Dummy" Hoy was not the first deaf man to play in the majors, but he was the first deaf baseball star, by a wide margin. His playing career, after all, ended in 1903 and still my own deaf undergraduate baseball fans all know his name.

And then some of them started telling me that Hoy was responsible for introducing umpire's signs to baseball. This has been a long-standing fact, practically a settled matter, within the deaf community. Deaf baseball fans will tell you that Hoy introduced umpire's signs to the sport because he could not hear their verbal calls.

In this particular instance, it was clear that these students were sharing this story with me in order to challenge me. They were expecting to correct me and they were prepared to defend their claim. Because, while the deaf community has long given the credit to Hoy, that claim has largely been rejected in the hearing baseball community. Hearing baseball researchers have, in fact, usually denied that Hoy had any influence on the development of the signs of baseball. I am a hearing person, but I teach in a deaf place. They were testing me to see which, and therefore whose, side I would take.

1

Preface

I seem to have surprised them a bit when I told them that I agreed with them, that Hoy deserves the credit. But then they recovered their nerve and quickly asked how I knew. What I told them, effectively, is that I trust the deaf community on this one. They have been passing down this story for more than a hundred years, and the consistency of that oral tradition, across generations of deaf fans, counts for quite a lot. Deaf people, I said, are telling us their history. As hearing people, we should be quiet and listen. We might learn something. We might also realize that the deaf community is giving us an important opportunity here: to see baseball history from a deaf point of view, a new angle of vision for most hearing people, one that might place the familiar contours of baseball history in a brand new light.

Finally, one student pressed even further: how did I know, as a historian? It was a great question, and one for which I had no answer. He was asking about proof, about sources, about historical facts and evidence. At that time, I had none from the period of Hoy's playing career to point to at all. I admitted as much. The student was crestfallen and I can't say that I was too happy myself. I told him to cheer up. It just means that we have to go searching for it. If the evidence is there, it will turn up eventually. How hard could it be?

Ten years later, I am here with this book. It took more time than I could ever have known. It also took the support of a community of scholars, researchers, and librarians, as it always does. I have accumulated many debts in writing this work and so owe many people my gratitude for their help along the way.

Many deaf researchers have been writing about Hoy, as well as other deaf players, in various places, in the press and in blogs. They have been taking the lead in fighting the good fight for more attention and recognition for these deaf athletes, again especially for Hoy. I extend my appreciation to the work of Matthew Moore, Steve Sandy, Brian Malzkuhn, Harry Lang, and the late Robert Panera. My thanks to Gary Kaschak and other members of the all-volunteer Hoy for the Hall Committee for their support.

For all their help in fielding my questions about their alumni, my thanks to Nancy Boone at the Ohio School for the Deaf, Rene Marra at the Kansas School for the Deaf, and Marene Clark-Mattern at the Illinois School for the Deaf. Marene put me in touch with some alums of ISD who kindly shared their memories of Dick Sipek with a stranger; much thanks, Bob Dramin and Ralph Reese. Additional research support for the Sipek chapter was provided by Alexandra N. Kyle. My thanks to her, and to Jim Baggett at the Birmingham Public Library, for introducing me to Andie. Organizations like the Friends of Rickwood Field, the Johnson County (Kansas) Genealogical

Society, the Kansas Sports Hall of Fame, the Ohio History Connection, and the Society for American Baseball Research (SABR) patiently answered my various research inquiries.

There were many archivists who extended their help to me to acquire photographs. My thanks to Lily Birkhimer at the Ohio History Connection, to Anne Jones and Andrew Gustafson at the Johnson County (Kansas) Museum, to John Horne at the National Baseball Hall of Fame Library, and to David K. Wilcox, the curator at the Kansas School for the Deaf Archive, as well as to Lorrie Shank and Chriz Dally at the Museum of the Deaf History, Arts, and Culture (MDHAC), both in Olathe, Kansas. My thanks to Warren Miller and Nancy Rourke. Thanks to Karen Christie, my now retired colleague here in Rochester at NTID, for her help with tracking down historical details that helped to greatly strengthen the chapter on Curtis Pride.

As I presented early stages of this work to audiences, I benefited enormously from their thoughtful feedback, probing questions, occasional compliments, and incisive criticisms. Participants in the Albion Tourgée Seminar, in Rochester, New York, graciously read and commented on an early version of Chapter 3; my thanks to all of them, especially to Dan Borus, Robb Westbrook, Michael Read, and Michael J. Jarvis. My attendance at baseball conferences, such as NINE and the Cooperstown Symposium on Baseball and American Culture, has brought me into a wonderful network of fellow baseball historians and researchers. Some of you offered extensive feedback on my fledgling efforts and some offered simply kind words of support. Both mattered enormously to me, and so I extend my gratitude, respect, and appreciation to the late Dorothy Seymour Mills, Jean Ardell, Steve Gietschier, Trey Strecker, Priscilla Astifan, and Geralyn Strecker.

The Giamatti Research Center at the National Baseball Hall of Fame has been an invaluable resource over the many years that I have worked to bring this project to a conclusion. The cheerful professionalism of the staff, even on a research trip undertaken during a wintry Cooperstown February, makes it an enormous pleasure to work there. I am grateful to Freddy Berowski and his entire crew of interns for all their help.

Most of the chapters here began their lives as conference presentations at the Cooperstown Symposium on Baseball and American Culture. The conference has provided a critically important venue for sharing and supporting my earliest ideas about this history. The audiences and presenters there have consistently been thoughtful, engaged, and curious. The National Baseball Hall of Fame and SUNY College at Oneonta jointly sponsor the conference. As scholars in the field, we owe both organizations a debt for providing us with this intellectual home for our work. My personal thanks to Jim Gates and Bill Simons for all of their work on and support for the Symposium.

Finally, I extend both my apologies and my thanks to my editors at Mc-Farland, Gary Mitchem and Charlie Perdue. Deadlines came and went as I struggled to bring this story together. They were never anything but patient and supportive. Thanks as well to the anonymous peer reviewers for their thoughtful comments and questions. Peer review is too frequently a thankless task in the academy; you should know that your labors here made this work better in the end and, for that, you have my appreciation.

This work was never meant to be a collective biography of deaf major league baseball players and readers should not expect to find that in the chapters that follow. Rather, these chapters offer a cultural history that explores the intersection of deaf history with baseball history. Deaf players began taking up the sport in earnest in the late 19th century and slowly broke into the professional ranks. Each era, it seems, had its deaf baseball player, and I have used that fact to take readers on a journey through the deaf history of the entire 20th century.

What follows is both a deaf history and a baseball history. Historically, deafness has been both a physical condition and a cultural one. A person can be physically deaf, with varying degrees of audiological hearing loss. There are some estimated 30,000,000 deaf and hard of hearing adults in the United States, a figure that includes previously hearing adults who have become increasingly hard of hearing as they age. Most Americans with some degree of hearing loss are only physically deaf. However, a physically deaf person can also be culturally deaf—that is, they can become members of the larger deaf community, which has its own distinctive culture, history, and language.

In the United States, that language is American Sign Language, which has its own linguistic characteristics, including a grammar and syntax unrelated to that of the English language. While deaf people do not choose their physical condition, most culturally deaf people are, in fact, people who have chosen to join the deaf community. Most deaf people, about 90 percent, have hearing parents. Therefore, only 10 percent of deaf people are born into and acculturated within the deaf community. Fewer than 1,000,000 use American Sign Language and identify as members of the deaf community.

This book largely focuses on the history of baseball within that distinctive deaf community. Chapter 1 begins where the deepest roots of deaf baseball can be found, in Ohio. The Ohio School for the Deaf was the first residential school to field a baseball team. The first men to make a living playing baseball came from Ohio. This is not to say that deaf men did not play baseball in other parts of the country. They did. There is good evidence to suggest that graduates of residential schools for the deaf in New York City took up the sport in the late 19th century.

Deaf players in the East also appeared on minor league rosters. Reuben Stephenson, who played for the first nine of the New Jersey School for the Deaf and went on to play for a variety of minor league teams, comes to mind. But in the beginning, the heart of deaf baseball was in Ohio. As researcher Brian McKenna notes, "Most deaf players ... came out of a much stronger baseball program at the Ohio Institute," including professional players.[1] To understand the history of deaf baseball, then, we must start in Ohio. Chapter 1 takes us into the Ohio School for the Deaf and introduces us to their influential baseball program and its key players, including the first deaf man to play in the major leagues, Ed Dundon (1859–1893).

Chapter 2 focuses on the most famous deaf baseball player of all, William Ellsworth "Dummy" Hoy (1862–1961). Hoy entered the majors after Dundon, but he was the better player with the longer career, and it is his name that is remembered and revered by deaf baseball fans today. Chapter 2 explores his entry into the majors. It explains how he became a symbol for deaf capability at a time when deaf people were increasingly under attack. Hoy reached stardom as eugenics was asserting that deafness was a deviant, abnormal condition that needed to be managed out of existence, perhaps even by forbidding congenitally deaf people to marry. Hoy stood as a power example of deaf achievement, pride, and even patriotism. What is more all–American than a ball player? Hoy proved a hero for his times and beyond.

Chapter 3 seeks to answer the question of whether or not Hoy had anything to do with the development of umpire's signs. Hoy's deaf supporters have long believed that his contribution to the sport has been unfairly neglected and rejected by hearing baseball fans and researchers. It turns out that they were right all along. Hoy did bring signs to baseball and umpires finally adopted his signs as their own. Most narratives have cited umpires Cy Rigler, Hank O'Day, and Bill Klem as the most significant of the early innovators with such gestures. In fact, none of these men was the earliest adopter of Hoy's signs. That honor goes instead to Francis "Silk" O'Loughlin (1872–1918). This chapter seeks to give credit to both Hoy and "Silk" for their pioneering work with the signs of baseball.

Chapter 4 explores the career of Luther Haden "Dummy" Taylor (1875–1958). Taylor is the only deaf pitcher of any note in major league baseball history. He was a key member of the pitching staff of the New York Giants in the early 20th century and pitched alongside such greats as Christy Mathewson and Joe McGinnity. Taylor's 1905 Giants claimed the National League pennant for the second straight year and were World Series champions. Taylor argued that the success of the Giants rested on their use of sign language, a surprising assertion, perhaps, but one that also turns out to be true. Taylor's New York Giants were the deafest team in major league history, with three deaf pitchers at one point. But they also stand out as the team most comfortable with sign language in major league history. Taylor was seen a champion of the deaf community, its culture, and its language in the early 20th century. But his sign language, and his hearing teammates' embrace of it, made the Giants champions too. Chapter 4 explains how.

Chapter 5 brings us Taylor's baseball discovery, Richard "Dick" Sipek (1923–2005), the first deaf player in major league baseball not to be nicknamed "Dummy." Sipek played for only one season in the majors, in 1945. The tendency to attribute the presence of men with disabilities in major league baseball at that time to the state of the sport in World War II has too often meant that Sipek's career has been overlooked. But Sipek was a politically aware player, and he very consciously seized the opportunity that the platform of baseball offered him to represent the deaf community in a positive light, especially for hearing audiences who were largely unfamiliar with deaf people. Sipek understood his personal moment of achievement—the first deaf man to break into the majors since Luther Taylor—as part of a larger quest for deaf people. His was a civil rights moment. He explicitly saw himself as being on a path quite similar to that of his peer in the International League, Jackie Robinson. Both men, Sipek believed, were trying to combat the social prejudices that they confronted, Robinson as a black man and Sipek as a deaf man. The story of Sipek's major league career is told in Chapter 5.

It should be noted here that there were two deaf men who very briefly appeared on major league rosters between Taylor and Sipek. The first was Reuben "Dummy" Stephenson (1869–1924). Stephenson came out of the New Jersey School for the Deaf and played extensively in the minors in the state, especially for the Camden club as a centerfielder. In 1892, he appeared for the Philadelphia Phillies for one week in September, when Ed Delahanty, one of the era's greatest players, went out with an injury. Delahanty holds a .346 career batting average, the fifth highest in major league history, and he hit over .400 in three different seasons. He was inducted into the Hall of Fame in 1945. Stephenson surely knew as well as anyone that he was not going to take Delahanty's place in the outfield for long. In fact, he came up on September 9 and departed on September 16. After hitting in five runs for the Phillies,

Stephenson was let go at the end of his week and never appeared on a major league roster again.[2]

The second was Herbert Courtland "Dummy" Murphy (1886–1963). Murphy was also brought up to the Philadelphia Phillies, in 1914. He appeared in nine games for them, hitting .154 and committing eight errors in the field. His first major league appearance was on April 14 and his last was on May 7.[3] Arguably his most successful season as a player was the one that had brought him to the attention of the Phillies in the first place. In 1913, Murphy played in Georgia, in the Empire State League, a Class D minor league, for the Thomasville Hornets. Playing at shortstop, he led the team with a batting average of .338. However, he also led the league in errors. Thomasville would go on to win the inaugural championship of the league and Murphy would find himself a position, however briefly,

Herbert Courtland "Dummy" Murphy. Murphy's break-out season with the 1913 Thomasville Hornets in the Empire State League in Georgia brought him to the attention of the Philadelphia Phillies. His major league career with the Phillies lasted for less than a month in 1914. This photograph of Murphy was taken in 1914. Library of Congress.

in the majors.[4] In this way, Murphy's brief career as a major leaguer mirrors Stephenson's experience with the Phillies of two decades earlier.

Finally, Chapter 6 considers the career of Curtis Pride, the first deaf African American to play major league baseball. Pride is currently the head baseball coach at Gallaudet University. As a player whose career spanned into

Preface

the early 21st century, as Pride last appeared in major league baseball in 2006, Pride came of age at a moment in deaf history very different from that of his predecessors. Hoy, Taylor, and Sipek were all connected to one another. Hoy and Taylor's careers briefly overlapped, and Taylor discovered and mentored Sipek. They each grew up signing at residential schools. Pride grew up wearing hearing aids and speaking. He attended his local public schools. Pride's story too, however, just as much as theirs, is an accurate reflection of the deaf history of his times, as we shall see.

Where that history goes from Pride is impossible to tell. Like every other baseball fan, I will be excited to watch it unfold.

1

Ohio—Field of Dreams

In the summer of 1901, the New York Giants boasted three deaf pitchers, George Leitner, Billy Deegan, and Luther Taylor.[1] That combination marked the most deaf men to play together for one professional team, either before or since. But, remarkably, they were not the only deaf players in baseball that year. William Ellsworth "Dummy" Hoy, by then playing for the Chicago White Sox, was still in the majors, nearing the end of his long career. He was just coming off an outstanding 1900 season, in which he led the American League in putouts, assists, and fielding average.

The year 1901 marks the deafest season in major league baseball history. Never again have so many deaf players appeared at once on major league rosters. On the one hand, the fact that the wave should crest in 1901 is no surprise, for it had been building since the 1870s. On the other hand, the prominence of deafness in baseball at the turn of the century demands explanation because that time, unlike our own, was far more hostile to deafness and to disability in public view. To give one example of this hostility to the sight of the disabled body in public space, in the early 20th century, at least three American cities, Chicago, Illinois, Columbus, Ohio, and Omaha, Nebraska, passed so-called "ugly laws," which forbid what the laws called "grotesque" people from appearing in public. Omaha did not repeal its law until 1967, Columbus until 1972, and Chicago until 1974.[2] How could a time arguably less hospitable to disability in American life prove to have been more accommodating than our own?

To trace the story to its beginnings, we must begin in the Midwest, specifically in Columbus, Ohio, at the Ohio School for the Deaf. Founded in 1829, the Ohio School for the Deaf is the fifth oldest school for deaf Americans in the country. It has the distinction of being the first deaf residential school to introduce baseball as a team sport to its male students. As historian Susan Burch describes it, "Particularly in the Midwest, strong athletic programs defined the school experience for many young boys."[3] This certainly proved the case at the Ohio School. Baseball was introduced to the school by

The Ohio School for the Deaf. The Ohio School was the first school for the deaf to field a baseball team. It sent the first generation of deaf players into professional baseball careers. Courtesy Ohio History Connection.

Parley P. Pratt, who had been hired as the master of the shoe shop in 1863, a position he held until 1887.

Born in 1838, Pratt went deaf at the age of three. His family moved to Columbus in 1848 and he was enrolled as a student at the Ohio School soon thereafter. He remained a student there until 1852. After a leave of absence, he returned to finish his studies and graduated in 1861. He was soon hired at the school as the foreman of the shoemaking department. His hire was seen as the key to the department's survival. As one administrator recalled, "The shoemaking department at Columbus had been practically a failure until placed in his hands."[4] Pratt was noted for his sense of humor, his "genial disposition" and "active, original mind."[5]

For his part, Pratt had been introduced to baseball when he was a student at the Ohio School. As he recalled, "During the superintendence of Mr. G.W. Weed [that is, George Weed, the fourth superintendent] and Mr. C.S. Perry [Charles Perry, the school's sixth superintendent], I took lessons in the base ball games with a nine called Stars, in vacations.... Then I introduced the games to the pupils. We always had lots of games with the city nines. When our old friend, Mr. G.O. Fay, was Superintendent, he took active interest in the national game and did much to encourage the boys."[6]

Gilbert O. Fay became the school's fifth superintendent in 1866. Fay

10

was the one who directly encouraged Pratt, who had been
hired as a teacher in 1863, to
introduce the sport, with the
school's blessing, to the student
body. By rights, Fay should get
the credit for encouraging the
Ohio School to make its mark
in the sporting world by embracing baseball. The school's
history described Pratt's critical role in bringing baseball to
the Ohio School, noting, "As a
lover of manly sports, he was
the first to introduce the game
of base ball at the Ohio Institution, and became manager
of the famous Independents,
which made a tour of the country, defeating nearly every club
with which they contested."[7]

The Ohio Independents
were a travelling team, drawn
from the ranks of the school's
own baseball nine. As Pratt

Parley P. Pratt. Pratt was the coach of the
Ohio School for the Deaf's baseball team. He
saw two of his players, Edward Dundon and
William Hoy, become the first two deaf men
to play baseball in the major leagues. Courtesy Ohio History Connection.

himself recalled, "In 1879 our boys began talking about a tour to the cities
in several States, and asked me to be their manager. I at once put the boys in
active practice and corresponded with many managers in the several States.
Some answered favorably and some were afraid to give us a game. They
thought we could not play on account of our deafness."

The Ohio Independents therefore had something to prove as they hit
the road. Pratt recounted their journey. "In June, 1879, we opened the game
with the 'Champions' of Springfield, Ohio, and beat them 6 to 0. Previously
they won a 6 to 5 game from the Chicago Club. We went to Cincinnati and
won a 1 to 0 game, and also won the next, but lost the last game. We then
took the train to Cleveland, riding all night, and won an 8 to 1 game from
the Forest City Club. We went to Buffalo for three games, but our opponents
backed out, so we went right to Rochester, Syracuse, Mexico, Utica, Albany,
Troy, and Hudson. The Troys beat us 2 to 0 in twelve innings. We won three

The Ohio Independents of 1879. This barnstorming team was made up of players from the Ohio School of the Deaf. This photo was originally in the possession of Coach Parley Pratt and he did not identify the individual players. However, Pratt is obviously the man in the suit. Players on this team included Edward Dundon, John Ryn, Isaac Sawhill, Collins Stone Sawhill, Joseph Leib, who served as team captain, and a token hearing player, remembered only as Short Stop Hunter. Courtesy Ohio History Connection.

straight games from the Syracuse Stars."[8] Their tour to that point had seen them play against several National League teams in exhibition games that summer, including Cincinnati, Cleveland, Troy, and Syracuse, against whom they compiled a 6–2 record.[9]

Their appearances garnered newspaper attention. In Rochester, for instance, the Ohio team faced the Hop Bitters, Rochester's professional nine at that time. They played in Hop Bitters Park on North Union Street in Rochester as part of the National Association.[10] As the *Rochester Times-Union* reported in July 1879, "A small audience attended the game yesterday between the Hop Bitters nine of this city and the Deaf Mute nine of Columbus…. The deaf mute players signal one another by pantomime and thus accomplish silently that which causes a great deal of chin music among players less afflicted."[11] The Hop Bitters won, 9–4.[12] The Ohio team had caught the Hop Bitters at just the right moment. They soon embarked on their own road trip, heading west, to Cleveland, to Chicago, to Dubuque, to Salt Lake City, and, finally, to San Francisco. A game there in October 1879 attracted a crowd of 10,000 spectators, an audience called the largest ever for a Pacific Coast game.[13] These kind of tours, such as the Independents were making, were quite common in the baseball world of the 1870s.

The Independents then headed south. Pratt wrote, "We went to New York City to play with the Jersey City Club, for three games, but they backed out. We had intended to go to Baltimore, Philadelphia, Washington and Pittsburg, but we found it impossible to keep the boys in good condition. Some were badly disabled with sprains and hurts. Remember, none of the boys ever wore a mitten in all games, so we agreed to come home for a good rest."[14] By "mitten," Pratt meant a baseball glove, as gloves were not common in the game until the 1890s.

Their rest did not last all that long. "In a few weeks," Pratt continued, "the boys wrote me to make another tour, and we met at Akron and lost the game to the Akrons. We next went to Cleveland and won the game. We played in Elyria, Norwalk, Findlay, Cincinnati, Cambridge, Ind., and Louisville." Effectively, the team played an Eastern route, followed by a Western route. "We won the majority of the games," Pratt was pleased to recall. "The Louisville Eclipses were generous and gave us the whole gate receipts for two games. We won three straight games from the Cincinnati Stars, and their manager told me that our boys were hoggish. Then we broke for home. I think the boys won 44 and lost 7 games on the first tour. Most of the nines were professionals. I had a diary and a large lot of clippings, which have become lost. You cannot imagine how much the papers praised our boys. We traveled over 3,500 miles and were absent from home from June till September. Our boys played for glory, as well as to show the people that we were as good players as hearing ones."[15]

As Pratt's commentary indicates, the deaf community faced discrimination from hearing people. Hearing nines sometimes assumed that deaf players simply could not play at all, or they assumed that deaf players were not "as good players as hearing ones." The Independents were out to challenge those stereotypes, but they also did not want to get taken advantage of. As a club of deaf nines out of the New York Institute for the Deaf (now the New York School for the Deaf), seeking summer games in Manhattan in 1877, put it, "While we are all deaf mutes, we do not ask from any club more than permission to have an impartial umpire and an interpreter to tell us his rulings."[16] They had discovered from "friends who could hear that in one game, an umpire, a member of the opposing club, the Jaspers, had given the Jaspers 11 runs in 4 innings in called balls."[17] The Ohio Independents apparently solved the problem of hearing teams trying to cheat the deaf players by adding a token hearing player to their team at shortstop. Years later, no one could recall his first name, calling him only Shortstop Hunter.[18]

Discrimination against the disabled was widespread in American culture. It was widely assumed that disabled people were not as capable as able-bodied people. Even one of the greatest champions of education for blind people, Samuel Gridley Howe, the director of the Perkins School for the Blind, had himself declared in the school's annual report of 1848, "THE BLIND, AS A CLASS, ARE INFERIOR TO OTHER PERSONS IN MENTAL POWER AND ABILITY" (yes, all caps in the original, to emphasize his view).[19] Given that the blind were inferior, it was no longer reasonable to expect society to work harder to accommodate their needs. Rather than social change, Howe recommended that sighted people should offer charity to the blind.[20]

Obviously this stance was deeply troubling not only to blind people but to disabled people more broadly. Deaf people did not believe that they were inferior to other persons and they certainly did not want hearing people to think that, either. Deaf people did not want charity from hearing people. They wanted inclusion in American civic, social, and economic life.[21] As Deaf Studies scholar Christopher Krentz reminds us, "Nineteenth-century deaf people were the first disabled American group to receive special education, the first to organize in a widespread way, the first to contest lack of access, prejudice, and pathological views of their difference, and as such pioneered the beginnings of disability activism in the United States."[22]

I suggest that deaf ball players, while certainly pursuing their passion for the sport, were also engaged in a kind of practical politics, a critical aspect of that larger effort on the part of the deaf community to contest hearing prejudice and demand inclusion. For as it would be for so many other minority groups, baseball was a vehicle for demanding inclusion in American life, by displaying passion for America's national pastime. For many such groups, as Lawrence Baldassaro reminds us, baseball "provided a passport to at least a part of mainstream American culture, making them more recognizably 'American' and less foreign."[23] Deaf players understood the politics of baseball quite similarly. They too could demonstrate their basic equality and humanity, as fellow American citizens, on the baseball diamond.

Deaf Americans were viewed as being outside the mainstream not only on account of their audiological difference but also their linguistic difference. In the 19th century, most educated deaf Americans used sign language to communicate. The first oral schools in the United States (that is, schools that exclusively used speech and lip reading to educate deaf children and forbid the use of the sign language) were not founded until 1867, when the Clarke School in Northampton, Massachusetts, and the New York Institution for the Improved Instruction of Deaf Mutes (later, the Lexington School) in Manhattan opened. Their appearance did begin to push some manual schools (schools that taught deaf students by using the sign language) to make classes in speech and lip reading available for those students who seemed to benefit from them, mostly those students who had gone deaf later in childhood. But the manual schools largely refused to abandon the sign language altogether and strongly resisted oralist calls to do so.

As the fifth oldest deaf school in the country, the Ohio School took a strong position in defense of sign language. In 1898, on the occasion of the school's 70th anniversary year, officials noted, "The sign language, like all other languages, is a growth. In its development it has followed the same rules that govern all other languages.... It has gone on steadily developing in terseness, significance, accuracy, copiousness and beauty, until now it is capable of rendering every phase of human thought. Like other languages it has its local dialects, its slang terms, its idioms and its value as a repository of forgotten usages. Being unwritten and having no lexicon its vocabulary, though rich and expressive and capable of infinite combinations, is necessarily short.... In this language all useless verbiage is ruthlessly doomed to extinction by the very necessities of its existence. The tendency is always to condensation and force of expression."[24]

Superintendent Fay remarked, "It has reached a clearness, an eloquence, a power as impressive to us as any spoken language is to any hearing audience, and which exercises over us, through the whole range of human thought, a supreme influence which no words, spoken, written or finger-spelled, can hope to equal."[25] The school was well aware that oralist challenges were mounting. The directors of the Ohio School nevertheless held firm. "It is the fashion, in some quarters, in this year of Grace, 1898, to sneer at the sign language; but it still maintains its sway among the deaf all over the world. They cling to it with hooks of steel and will not abandon it—and it will never be abandoned so long as a single deaf man is alive on earth. Those who sneer at it are found to be of two classes—those who do not or cannot understand it and those who find that it is an insurmountable barrier to their self-conceived theories.... To deprive so large a number of the deaf of these advantages simply to bolster up a theory would be no less than a crime against them, at which the deaf all over the State would unanimously rebel."[26]

Speech lessons, of a half an hour each day, had been offered to all students at the Ohio School as part of their regular school day since 1869. The rest of the school day's lessons were taught in the sign language. That was the curriculum that prevailed when Pratt's baseball players were attending the Ohio School.[27] The result was that, while some of Pratt's players may have acquired speech skills, all of them would have signed fluently.[28] The students would not have been segregated by their linguistic skills, divided into speakers and signers. All of them would have learned the sign language, together. That language bound them together.

It also marked them as deaf in the wider world. Their signing was a visible indication that they were not hearing. While their deafness was an invisible disability, their sign language was not. Hearing onlookers were frequently taken aback by signed conversations. As an account out of New Hampshire put it in 1879, "Two baseball clubs composed of deaf mutes have been playing in Ohio. They say it is sad to see the club that loses swearing at the umpire and calling him 'a hide-bound, lily-livered, black-hearted liar' with their thumbs and fingers."[29]

As another paper, reporting on deaf ballplayers in 1888, noted, "They play with great spirit and animation, and a foreign exuberance of gesticulation, and sometimes with those strange, inarticulate sounds that the dumb make. To the uninitiated, it is difficult to comprehend the slight, almost imperceptible, signs by which the Captain conveys his commands, but their keen, trained eyes never miss them. The regulation protests and expostulations to the umpire are conducted with fiery animation and although he receives them in silence it is far from being a stoical silence. Hands and fingers fly in a perfect pyrotechnic display, and it is very evident one can be just as mad in deaf and dumb talk as in the choicest vocal vocabulary of profanity and slang."[30] Here, the coverage moves from perceiving deaf people and their sign language as "foreign" to seeing the deaf ballplayers as being very similar to hearing ones. After all, regardless of audiological status, everyone can, and apparently will, curse out the umpire.

This is exactly the impact that the deaf community hoped embracing baseball would have. By playing baseball, they could demonstrate that, even though they used sign language, they and their fellow hearing citizens were more alike than not. Baseball provided a path for deaf people to break into the mainstream of American life. Parley Pratt was understandably proud of the legacy of the Ohio School's baseball program. The boys that he coached went on to become the first deaf professional baseball players in American history.

Significantly, observers at the time also recognized Ohio's special place in the early history of deaf players in baseball. As the *Indianapolis Journal* noted in 1889, "Ohio has the honor of having furnished all the deaf mute players to the profession. Hoy, Dundon, Ryn, Gillespie, and Sawhill all came from the Buckeye State."[31] With the exception of Gillespie, who has proved elusive, we will meet the rest below. Ohio's place as a foundational home for deaf baseball may also result from the fact that the Midwest seems to have constituted a deaf heartland of sorts in the late 19th century. A study of 1880 census data reveals that in Illinois, Indiana, Michigan, Ohio, and Wisconsin, the deaf population was notably greater in proportion than the hearing population. These states contained 29.07 percent of the deaf population in 1880, but only 22.37 percent of the hearing population.[32]

Edward Dundon

The team's star pitcher was Edward Dundon (1859–1893). Dundon's parents, John and Mary Dundon, were Irish immigrants. They had 10 children, three of whom were deaf, suggesting that congenital deafness ran in the family. All three deaf siblings attended the Ohio School. Dundon had studied book binding as his trade at the school. He was also the class valedictorian when he graduated in 1878. As Pratt indicated, Dundon went on to a brief professional baseball career, the first deaf man to appear in major league baseball.

He pitched for two years for the Columbus Buckeyes, an American Association team, in 1883 and 1884, posting a two-season record of 9–20. This was not the extent of his time in baseball, however. After the Columbus franchise folded, Dundon headed south to play for Atlanta in the Southern League. There, he posted a 21–11 record with 210 strikeouts and a 1.30 ERA in 37 games pitches.[33] In 1886, he was in the same league, now playing for the Nashville team. He attracted a lot of attention from the deaf community there. As one paper reported, "Dundon has made the acquaintance of all the deaf mutes in Nashville. They make a great deal of him."[34]

Dundon continued on to play in various minor leagues, and by 1886, he was playing in the Gulf League. There in Mobile, Alabama, Dundon was called on to umpire a game. This is believed to have been the first time that a deaf man acted as an umpire in a game between two professional nines.[35] As

The Sporting News reported, "It seems impossible that a mute should be able to umpire, and yet Dundon did so satisfactorily. He used the fingers of his right hand to indicate strikes, the fingers of his left to call balls, a shake of the head decided a man 'not out' and a wave of the hand meant 'out.'"[36] Presumably, this is the same system that the Ohio Independents had used, one that they had most likely developed at the residential school.

As deaf baseball researcher Brian Malzkuhn notes, when the boys played together at the Ohio School for the Deaf, "it would be safe to assume that there was a mechanism that deaf players used to signify certain calls."[37] Indeed, it seems like a most reasonable assumption. They had to have called the game with gestures and the Ohio School for the Deaf was the first residential school for the deaf to field a baseball team. It seems entirely likely that deaf baseball players created and introduced system of gestures at the Ohio School for the Deaf, gestures which eventually made their way, in modified forms, more widely into baseball.

Dundon's own umpiring system directed signs to the baseman. A shake of the head "no" meant that he had not made the play and so the runner was safe. A wave of the hand indicated to the baseman that he had made the play and so the runner was out. Eventually, all of that information was condensed into one sign, and the wave of the hand would come indicate "safe" to both baseman and runner.

In 1888, Dundon finally ended up in Syracuse, New York, playing for the Syracuse Stars in the International League. Today, that Syracuse team is best remembered as the team of Moses Fleetwood Walker, baseball's first African American professional

Edward Dundon. A graduate of the Ohio School for the Deaf, Dundon was the first deaf man to play baseball in a major league. Courtesy Ohio History Connection.

player. He is standing in the back row in the team photo, next to Edward Dundon. Walker got his start in baseball at Oberlin College, a member of their first varsity squad in 1881, along with his brother, Weldy. Walker was deeply attracted to baseball. As David W. Zang puts it, "Of all the different arenas in which to seek equality and success—political, economic, social, intellectual—baseball was the only one that offered to Fleet Walker not only an interregional, highly visible platform, but also an irrefutable, competitive disproving ground for the fiercely held racial beliefs that were embedded in

The 1888 Syracuse Stars. The Stars were a prominent team in the International League, a minor league. The 1888 Stars were both a racially and audiologically integrated team. The Stars had been roiled with racial unrest during the 1887 season, as white teammates turned on their own pitcher, Robert Higgins, another of the earliest black professional baseball players. Management brought in a new manager, Charlie Hackett, for the 1888 season. Hackett determined that bringing another black player to the team to catch for Higgins would settle things down. Hackett brought Moses Fleetwood Walker with him to Syracuse from Newark. The move produced results. The team won the International League championship in 1888. Back row, from left to right: Moses Fleetwood Walker, Ed Dundon, Mox McQuery, Bones Ely, Bill Higgins. Middle row, from left to right: Ollie Beard, Con Murphy, Rasty Wright, manager Charlie Hackett, Joe Battin, Ed Mars. Seated, left to right: Robert Higgins and Al Schellhase. Courtesy Robert Edward Auctions.

anatomy and physiology—that presumed blacks to be an inferior race be-cause of their physical attributes."[38] Baseball, in that way, held out the same attraction for Walker as it did for Dundon—it was an arena to challenge the prejudices against them, on account of the blackness of the one and the deafness of the other.

The quality of his play in the minor league International League earned him a spot in the major league baseball in 1884. Walker joined Toledo Blue Stockings of the American Association, a league which had attained major league status in 1882. Walker had the first base hit for To-ledo to kick off their major league debut and he scored their first run.[39] The hometown's leading newspaper, the *Blade*, mostly concerned with winning, supported Walker throughout the season, as did the national *Sporting News*. But papers in the South engaged in a campaign to discredit Walker.[40] White players sometimes refused to play against him. His own star pitcher on the Stars, Tony Mullane, refused to take signals from him. Instead, Walker managed to catch him without ever knowing what pitch was coming where.[41]

Like Dundon, Walker took a turn behind the plate as an umpire, in 1887. "A catcher standing in as umpire was not earthshaking in 1880s baseball," notes David W. Zang. "Still it would have been a bold move for any mulatto less self-assured and less drawn to the spotlight than Fleet Walker."[42] De-spite his personal sense of strength and self-assurance, the pressure on Fleet Walker and other black players increased. Those players included his brother, Weldy, who had joined him on the Toledo team, becoming the second black player in major league baseball in the process.

White players, led by Adrian "Cap" Anson, agitated to get black play-ers banned from baseball. Anson had enormous influence in major league baseball. He played 27 seasons at first base for the franchise now known as the Chicago Cubs (then known as the Chicago White Stockings), was the first player to amass 3,000 hits, and led his team to six National League pennants in the 1880s. Anson was also a segregationist. He refused to take the field against integrated teams and, in fact, demanded assurances that Fleet Walker would not be on the field when Chicago played an exhibition game against Toledo.[43] Anson was quoted in the Toledo press as having declared, "We'll play this here game but won't play never no more with the nigger in."[44]

Walker played only one season at the major league level. Toledo re-leased both him and his brother at the end of the 1884 season. Walker con-tinued to play baseball professionally, however, for several more seasons, finding places on teams in various minor leagues. He was offered a position as catcher for the Newark Little Giants in the International League in 1887. There, he formed one half of the first all-African American battery, catching for pitcher George Stovey.[45] Walker went on to the Syracuse Stars in 1888, where he crossed paths with Dundon. The International League was still hospitable to black players. Walker had a black teammate on the Stars, the pitcher Robert Higgins. In the 1887 season, Higgins went 20–7 for the Stars, and in 1888, he helped pitch the team into its International League title.[46] Meanwhile, another early black player, the Buffalo Bisons' Frank Grant, was the International League's leading hitter. Grant is widely acknowledged to have been the best black player in 19th-century baseball, as well as one of the best second basemen of 19th-century baseball. Grant was inducted into the Hall of Fame in 2006, one of the few pre–Negro League black players to be so honored.[47]

It was perhaps the success of these black players that was most galling to Cap Anson and to fellow whites. Far more than white owners, many of whom wanted to secure players who would bring their respective teams success, it was white players who led the charge to draw the color line in the International League.[48] As the 1888 season opened, it was understood that black players would be increasingly restricted, held to an informal quota of no more than one per team, but not entirely banned.[49] Syracuse managed to retain both of its black players on the Stars only because it had acted early, signing Walker four months prior to the season opening.[50]

Despite the mounting turmoil within the league over race, player relations on the Syracuse team itself were largely good. For one thing, the team won a lot, which surely helped. They were also well paid, by league standards. The team's payroll was $20,000, a rather stunning amount for the times. Black citizens of Syracuse rallied around the team. And one of the team's white directors, J.C. Bowe, was personally supportive of Walker.[51]

It may also have helped that one of Walker's Syracuse teammates, namely Edward Dundon, had previous experience with racial integration. The Ohio School for the Deaf was racially integrated. The school reported in 1898 that "something like thirty colored pupils have been educated at the Ohio School during its career, a number of them making good records as students and afterwards as citizens."[52]

It is not clear from the records what precise years all 30 of these students of color attended. However, all of the Ohio School ballplayers under discussion here went to school with at least one black deaf classmate. *A Historical and Biographical Souvenir of the Ohio School for the Deaf. Seventy Years' His-*

tory of a Notable Seat of Learning, with Personal Recollections of Its Founders and Early Officials. The Institution of the Present Day. Official, Education, and Industrial Departments, Domestic and Social Life. Portraits and Biographical Sketches of Representative Alumni, published in 1898, in celebration of the school's 70th anniversary, included two biographical sketches of black deaf women among those representative alumni. They were Jennie Stewart and Mary Florence Fowlis.

Edward Dundon and Mary Florence Fowlis had been classmates together at Ohio. Mary Florence Fowlis attended from 1874 to 1884. She would have seen Dundon rise to the rank of class valedictorian in 1878. Every other deaf baseball player from the Ohio School in these years would also have gone to school with Fowlis. Jennie Stewart attended the school from 1887 to 1897, overlapping in years with another deaf ballplayer, George Kihm, under discussion below. Both women were trained in book binding and both were supporting themselves as folders in the state bindery.[53] Interestingly, the pictures and biographies of both women appear on the same page with Edward Dundon. Any readers looking for information on the first deaf baseball player in the major leagues would have been obligated to meet these two black deaf women in the process of finding his entry.

Additionally, with the exception of Kihm, the rest of the men would have attended school with James Gilbert, Jr., of Cincinnati. Gilbert was a member of the class of 1880. He was the only black deaf graduate of the Ohio School for the Deaf to attend Gallaudet College (now University), the world's first college for deaf people. Gilbert arrived on the campus in the fall of 1880. Founded in 1864, Gallaudet was open to both white and black deaf students during the 19th century. Fourteen black deaf students attended Gallaudet in those years.[54] The racial integration of Gallaudet, however, would barely survive the 19th century. Gallaudet's president was Edward Miner Gallaudet. He was the son of Thomas Hopkins Gallaudet, the hearing co-founder of the American School for the Deaf, the first school for deaf Americans, which opened in 1817. The college was named in honor of Thomas Hopkins Gallaudet. The American School for the Deaf had also been racially integrated; its first student of color enrolled in 1825. In his history of Gallaudet College, Gallaudet recalled that even the school's limited integration efforts met with increasing resistance as the nineteenth century wore on. Not only were there very few black students, but they also lived in separate housing from the white students and sat at separate tables within classrooms.[55] Nonetheless, there was white resistance, as Gallaudet reported. "On a good many occasions," he wrote, "we had complaints from the parents of white children and protests against the mixture of the races in our school. Some difficulties also arose, growing out of the treatment of the colored students by the white."[56] It would seem that Gilbert himself was a victim of those racial troubles on campus. He was at the college for only one year, leaving when the 1880–81 academic year came to a close. The next black student to follow him, in 1883, Ennal Adams, lasted only for three months of his first year.[57] Gallaudet finally capitulated to the racism of white parents and students. He removed the remaining black students from the campus in 1905, making arrangements to send them to the Maryland School for Colored Deaf-Mutes in Baltimore.[58] Gallaudet College would not welcome black deaf students again for another 45 years. The first black student to complete his studies and graduate from Gallaudet was Andrew Foster in 1954. In his telling of the history of Gallaudet University, David Armstrong concludes that there was "no evidence that white deaf people at Gallaudet felt a sense of solidarity with deaf African Americans."[59] It is not clear, however, that the racial conflict found at Gallaudet was typical within the larger deaf community of the late nineteenth century. Unlike Gallaudet College, for instance, schools like the American School, the New York School, and the Ohio School never segregated. At the regional level, there is evidence to suggest that white and black deaf people experienced some level of social integration. It may well have been that the ballplayers under consideration here crossed paths with black deaf people outside of school. Deaf African Americans seem to have been included in the social world of Ohio School alumni, as this photograph of a gathering of such alumni taken at the World's Fair in Chicago in 1893 indicates. Dundon, for one, surely had more experience with African Americans as peers and schoolmates than most of his white teammates in Syracuse.

In spite of their success as a team, these years with Syracuse proved the last for both men. Dundon was released from Syracuse at least in part because he had developed a drinking problem. It was reported that "Syracuse has released pitcher Dundon, the deaf-mute. Dundon is a good twirler but he imbibes too freely."[60] His career in baseball was over by 1889.[61] Walker played for one more season in Syracuse, appearing in the 1889 season.

When he was let go, in August 1889, the color line fell across organized baseball, forcing black players out of the sport and bringing the age of integrated professional baseball, at both minor and major league levels, in the United States to an end. Walker was the last African American to play in either the major leagues or in the International League until Jackie Robinson's arrival in baseball in the mid–20th century.[62]

Using baseball to prove one's worth as an American and as a citizen was

Gathering of Ohio School for the Deaf Alumni at the World's Fair in 1893. The Ohio School for the Deaf was racially integrated. This picture of alumni suggests that the social world of the school's graduates remained one where white and black adults continued to enjoy social ties with one another. Courtesy Ohio History Connection.

a strategy that failed to overcome racism in the 1880s for African Americans. Walker himself became increasingly pessimistic about the future of race relations in the United States. In 1908, Walker published a book called *Our Home Colony: A Treatise on the Past, Present, and Future of the Negro Race in America.* Anticipating in some ways the views of Marcus Garvey, Walker explored the idea of black Americans emigrating back to Africa, arguing that, in the United States, African Americans "are treated as though they were non-assimable aliens." He concluded, "We see no possible hope that the Negro will ever secure the enjoyment of this social freedom or equality."[63] Walker died in 1924.

For deaf Americans, however, the effort to use baseball to gain social acceptance from hearing people. But not for Edward Dundon. Ill health finally forced his retirement, and Dundon died from tuberculosis in 1893 at the age of 35.[64] Scarcely remembered today, Dundon was nonetheless an early sports hero within the deaf community. As his alma mater remembered him, "Since his day other deaf ball players have won distinction on the diamond but he was practically the first one to enjoy a national reputation along this line. In the athletic annals of the Institution his name and memory will always remain illustrious."[65]

Walker suffered much the same fate. Like Dundon, his time as a professional baseball player was long forgotten, until historians went digging for antecedents to Jackie Robinson. Dundon was, at best, a decent pitcher with occasional flashes of real brilliance. And Walker? He was an adequate offensive player but a truly gifted defensive catcher. He faced racism from fans, from the press, from opposing players, and sometimes from his own teammates. As his biographer David Z. Wang concludes, "Perhaps it is enough to know that in an age of surging racism, where umpires admitted to making calls and teammates admitted to subverting their play on the basis of color, with the alternative of all-Negro teams beckoning, and despite the physical demands on an aging catcher, predominantly white teams in competitive leagues had, for seven years, paid Moses Fleetwood Walker to play baseball. That's how good he was."[66]

Dundon was but one example of the deep roots of deaf baseball. Indeed, in 1893, five Ohio School graduates reported that they were earning a living playing baseball, or as the school's own employment records put it, "base ball players (professional): 5."[67] By 1893, the school had welcomed 2,523 pupils. The overwhelming majority of them, 152 in all, were working in a very different field, as farmers.[68] Officially, the school offered students training in shoemaking, printing, bookbinding, carpentry, tailoring, and dressmaking.[69] Baseball, as a trade, seems to have emerged more organically.

As Peter Morris notes, the Ohio School for the Deaf was something of a baseball powerhouse. He writes, "The school had a prominent baseball team in the 1870s and 1880s, and went on a tour of the state in 1879. Several of its players made the leap to professional ball."[70] In fact, six men, all of whom had played originally at the Ohio School for the Deaf, would begin to appear on professional baseball rosters in the late 19th century: Edward Dundon, Isaac "Ike" Sawhill, William Lorimor Sawhill, John Ryn, George Kihm, and William Hoy.

Isaac Sawhill

Isaac "Ike" Sawhill attended the Ohio School from 1872 to 1878. His parents, William and Amelia Sawhill, had also attended the Ohio School for the Deaf. The couple had seven children, all hearing, save for Ike. He was known as "a brilliant student." He was "not only ambitious in his studies but excelled in all kinds of manly sports." He played on the Independents, where his coach praised him for his "very sharp eye on fouls."[71] Ike went on to be "regarded as the finest catcher in Columbus, being at the top of the ladder in 1865, '76, '77, and '78. No pitcher was too speedy for him." He played as a professional, in Ohio, "with the Mansfield Club; in 1882, he caught 37 consecutive games without a mask or gloves."[72]

Isaac "Ike" Sawhill. An 1878 graduate of the Ohio School for the Deaf, Sawhill played baseball professionally in leagues in Ohio after his school days. Courtesy Ohio History Connection.

William Lorimor Sawhill

William Lorimor Sawhill, Ike's cousin, was born in Pennsylvania in 1865 to deaf parents. They were originally from Ohio and had been educated at the Ohio School for the Deaf. They moved back to Ohio when their son was a boy. He enrolled at the Ohio School as well, in the fall of 1873. He was at school for seven years and was orphaned during that time. When he graduated, he was on his own, fending for himself. He worked as a laborer in steel works in Pennsylvania and then worked in a freight yard in Missouri.

In the spring of 1885, he decided to try baseball, having learned the sport at the Ohio School, playing in the Ohio League in Akron at first and then, in 1888, for Lafayette, which was at first in the Indiana State League and then in the Central Interstate League. "He played ball in the springs and summers of 1886–88, when he found time was being wasted without work in the winter, and determined that steady employment would, if he could get it, be the wisest movement for the rest of his life."[73]

William Lorimor Sawhill. Isaac Sawhill's cousin, William Lorimor Sawhill played professionally in the minors in the Ohio League in the late 1880s. Courtesy Ohio History Connection.

He returned to Pennsylvania, "where he was given employment as assistant carpenter in the oil fields. It was in the winter of 1888 and today he enjoys the reputation of being the only mute oil man that can take care of four boilers and eight engines that run eight wells. He is well known among the sportsmen of Western Pennsylvania and West Virginia as one of the best ballplayers."[74] Sawhill married a fellow Ohio School graduate, Emma Kob, in 1888. This transition to the role of husband and father may have finally persuaded him to hang up his spikes. The couple had three children, one daughter and two sons, by 1895.[75]

John Ryn

John Ryn was born in 1862 to hearing parents. However, three of their seven children were deaf, John and his two older sisters, Mary and Annie. All three deaf siblings attended the Ohio School for the Deaf. Ryn joined his sisters at the school in 1870, when he was eight years old. He learned to play baseball there and was on the school's baseball team, mostly as a pitcher and catcher. Coach Pratt said, "Ryn was a natural hitter."[76]

During summer breaks, Ryn began to join mostly hearing nines in the area to play baseball. In 1882, he was among the first members of the newly formed Marion Mohawks. He later joined Ed Dundon on the Columbus Buckeyes, in 1883. Dundon got the call to go up to the majors from there. Ryn, unluckily, had suffered a hand injury behind the plate and remained in the minors. That was as close as he would get to the major leagues. His injury probably cost him his chance to go up with his teammate. It was caused by the fact that he caught gloveless. As the *Marion Star* noted, "When he caught he wore only a common leather driving glove on his left hand and a canvas glove with the fingers cut on his right."[77]

Baseball chronicler Peter Morris notes that, while modern fans might find it unusual for deaf teammates to play together in the minors, the 19th-century students at the Ohio School for the Deaf were quite accustomed to seeing their classmates break into baseball. He notes that "when the school reopened for the 1883–84 academic year, the school newspaper noted matter-of-factly that students John Ryn and Ed Dundon had spent their summer vacations playing baseball."[78]

In 1884, Ryn signed with the Portsmouth team in the Ohio State League. In 1885, Ryn and Dundon were reunited in the Southern League, Ryn with Chattanooga and Dundon with Atlanta. He left the South and did not play organized baseball at all in 1886, finally reappearing on the rosters in the Ohio State League in 1887. In July 1888, the *Daily Inter Ocean* noted, "All of the deaf mutes are distinguishing themselves this year. Ryn, the right fielder of Sandusky, is playing in a way to rival the king of the mutes, Hoy, of Washington, and Dundon is doing good work for Syracuse."[79] It is fascinating to see their names in print together. Hoy, referenced here in 1888, was just starting his major league career. It is a reminder to us that the lines between leagues were thinner than we might imagine. Here, the three men were seen as comparable on the sports pages, though Hoy was the only major leaguer among them.

Ryn proved a sought-after player in the minor leagues. He was brought to Canton of the Tri-State League in 1889, where he played 102 games, all of them at first base. He led the league with 150 hits and a .358 batting average. He was instrumental in the team's drive to the pennant, which they secured by 10.5 games. That attracted the attention of Minneapolis of the Western Association and they brought him in for the club's last seven games of the season. Ryn overperformed in those games, batting .414 with six doubles. They signed him for the following season.[80]

As he reported in 1890, the expectations were high. "Ryn is in excellent health and will play first base as it has never been played before in this city. The 'Dummy' is not much of a coacher but when it comes to stealing bases or hitting the ball he is always on deck. Ryn played a few games in this city last season and his stops and throws were wonderful."[81] Ryn did not disappoint. In 117 games for Minneapolis, he hit .286 and played solidly at first. The club fell, painfully, one game short in the race for the Western Association pennant.[82] Ryn's work for the team drew attention from *The Sporting Life*. "Ryn, in addition to his terrific hitting, is putting up an almost perfect game at first, and it is safe to wager that he will lead the first baseman at the close of the season."[83]

After falling just short in the race in 1890, Ryn returned to Minneapolis for the 1891 season. But disaster struck when he suffered a knee injury in June that refused to heal. By July, he had been laid off from the team, at his own request. He headed home, to Ohio.[84] He kicked around with various teams there, including another turn with Sandusky, this time with a more recent graduate of the Ohio School for the Deaf, George Kihm. But, much like Dundon, Ryn had taken to drinking, perhaps in response to his frustrations with his injury. He continued to play semi-pro ball in Ohio into the 1895 season but never recovered his early form. He retired from the sport for good at the age of 33.

His later years indicate the struggles that deaf men faced in the social and economic settings of the early 20th century. Ryn had been a celebrated minor league baseball player. But by 1900, he found himself a "day laborer," as baseball chronicler Brian McKenna notes for Ryn's entry in the SABR Biography Project. He remained a "common laborer," as census records show, for the rest of his life. He lived with his deaf sister, Anna, after his retirement from baseball and never married. He died in 1928, in Marion, Ohio.[85]

George Kihm

George Kihm attended the Ohio School with his brother, Anthony. They were the only deaf children among their parents' brood of seven. They arrived at the school together in 1880, when George was seven and Anthony was 10. Kihm graduated in 1891, nearly 18, six feet tall and a good infielder. He soon caught the attention of a local team, the Delphos Reds. He played for both the Reds and the Sandusky team, where he played with John Ryn, in 1892. The Reds started slow the following season, in 1893, opening 1–3, but suddenly caught fire and won 21 of their next 23 games. They finished the season at 33 and 12 and were recognized as "the champions of Northwest Ohio."[86]

A big, strong guy, Kihm was also a fixture on the local boxing circuit in northern Ohio, where he was billed as "The Mute" or the "Delphos Cyclone."[87] He continued to develop as a ball player, jumping from team to team. Kihm attracted increasing attention for his play. As the *Tacoma Daily Ledger* noted in 1896, "Kihm simply electrified the fans" with his play at first.[88] In 1897, Kihm found himself playing for Fort Wayne in the Interstate League. He excelled, finishing the season among the league's batting leaders. He also gained a deaf teammate, Jake Funkhouser, at third base. Kihm hit .350 in 124 games and led the league with 17 home runs. While some papers suggested that "Kihm is not fast enough for the National League, although he is a very good minor league player," there is some reason to think that his career was held back on account of his deafness.[89] As Brian McKenna points out, "The Fort Wayne team was a farm club of the National League's Cleveland Spiders, and many of the team's players played at least briefly for

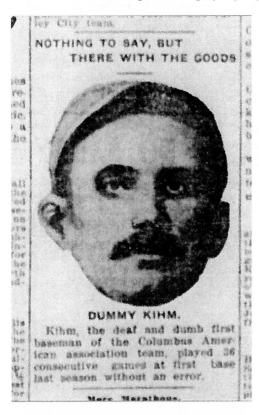

NOTHING TO SAY, BUT THERE WITH THE GOODS

DUMMY KIHM.

Kihm, the deaf and dumb first baseman of the Columbus American association team, played 36 consecutive games at first base last season without an error.

More Marathons.

George "Dummy" Kihm. Kihm was another product of the Ohio School for the Deaf who played baseball professionally. Kihm was argu-ably the finest deaf player who never made it to the majors. This image appeared in *The Seattle Star* on 17 December 1908.

the major league team. Though Kihm was one of Fort Wayne's most accomplished players, he never appeared in a regular season game for Cleveland."[90]

Kihm went from Fort Wayne to Troy, New York, to Delphos to Los Angeles to Indianapolis. There, he played with the 1902 Indianapolis Indians, a minor league team often listed among the top minor league teams in baseball history, ranked 27th by Bill Weiss and Marshall Wright for www.milb.com. Associated with the minor league American Association, the 1902 Indians went 96 and 45. Kihm played first for them, hitting .296 in 134 games. "Over the space of 95 years," Weiss and Wright write, "the American Association reigned supreme over the minor league world in the midsection of the country. Getting this league off to a strong start was a strong team from Indianapolis, a team well worthy of inclusion on the list of great minor league teams."[91]

In 1904, Kihm joined up with Columbus in the American Association, a team he stayed with for the next four seasons. The team won three pennants. Kihm had a loyal following. "Every time Dummy Kihm plays here, [owner] Tebeau's pockets profit by about ten prices of admission paid by that many mutes who live in Louisville. Kihm is naturally a great favorite with them, as well as everyone else, and after each game the mutes gather round the main entrance and enthusiastically go through all kinds of fantastic motions indicating that part the great first baseman took in the game."[92]

Kihm was not only deeply attached to and included in the larger deaf community. He was a true member of his various teams. His deafness was seen as the major factor "that makes him the brainy player that he is."[93] Kihm was outgoing, bright, and friendly. As *The Dayton Herald* noted, "Deprived of the power to speak and hear, he ranks among the most intelligent men in the game today. He is a close student of baseball and of the current events of the world." His hearing teammates liked Kihm, the man, and seemed to truly enjoy his company. The paper continued, "He is handicapped on account of being a deaf mute, but he does not lack for company. The players like to talk with him, either by the sign language or by writing sentences. 'Dummy' has adopted a novel plan of teaching his fellow players to talk the sign language. Whenever a new player joins the team on which he is playing, he gives him a card … containing pictures of the finger alphabet. Every member of the Grand Rapids club has one of Kihm's cards and most of the Stags can talk with their fingers. Other players in the league with whom Kihm comes in contact receive cards with a request to learn the language he talks. Several members of the Soldier team are learning to talk on their fingers, so they can 'fan' with 'Dummy,' one of the most interesting talkers on the circuit."[94] Sign language proved the way to integrate Kihm into his hearing teams in the minor leagues, just as it later would for the deaf players who at last made it into the majors.

Kihm found himself an integral part of another great minor league team, the 1905 Columbus Senators, who went 100 and 52. "In starting the American Association's first dynasty," Weiss and Wright write, "the 1905 Columbus Senators became the first league club to reach the century mark in wins."[95] Kihm was an important part of this team. "One key player of the Columbus club never saw the light of the majors," Weiss and Wright note, their 32-year-old first baseman, George "Dummy" Kihm, who hit .285 that year. "During his playing days," they explain, "spent mostly in the high minors, Kihm amassed 2,245 hits while compiling a .293 average."[96] He also stole over 300 bases.[97]

Columbus won 91 games in the 1906 season and 90 games in the 1907 season, clinching three American Association pennants in a row. Kihm "had

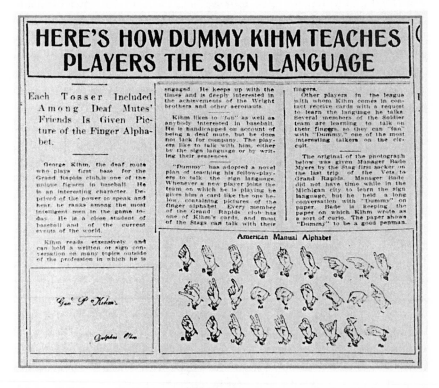

Kihm's alphabet card. Kihm gave his hearing teammates cards with the manual alphabet printed on them, so that they would be able to communicate with him. Deaf players who made it to the majors brought this very same practice with them. This image appeared in *The Dayton Herald* on 10 July 1909.

a string of 51 consecutive errorless games in 1906. He ran off another errorless streak two years later, 36 that time. In 1908, the club sipped to third place; likewise, Kihm's average dipped to .240."[98] He was let go at the end of the season. In 1909, he joined Grand Rapids, seen as a farm team to Columbus. His hitting improved to .260, and his fielding remained as sharp as ever.[99]

By 1910, Kihm was a fixture in the world of minor league baseball and an enormously popular player. His deafness was always acknowledged, as his nickname "Dummy" never let fans forget that he was deaf. But press coverage portrayed him in far more well-rounded terms as his career went on. One of the more humorous examples of that can be seen in a series of stories not about his ears but rather his mustache.

In Ohio, it was reported in 1910 that Dummy, "the tall and noiseless first sacker," was in "an off year" in regard to facial hair: "its absence makes Dummy look five years younger than he did last season." He apparently played younger too: "his hits this year according to his boss are all good hard raps that leave a trail of smoke behind them."[100] A headline out of Indiana similarly explained that "Dummy Kihm Wears His Mustache Every Other Season." Manager Joe Raidy explained to the reporter that "Kihm wears his mustache every other year and that this is one of his off years. Dummy will appear next year with a nice crop of black hair on his upper lip but this season it will remain clean." While not claiming causation per se, the paper noted that, with his hairless lip, Kihm's playing seemed to have improved. Raidy offered that Kihm was "playing even better ball now." While holding down first, "all the infielders have to do is to get the ball somewhere near the bag and he'll do the rest." The paper concluded, "With his mustache off, Dummy looks and acts a great deal younger, and all indications point to his having one of his best seasons on the diamond this year."[101] It is a classic sort of minor league story, a public interest piece meant to drum up interest in the upcoming season, while hyping the return of a veteran player to rare form. But it is rarer still to see a deaf player featured like this, and with a storyline that has absolutely nothing to do with his deafness. It surely speaks to the way that, after nearly two decades in the minors, Kihm was truly seen by his peers as the player that he was.

Kihm finally called it a career in 1911, at the age of 38. He had appeared in over 2,100 games, amassing 7,661 at-bats on his way to his .293 lifetime batting average.[102] As one headline said of Kihm, "Nothing to Say But There with the Goods."[103] The *Silent Worker* lamented the fact that Kihm had never made it to the majors. "Kihm, a splendid ball player and batsman, and one of the boys who couldn't say a word or hear the roar of applause or abuse, was a star in the big minor leagues for many seasons. A wonderful first sacker was

Kihm, and a terrific hitter, but he never reached the big league."[104] He lived out the rest of his life in Delphos, Ohio, working at the Schaffer Sawmill and Handle Factory, owned by his brother-in-law. He died in Delphos in 1936 at the age of 63, on his 43rd wedding anniversary.[105] *The Cincinnati Enquirer* put it simply, in their 1936 headline: "Ball Player Dies."[106]

Collins Stone Sawhill

Though he never moved further into the professional ranks, there is one other Ohio School ball player worth noting and that is Collins Stone Sawhill. Collins was William Lorimor Sawhill's brother. Collins was "well known in the deaf circle as the funny sign maker and story teller."[107] His reputation as a humorist may have been well known in his community, but it was unlikely that Collins would have been perceived that way outside of "the deaf circle." Even in the 19th century, deaf people knew that their humor was frequently lost in translation. "And here it may be added, a joke exquisitely funny as expressed in signs is utterly untranslatable. It loses its pith when translated into English or any other language, just as a joke or pun in one language loses its point when translated into another."[108]

Collins had been the Independents' left fielder but that is as far as his baseball career went. He went to work in Pennsylvania, promoted from a position as laborer at the Edgar Thompson Steel Works, where his brother

Collins Stone Sawhill. Collins was William Lorimor Sawhill's brother. Collins played with the Ohio Independents in 1879. Courtesy Ohio History Connection.

also worked, to "the position of assistant boss heater. He has not only won the confidence of his employers but is a favorite among the mill men."[109]

Though he never made a living as a baseball player, the example of Collins Stone Sawhill still helps us to see how deaf people, once scattered in mostly hearing families across the country, were brought together and trans-formed into a tight community by the residential schools of the 19th century. His very name displays an awareness of important figures in the history of the deaf community. He was named for Collins Stone, an early teacher of the deaf, who began his career at the American School for the Deaf, the first perma-nent school for deaf people in the country, starting there as a teacher in 1833. He became the superintendent of the Ohio School in 1852 but returned to Connecticut in 1863 to become the fourth president of the American School.

As it turns out, Sawhill's deaf parents had attended the Ohio School when Stone was superintendent. They named their son in his honor, demonstrating in their own way their gratitude for their education. Their choice of name for their son also highlighted what Deaf Studies scholar Christopher Krentz has pointed to as a distinct part of American deaf education. Unlike blind edu-cation, where the sighted reformer Samuel Gridley Howe worked exclusively beside sighted people and could come to impose a project of sighted charity for the blind upon his blind students, deaf education was, in Krentz's phrase, "a symbiotic deaf-hearing collaboration."[110] The first permanent school for the deaf in the United States, after all, had both a deaf (Laurent Clerc) and a hear-ing (Thomas Hopkins Gallaudet) co-founder, and the school hired its own graduates as teachers, establishing the practice of hiring deaf teachers as an expectation for the emerging profession of deaf education as a field. Collins Stone worked beside deaf peers regularly, both at the American School and at the Ohio School. Sawhill's deaf parents experienced the benefits of that deaf-hearing collaboration for themselves. Naming their deaf son for a hear-ing man was a very 19th-century gesture of appreciation for the fruits of that collaboration.

The school had done far more than provide them an education. It had brought Collins' parents together and, in a real sense, had allowed them to lay claim to what was a perfectly average adult experience in the hearing world, namely, marriage. Deaf men and women would not likely have been seen as suitable marriage partners by their hearing peers. Had each of them remained isolated in hearing families, surrounded by hearing people, they might well never have married. By attending the Ohio School for the Deaf, the Sawhill brothers' deaf parents were empowered. They not only received an education. They were able to lay claim to the life most hearing people expected to experience when they grew up, getting married and raising a family of their own.

Additionally, attending a school for the deaf brought deaf individuals together into a larger deaf community. Most deaf people, in the 19th century and still today, are born into hearing families. Fewer than 10 percent have deaf parents. Coming into the residential school, many newly enrolled deaf students met large numbers of other deaf people for the first time. When they all graduated from school, those educated deaf people would form the heart of the emerging deaf community in the 19th century. By the 1850s, there was a large enough number of such educated deaf people, a critical mass, as it were, that a recognizable deaf community was visible on a national level in the United States for the first time in its history. The deaf community, by that decade, had its own schools, language, newspapers, journals, churches, and organizations, all the things that marked the emergence and existence of other ethnic groups.[111]

Collins Stone Sawhill came to adulthood within that larger deaf community and he participated actively in organizations that were particular to his community. In 1895, he was elected vice president of the Ohio School's Alumni Association.[112] It was founded in 1870, as the number of alumni had finally reached a critical mass. Parley P. Pratt, Sawhill's old coach, called to order the meeting that culminated in the creation of the alumni association, its constitution, and its by-laws, and he was named the Ohio Deaf Mute Alumni Association's first treasurer. The object of the association, according to its constitution, was "the promotion of our own improvement by holding stated meetings, and in other ways looking to that object."[113] The first meeting of the association drew 143 attendees and the ninth, in 1895, when Collins Stone Sawhill assumed office, saw 220.[114]

Sawhill did not stay in Ohio. He spent two years as a student at Gallaudet College, from 1878 to 1880, though he did not graduate. He was ordained as a preacher in 1924. He died in Birmingham, Alabama, in 1934, at the age of 77.[115] Collins Stone Sawhill was indeed known as a ball player, but only within the deaf community, where some still remembered his play in left field for the Ohio Independents. Sawhill is an example of how much the deaf community grew and thrived over the course of his lifetime, a time when a deaf man with deaf parents could be proudly named for a hearing man who had devoted his professional life to deaf education, a time when baseball came to deaf boys, and a time when deaf graduates built the social organizations and networks that would lead the deaf community solidly into the 20th century.

William Ellsworth Hoy

That leaves us to consider the Ohio School's most famous baseball alumni, William Ellsworth Hoy. Hoy was there in the thick of things, in the heyday of the Ohio School's time as a baseball powerhouse, as he attended the school from 1872 to 1879. As superintendent of the Ohio School Gilbert O. Fay recalled, "The athletic tone and bearing of the boys during those years was a matter of general admiration and pride. The Independent Base Ball Club won for itself a state and national reputation.... Nor was the general scholarship of the school lowered or crowded to the wall. I remember well the very creditable valedictory of W.E. Hoy, at the graduating exercises of June 24, 1879."[116] Parley Pratt explained, "Mr. Hoy was a member of the club, but we did not take him on the tour on account of his size and youth."[117] Rather than go out on the tour in 1879, Hoy went home.

We turn to his story in the next chapter.

William Ellsworth Hoy. The most famous graduate of the Ohio School for the Deaf, and the valedictorian of his 1879 class, Hoy would become the first deaf star in major league baseball. Courtesy Ohio History Connection.

2

The Radical Deafness of William "Dummy" Hoy

When the Ohio School's baseball team went out on its summer tour in 1879, Hoy did not accompany them. Coach Parley Pratt thought him too small in size (barely 5'5" and 145 pounds) and too young (17). Instead, Hoy went home. In spite of his obvious intelligence, as evidenced by the fact that he graduated as class valedictorian, his hearing parents assumed that his future would be severely limited by his deafness.

When Hoy's hearing sister reached 18, their father gave her a cow and a piano as her dowry. When his hearing brothers reached 21, their father gave them each in turn a new suit, a buggy, a harness, and a saddle. But Hoy remembered, "When I turned 21, my father gave me a suit of clothes and a promise of free board until I turned 24."[1] His parents had apparently determined he would have to live at home for a time, unlike his hearing brothers, on account of his disability.

Hoy had other ideas. He wanted to pursue a career in baseball. Soon, he took off for Oshkosh, Wisconsin, where landed a minor league contract in 1886. He was brought into major league baseball by Washington in 1888, and he promptly led the league that year in steals, with 82 thefts to his name. He joined the upstart Players' League in 1890, where he played for the Buffalo Bisons. In 1891, he played for the St. Louis Browns in the American Association. But he was soon back in the National League, in 1892, where he played through the years in Washington (1892–1893), Cincinnati (1894–1897, 1902), and Louisville (1898–1899). He again took a chance on a new league in 1901, heading for the fledgling American League and the Chicago White Stockings. He ended his career in the Pacific Coast League, where he played for Los Angeles in his final season as a professional ballplayer in 1903.[2] That 1903 team, incidentally, is considered one of the best minor league teams of all time and Hoy one of its most celebrated members.[3]

Like Dundon before him, Hoy had a brief experience with racially in-

1887 Oshkosh Base Ball Club, Hoy's first team as a professional baseball player. Hoy is seated crosslegged on the floor, on the left. Back row, from left to right: John Doran (third base), P.H. O'Connell (first base), James Burns (left field), G.H. Crock (pitcher), Edward Gastfield (catcher), W.B. Burdick (pitcher). Middle row, from left to right: Joe Wilson (catcher), Thomas Lovett (pitcher), Frank Seele (manager), Tom McCarthy (right field), Taylor Shafer (second base), Dan Shannon (captain and short stop). Seated, from left to right: Hoy (center field), Con Murphy (pitcher), James Cooney (short stop). Courtesy Robert Edward Auctions.

tegrated baseball in 1895. While playing for Cincinnati, the team agreed to a couple of pre-season games with a barnstorming black baseball team out of Adrian, Michigan, called the Page Fence Giants. The team name referred to their sponsor, J. Wallace Page, and his fence company. The Giants were founded in 1894 by the legendary 19th-century player Bud Fowler. Fowler was the first black professional baseball player, debuting in the International Association, arguably the first minor league, in 1878. He made his living in baseball professionally at nearly every level, with the exception of the major leagues. Fowler played initially in the racially integrated minor leagues of the 1880s and later played for, founded, and managed black barnstorming teams until around 1908.[4]

Fowler brought together an all-star team, featuring Sol White, Grant Johnson, and George Wilson.[5] King Solomon "Sol" White was a talented in-fielder, a successful manager who managed the Philadelphia Giants to four straight black baseball championships, and author, who would write the first history of black players in baseball in 1907. He was inducted into the Hall of Fame in 2006. Grant Johnson played on White's Giants in 1905. George Wilson started his baseball career with the Page Fence Giants and went on to pitch for black teams until 1907.

Scores of black fans came out to see the Page Fence Giants. "Every colored barber, every palace car porter, and every member of the local colored population of the male gender who could get off … was on the seats of the Cincinnati Park." Cincinnati had, in fact, fallen behind the Giants until the fourth inning, when Hoy hit a triple to tie the game up. Seizing the momentum from there, Cincinnati would eventually go on to win 11–7, but not before the Giants staged a late game rally that briefly threw a scare into the home team.

The local paper admitted that Bud Fowler's reputation had preceded him and it noted that he had "put together a great team of players" who had "batted and fielded in a way that surprised and delighted everyone."[6] The quality of play in the first game inspired the local paper to urge baseball fans to come out for the second game. That one, however, was never close, with the major leaguers running away with it, 16–2.[7] Of all the white players that the Giants faced for that two-game stand, Hoy was surely the only one who had attended a racially integrated school.

Hoy and Fowler had much in common. Like Hoy, Fowler played on integrated teams. Hoy was used to being the only deaf player on hearing teams and Fowler broke into the minors as the only black player on otherwise white teams. As Brian McKenna states unequivocally, "In black baseball history, he is *the* pioneer."[8] Like Hoy, Fowler fought against the stereotypes of his day, challenging the racism of white players and fans through his phenomenal baseball skills. Like Hoy, Fowler had a long career in baseball, spanning some 30 years, first as a player and then as a manager and promoter of black barnstorming teams.

Like Fowler, Hoy believed that baseball, potentially, had the power to change minds. As Susan Burch notes, "having Deaf athletes compete on the national scene—particularly in baseball, 'America's pastime'—challenged important stereotypes."[9] And like Fowler, Hoy was a minority in baseball at that point, a minority of one. When Hoy's path crossed briefly with that of Fowler in 1895, Hoy was the only deaf player in all of major league baseball, trying to prove himself to his hearing counterparts.

He earned their respect with his play. In 1891, *Sporting Life* reported, "[Charles] Comiskey says Hoy is the best man to lead off he has ever had, and that is saying a good deal when one remembers Latham in his prime."[10] By 1900, Hoy had agreed to play again for Comiskey, by then in Chicago. *The Chicago Tribune* reported, "Comiskey is much pleased at his success in landing Hoy. This player, he declares, is one of the best all-around men in the business. He is a good batter and fielder and is a gentleman on the field.... His physical handicap has always made him an interesting object to the fans, and he has repaid this interest by brilliant playing. Hoy probably has the best eye for a fly ball of any player now on the field ... hardly excelled by either Welch or Fogarty."[11]

Of his time with the Los Angeles LooLoos in 1903, Hoy's last year in professional baseball, the *Los Angeles Times* reported, "Hoy proved a ball player of great heart last year. His batting was consistently good and he usually came through with the little hit to right field when needed. His ability to lay down a bunt any time a man could be advanced by it, his fielding, and his successful work on the bases made him, while not a sensational player, an outfielder who could be relied upon to do the right thing at the proper time, and that is what counts."[12]

Finally, Honus Wagner remarked in 1916, "Dummy Hoy, the deaf mute, who played with Louisville and Cincinnati in my early days in the majors, was a most

HOY, C. F., Washington
Copyrighted by GOODWIN & CO. 188?
OLD JUDGE
CIGARETTES.
GOODWIN & CO., New York.

An early Hoy baseball card, from his time with Washington. Created by Goodwin & Co., between 1887 and 1890. Library of Congress.

wonderful player, on whose ears were lost any benefits that others could receive though oral coaching.... He never became entangled in a mix-up nor did he lose any short ones or long ones through misunderstanding.... How Hoy handled his position without hearing and without blunders is a sad commentary on some outfielders who can see, hear, and yell, but still go piling into each other. Considering his handicap and giving him credit for lots of ability, I regard Hoy as one of the greatest outfielders I ever played with."[13]

Due in part to his longevity as a player, Hoy remains the best-known deaf player in baseball history. Despite the fact that no deaf fan living today ever saw him play, his name still has commands near instant recognition in deaf circles, more than one hundred years after his playing career ended. This is surely due to the fact that Hoy has become an iconic figure within the deaf community.

Deaf artists have had a hand in memorializing Hoy. Deaf artist Nancy Rourke studied graphic design at the National Technical Institute of the Deaf at the Rochester Institute of Technology. She is closely associated with the deaf art movement known as De'VIA (Deaf View/Image Art). The celebration of deaf history has long been an important theme in Rourke's work, and she has painted portraits of many important figures from transatlantic deaf history. She painted Hoy in 2012 to mark the 150th anniversary of his birth.

This painting of Hoy honors his powerful presence in the memory of the American deaf community. Image courtesy of the artist, Nancy Rourke.

Warren Miller, a Deaf artist who also studied graphic design at the Rochester Institute of Technology, seeks to produce artistic work that "illustrates my views of deaf culture and the deaf experience. I want my art to serve as a bridge between the deaf and hearing world."[14] He produced this striking image of Hoy, emphasizing his status as a deaf player. Visually, Hoy's deafness is indicated by his lack of a mouth, to indicate his muteness, the source of his nickname,

"Dummy." In Hoy's lifetime, "dumb" still meant "mute" and deaf people were largely referred to as "deaf and dumb." Deaf people largely emphasized that they were "mute" or "signing people," and referred to hearing people as "speaking people," well into the middle of the 19th century. The term "speaking people" is a more accurate translation of the ASL sign HEARING PERSON, which is usually rendered in English as "hearing," but which is made at the mouth and not at the ear. "Speaking people" implies that hearing people speak, while deaf people sign. Speaking becomes more clearly delineated as a hearing behavior.[15]

This illustration of Hoy emphasizes his status as a deaf player by focusing on his eyes. By portraying him without a mouth, Hoy's preference for sign over speech is made clear to viewers. Image courtesy of the artist, Warren Miller.

The nickname "Dummy" was always meant to refer to Hoy's lack of speech. He was, to hearing players at the turn of the century, colloquially speaking, deaf and dumb. As *Time* magazine explained to readers in Hoy's obituary in 1961, "in the blunt innocence of a bygone age, [he] was affectionately dubbed 'Dummy' by his teammates."[16] Hoy himself insisted that people continue to use his nickname throughout his career, even as "dumb" acquired more pernicious meanings. He knew the spirit in which it was originally given to him by his teammates.

But the deaf community was not universally as sanguine about this nickname. They knew that "dummy" was on its way to signaling not simply muteness but stupidity. They did not find anything innocent or affectionate about that.

For Alexander Pach, a fiery deaf journalist who contributed a regular column in *The Silent Worker*, the leading deaf press of the time, the nickname rankled. He complained bitterly that the effect of calling deaf baseball players by this nickname was that "every other deaf man who comes within the focus of the public eye is a dummy." This was clearly an "insult." He urged the deaf press to protest the use of this word in all sports coverage.[17]

By 1914, though, Pach had thrown in the towel. "I suppose the word 'Dummy' is here to stay," he conceded. "I used to fight it, but it was not any use. As an epithet carrying a contemptuous meaning I think it has passed except among the very ignorant. Baseball players fairly revel in nicknames … 'Rube,' … 'Chief,' … 'Slim,' … so it was natural and to be expected that deaf players come to be known and in a great sense loved as 'Dummy' Hoy." Besides, he reasoned, "there's a million miles of difference between 'Dummy' malicious and 'Dummy' affectionate."[18]

Alexander Pach was a fascinating figure to take up this cause. He had lost his hearing in 1879, at the age of 15, to meningitis. He immediately enrolled in the New York School for the Deaf and in 1882 graduated as valedictorian. He

Prominent deaf journalist Alexander Pach. Pach wrote a regular column for the deaf newspaper, *The Silent Worker*. He fought against the use of the nickname "Dummy" for deaf ball players, arguing that it was demeaning and insulting to the deaf community. Image courtesy Gallaudet University Archives.

entered into the family business, Pach Brothers, one of the oldest photography studios in New York City, which opened in 1867 and specialized in portraits.[19] An American-born deaf man of German Jewish descent, Pach chose to embrace a deaf identity above all others. Despite how late deafened he was, Pach embraced his deafness and became a leading figure within the deaf world.

In many ways, Pach's turn of the century life exemplifies the 21st-century idea of deaf gain. In their recent book *Deaf Gain: Raising the Stakes for Human Diversity* (2014), editors H-Dirksen L. Bauman and Joseph J. Murray advance their theory of deaf gain. The pair coined the term "to counter the frame of hearing loss as it refers to the unique cognitive, creative, and cultural gains manifested through deaf ways of being in the world."[20] In other words, they challenge us to think not about losing one's hearing, but about gaining one's deafness. Seen in that light, what would it mean to gain deafness?

2. The Radical Deafness of William "Dummy" Hoy

Bauman and Murray view deaf gain as having three distinct inflections, with three lines of exploration and explanation. The first is "deaf benefit," by which they mean to draw attention to the benefits of deafness to the individual deaf person, cognitively, socially, and psychologically. The next is "deaf contribute," where the pair direct attention to the benefits that the existence of a deaf/sign language using community provides to humanity as a whole. Finally, we have "deaf ahead," or the alternate English translation, "taking the lead," by which Bauman and Murray indicate the ways in which deaf people have, can, and will transform the public sphere with thinking that is ahead of that of hearing contemporaries.[21]

Pach was one such person who did not see himself as losing his hearing but as gaining his deafness. Deafened at 15, he might have attempted to pass as hearing. After all, by 1879, the year he became deaf, the deaf educational system in the United States was torn by a major pedagogical battle. Manual schools (schools that taught with the use of the sign language) were challenged by oral schools (schools that taught all deaf children with speech and lip reading, and in most cases forbid the use of any gestural communication, including both sign language and fingerspelling, in its schools for the deaf).

HOY, C. F. Washington

OLD JUDGE
CIGARETTES.
GOODWIN & CO., New York.

Another early baseball card image of Hoy, this time showing off his throwing arm. Created by Goodwin & Co., between 1887 and 1890. Library of Congress.

45

As the 20th century opened, oralism was gaining the upper hand in deaf education.[22]

As an educational philosophy, oralism aimed to make it possible for deaf people, and particularly late deafened people like Pach, to pass as hearing. Oralist teachers hoped that deaf people would no longer sign to communicate, but rather would talk and read lips. In this way, oralists imagined, deaf people would be rescued from their own community and culture and would be fully assimilated into hearing society, as people who, if they did not hear, could at least communicate like hearing people. Oralists encouraged deaf people to act like hearing people.

Oral education not only focused on getting deaf people to communicate with speech like hearing people, it also tried to get them to use sound more generally in an acceptable hearing way. Remembrances of the heyday of oral education find deaf adults recalling how hearing teachers tried to teach them how to laugh like a hearing person, to sound "normal."[23] It was not enough that deaf people would communicate like hearing people. Their use of the voice must in all cases be made to approximate hearing norms. The project of passing went well beyond mere speech.

By the late 19th century, oralism's greatest champion was Alexander Graham Bell. Bell used the funds from his 1880 French Volta prize for the invention of the telephone to promote the oralist cause. His involvement in this cause drew other wealthy patrons to take an interest. Both Thomas Edison and Andrew Carnegie joined the leading oralist organization of the day, the American Association for the Promotion and Teaching of Speech to the Deaf (founded in 1890 by Bell and renamed the Alexander Graham Bell Association for the Deaf in 1956).

The oralist cause benefited from this influx of support. "Such financial and institutional support," historian Susan Burch writes, "enabled oralists to initiate a massive public education campaign. Public speeches, meetings between oralists and influential politicians, and numerous articles in mainstream publications and professional journals helped to spread the concept of oralism to school boards, doctors' offices, and state legislatures' appropriations committees."[24]

Oralism, its supporters argued, would make deaf people over in a hearing image. With Bell's powerful support, oralism came to dominate the field of deaf education by the early 20th century.[25] In a painful twist, the very existence of the deaf community was invoked as proof that deaf education needed to embrace the oralist philosophy. Deaf people saw their community, with its language, schools, newspapers, journals, churches, social clubs, and political organizations, as a point of pride. They had built a collective life, together, one that allowed deaf people to live full, rich, satisfying lives as deaf American citizens. Oralists saw it quite differently. As historian Douglas Baynton puts it, "The image of an insular, inbred, and proliferating deaf culture became a potent weapon for the oralist cause."[26] Deaf people were shocked to see the community they had worked so hard to build, the community in which they took such pride, depicted as nothing more than an insular, inbred, eugenic dystopia. Just as oralism's attacks on the deaf community were arguably reaching their peak, William Ellsworth Hoy emerged as a deaf hero who stood up for his embattled community, the deaf community, and its language, during this dangerous time.

Alexander Pach did likewise, voluntarily aligning himself with this community and actively defending it. He contributed a regular column for *The Silent Worker*, writing "The Silent Worker with the Silent Workers" from 1896 to 1929. *The Silent Worker*, published monthly out of the New Jersey School for the Deaf, was arguably the most prominent national newspaper of the deaf community of its day. It was published from 1888 to 1929.[27] He was a member of the National Fraternal Society of the Deaf, founded in 1901. By 1930, the NFSD was the "largest and strongest organization of the Deaf in America."[28] Pach became an outspoken champion of the NFSD, as it welcomed both Jews and Christians as members. He was critical of the notion of a separate deaf Jewish identity because, as Sarah Abrevaya Stein puts it, he "worried that an articulation of deaf Jews' difference might alienate them from deaf America and even put their patriotism in question."[29]

Pach's concerns were hardly overblown. Jewish Americans faced anti–Semitism, and increased Jewish immigration in the period collided with cultural concerns of native born Americans over the nation's ability to assimilate newcomers. The question of who could be a good American, however, was the same one that fueled increasing support for oralism. The deaf community faced the same complaint from oralists, namely, that their separate community, with its distinct language, was a threat to the unity of the United States. And their deaf children posed a eugenic threat to the hearing variety of the human race.

Pach's unqualified support for the unified Frat must therefore be seen as a reflection of his times. He wanted all deaf people to join together, to combat the forces that threatened their community and their language. Just as he had done, Pach wanted all deaf people, regardless of when or how they had acquired their deafness, to choose a deaf identity, to join the larger deaf community, and to defend it.

Pach's concern about deaf ballplayers and how they were perceived and treated by the larger hearing public now makes more sense. Given that the oralist cause was at its peak during the turn of the century, the cultural importance of William Hoy for the larger deaf community as countervailing public symbol of the benefits of sign language comes into sharper focus.

Few deaf people were well-known in the hearing world, either then or now, for that matter. Hearing oralists like Bell preached that the best way for deaf people to function in the hearing world was to act like hearing people. While oralists praised the image of a speaking deaf person passing as hearing, Hoy made no effort to pass. Instead, Hoy demonstrated that the best way for a deaf person to guarantee success and acceptance in society was as to embrace one's deaf identity. In a time when the larger deaf community was under attack, the deaf press unsurprisingly seized on Hoy as both a representative and a role model—he was the right man to project a proud vision of deafness for hearing fans.

As historian Susan Burch puts it, "Hoy embodied the American dream for the Deaf.... As a noncollege graduate who communicated only in signs and in writing, he displayed the abilities of common Deaf people."[30] The deaf press unsurprisingly emphasized Hoy's silence, highlighting his use of the sign language precisely at a moment when the communication preferences of the deaf community were being challenged by oralists.

For despite oralist fantasies to the contrary, the reality was that most deaf people did not pass as hearing. They simply couldn't; the task of acquiring speech was too arduous and the practice of lipreading was too unreliable. The deaf community continued to value sign over speech throughout these oralist years. Increasingly, the deaf community fought back against the hearing assumption that if you cannot speak, you must be stupid.

This was an assumption stoked by oralist educators themselves. Oralists described "nonvoicing Deaf people as 'oral failures,' somehow defective, deviant, even un–American."[31] For these so-called failures, oralist teachers recommended a transfer to a manual program which permitted the use of the sign language. That recommendation pointed to one unmistakable conclusion—namely, only less intelligent deaf people would sign to communicate.

For deaf people, this harmful oralist propaganda was all the more reason to praise non-speaking, signing sports stars as potent examples of what the deaf community wanted the hearing community to understand: You can succeed in the hearing world without speech and the best way to make your way as a deaf person in the larger hearing world is with sign language. Having a signing, nonspeaking deaf man like Hoy as a prominent public figure was electrifying for the deaf community.

Hoy made his way in the world as a deaf man and insisted that his teammates accommodate him as such. The hearing ballplayers were not going to be able to communicate with him in a hearing fashion. Yet, to function as a team, they would have to find some reliable ways to communicate. Hoy pioneered the way here, using a combination of fingerspelling and a distinctly deaf voice.

Hoy employed fingerspelling extensively with all of his teams. It was a deaf way to communicate, to be sure. Left to their own devices, after all, most hearing people did not take up the manual alphabet. The knowledge and easy use of fingerspelling tended to mark one as a member of the larger deaf community, or at least as someone culturally in the know, familiar with that community's linguistic preferences. Fingerspelling, like signing in public, made the hidden physical difference of deafness visible. Yet, in another sense, it was a hearing-friendly way to communicate. In fingerspelling, one reproduces English letters on the fingers. In this way, it represents a good compromise for both sides. It is a manual style of communication, more reliable for deaf people, but, unlike American Sign Language, fingerspelling can be used to reproduce the grammar and spelling of English, more comfortable for the hearing people.

Press coverage of Hoy's career is full of examples of this widespread use of fingerspelling in major league baseball. The manual alphabet appeared in use on all of the teams and in all of the cities where he played. Hoy played for the St. Louis Browns in the American Association in 1891. Their first baseman and manager was Charles Comiskey. On a road trip, it was reported that "every day at dinner the boys studied Hoy as he wiggled his fingers. He was teaching them the deaf and dumb alphabet and spent hour after hour doing it, until he had every man on the team talking the finger language fluently."[32]

The road trip continued.

In Baltimore, Comiskey was taken for a mute by one of the guests of the hotel. As he was walking out of the dining room, he heard some one behind him say, "See that long, lean, lank fellow going out there? He is one of a deaf and dumb party that arrived here this morning." "Get out, that's Comiskey, the captain of the Browns," responded another voice. The first man replied, "I'll bet you five it isn't." Comiskey, of course, overheard the entire exchange; he decided to have a little fun. With the bet on, one of the men approached him. "Ain't you Charles Comiskey of the Browns?" said the positive guest, tapping Comiskey on the shoulder. Commie produced a pad and pencil and wrote: "You'll have to write it; I am deaf and dumb." Comiskey said he never saw a man look so cheap in his life as the fellow who lost the five. "That big dummy is the best ringer for Comiskey you could pick out of a million," said the crushed fellow to himself as he walked off.[33]

When Hoy played for the Cincinnati Reds, from 1894 to 1898, it was reported that "[he] was so admired by his teammates that the Reds all learned sign language ... [there were] times when the players would be having dinner and would communicate exclusively by sign language to avoid being interrupted by autograph seeking fans."[34]

When Hoy went to Chicago, manager Clark Griffith, a hearing man, learned how to fingerspell and the team used the manual alphabet to send in signals, that is, until the opposing team figured them out. As Griffith put it, "The letter S meant steal.... H was the signal for the hit and run. And B was the bunt sign. I'd make some meaningless motions with my fingers, of course, to cover the signals."[35] Here again, Bauman and Murray's theory of deaf gain comes to mind. Clark Griffith saw the ways in which the deaf both contribute and are ahead of the hearing people. He quickly saw the power of gestural communication and the advantages that it could give him over rival teams if he adopted it for himself.

Sign language proved the key to incorporating Hoy into every team for which he played. He was regarded as a pretty good lipreader, but he did not speak. (Actually, it is not clear that he communicated only in those ways. *The Sporting Life* reported in 1893 that Hoy was learning to talk. "So far," the reporter noted, "his vocabulary consists solely of swear words for use against umpires."[36]) In fact, by the time that Hoy attended the Ohio School, the school had already abandoned the practice of teaching what were then called semi-mutes exclusively by oral methods.

Terminology regarding audiological differences has changed over the years. Then as now, there were deaf people and hearing people, though in the 19th century, deaf people sometimes referred to hearing people as "speaking people," while calling themselves either deaf people or "mute people." Such terminology was meant to underscore that the difference between hearing and deaf people, from a deaf point of view, was not their audiological status but rather their communication preferences. Speaking people talked, while mute people signed to communicate and did not speak.

Additionally, there were people with varying degrees of hearing loss. The 20th century would come to label all of those people as "hard of hearing," implicitly claiming them as audiologically challenged members of the hearing community. Nineteenth-century deaf people, on the other hand, used such terminology to indicate that they understood an audiologically diverse range of people as being of varying degrees of deaf and not as deviating from a hearing-centered norm, as the phrase "hard of hearing" would imply. So they referred not to "hard of hearing" people but rather to "semi-mute" or "semi-deaf" people, again identifying such people in terms of their communication preferences.

Semi-mute referred to those profoundly deaf people who knew sign language but who also used some speech to communicate. They were no longer fully mute people, but semi-mute. Semi-deaf generally referred to hard of hearing people. Semi-deaf people typically would not know any sign language. If they were very late deafened and completely without sign language, deaf people might refer to them as "only deaf," a term meant to refer to those people who had lost their hearing well after they had learned how to speak—that is, they were not "mute" at all and they were now "only deaf."[37]

The Ohio School had experimented with a separate system of oral-only instruction for 31 semi-mute students in the 1869–70 academic year but had abandoned it the following year. For 1870–71, they were instead offering classes in articulation to semi-mutes. However, these classes were not limited only to semi-mute students but were open to any other deaf student who wanted to try speech lessons. There is no evidence that Hoy ever took speech classes when he was a student at Ohio.[38]

Yet, to communicate with his fellow outfielders during a game, Hoy routinely used his voice. When he joined the Washington Nationals, he posted an explanatory note on the clubhouse wall. "Being totally deaf as you know and some of my teammates being unacquainted with my play, I think it is timely to bring about an understanding between myself, the left fielder, the shortstop and the second baseman, and the right fielder. The main point is to avoid possible collisions with any of these four who surround me when in the field going for a fly ball. When I take a fly ball I always yell 'I'll take it'—the same as I have been doing for many seasons…. Whenever you don't hear me yell, it is understood I am not after the ball."[39]

While his system of signaling his intentions worked well over the course of his career, Hoy did not actually yell out this phrase as described. In truth, Hoy did not speak English, though he did regularly use his voice in the outfield. As Tommy Leach, Hoy's teammate in Louisville, recalled, "When you played with him in the outfield, the thing was that you never called for a ball. You listened for him, and if he made this little squeaky sound, that meant he was going to take it."[40] This was oral communication, to be sure, but this "little squeaky sound" wasn't what oralists had in mind when they urged deaf people to use their voices to communicate. But Hoy quickly realized that he had to communicate in ways that would be successful and not simply conform to hearing ideas about the appropriate use of sound and the voice.

Hoy was keenly aware that he had to convince his hearing teammates that a deaf centerfielder could actually work with them, not merely pass as one of them. He knew that he faced prejudice on account of his deafness. As he put it, "deafness is such a heavy handicap, at least in the eyes of his manager and his team-mates, that he is obliged to demonstrate in every play he makes that he has superior judgment, wonderful observation, and quick wit in order to overcome their natural aversion at having a deaf player hold an important position on the team."[41] Using his voice effectively, though in a clearly deaf way, as a part of the team, was one way to overcome those prejudices.

Elsewhere, Hoy went further, directly challenging the so-called "natural aversion" that hearing players had to a deaf baseball player. Hoy believed that his deafness gave him an edge as a ball player and offered him an advantage over hearing players. Hoy provided an extensive analysis of how his deafness positively affected all parts of his game:

> In batting there is really little handicap for a mute. I can see the ball as well as others.... I think, perhaps, the fact that I have to depend so much on my eyes helps me in judging what the umpire will call a strike, and if the ball delivered is a little off I wait for four bad ones. In base running the signals of the hit and run game and other strategies are mostly silent, the same as for the other players. By a further system of signs my teammates keep me posted on how many are out and what is going on about me.... Because I can not hear the coaching I have acquired the habit of running with my neck twisted to watch the progress of the ball. I think most players depend too much on the coachers and often a man is coached along too far or not far enough, when, if he knew where the ball was himself, he would know what chances were best for him to take. In judging fly balls I depend on sight alone and must keep my eye constantly on the batsman to watch for a possible fly, since I can not hear the crack of the bat. This alertness, I think, helps me in other departments of the game. So it may be seen, the handicaps of a deaf ball player are minimized.[42]

We get a rare glimpse here into how Hoy himself understood the ways in which his deafness made him a better ballplayer. Hoy's self-reflection makes it clear that his deafness made a significant contribution to his own game. In discussing the advantages provided to him by his deafness, Hoy anticipated the work of Bauman and Murray. He experienced what many hearing Americans might perceive to be a hearing loss instead as his deaf gain.

Furthermore, the deaf gain model underscores that a culturally deaf position has always been one that needed to be actively claimed and defended. The hearing majority has never been particularly open to the idea that being deaf is a physical characteristic to cherish, one that adds a beneficial diversity to our society. Deaf people themselves have had to take the lead in demonstrating this understanding of deafness to hearing people. For the entirety of Hoy's career, he represented to the hearing public a specifically deaf claim to the mainstream of American life, as he played as a recognizable deaf athlete in a hearing league and as one who regarded his deafness as a benefit to his performance as a ballplayer.

His alertness in "other departments of the game," as Hoy put it, is reflected in the sense of many of his peers that Hoy was a brainy player. He thought deeply about the game and paid close attention to it. Third baseman Lave Cross recalled Hoy as a player who "introduced many curious and wonderful innovations into the game in his day." Cross remembered one game where he faced Hoy.

> In the first inning, the man ahead of me in the batting order sent a long, low fly to Hoy, which he caught after a hard run and we all noticed that he held the ball for a long time after it was in his hands. When the ball finally came back, the pitcher picked it up carefully, looked at it, as if he were searching for something, and then gave me two low in curves, at which I made futile swings. Out of sheer curiosity, I stepped on the plate and asked to see the ball. The catcher handed it over, and there on its new white surface was scratched in Hoy's well-known hand: "Low in curve." The pitcher had followed Dummy's tip and already had me 0–2. And even then Hoy had not exhausted his ingenuity, for he lifted his hands and gave [pitcher Billy] Rhines a sign signal, which I interpreted as meaning "fast one, straight across," but which really was a "slow one" and I struck out, greatly to Hoy's delight.[43]

By the time Hoy retired from the sport, he had been playing professional baseball for a living in a variety of major leagues as a centerfielder for 14 seasons. In 1,796 major league games, he amassed 2,044 hits, 248 doubles, 121 triples, 40 home runs, scored 1,426 runs, stole 594 bases, had 274 career assists, had a career fielding percentage of .915, and had a career batting average of .288. His batting average exceeded the league average of .281. His combined on-base and slugging percentage of .759 exceeds the league average of .725.[44] As Ed Koszarek points out, "In period stats 1890–1899, [Hoy] ranks: third in games, sixth in at bats, eighth in runs, third in walks, sixth in hit by pitches, fourth in stolen bases, second in sacrifices."[45]

In 1901, with the Chicago White Stockings, and nearing the end of his career, Hoy recorded his highest fielding percentage, .958. He hit lead off for the White Stockings and led the team in doubles (28), on base+slugging percentage (.807) and OPS+ (126). He hit .294 for the season. He also holds the distinction of being the first player in the American League to hit a grand slam, which came in a game against the Detroit Tigers on May 1, 1901.[46] His performance helped propel the White Stockings to the first American League pennant, making the team the first champions in League history. In 1903, at the age of 41, playing for the Los Angeles Angels in the newly formed Pacific Coast League, he hit .257, stole 48 bases, and led the league in runs batted in (157). Hoy was the only player to appear in all 211 games, coming to bat 808 times. The team compiled a record of 133–78 and won the first PCL pennant.[47] Hoy retired from the sport on top.

For a player who last played in the majors in 1902, Hoy still appears within the top 100 of several career records' lists. His 596 career stolen bases rank him 19th on that list, and he finished in the top 10 for basestealers five times over the course of his career, in 1891, 1892, 1893, 1895, and 1898. His 72 career double plays turned as an outfielder puts him eighth on that list; he also appeared in the top 10 for double plays turned in eight seasons in his career, in 1888, 1890, 1893, 1895, 1897, 1898, 1899, and 1901. His 274 career assists as an outfielder puts him at 14th on the all-time list, with four seasons in the top 10, in 1888, 1889, 1891, and 1894. His 3,964 career putouts as an outfielder puts him 77th on that list, and he was top 10 as a league leader 10 times in his career in this category, from 1888 to 1901.[48] His 1,429 career runs scored puts him 84th on that all-time list. He appeared three times on top 10 lists here during his career, in 1891, 1899, and 1901, his last year in the majors. He is still, just barely, holding onto a spot in the top 100 players with career triples, coming in at number 98 with 121.

Finally, his career on-base percentage of .386 has him at number 126, nestled between Albert Pujols and Larry Doby. He also appeared in the top 10 for four seasons for his on-base percentage, in 1888, 1890, 1891, and 1901. His numbers have held up well, particularly given that his major league career ended more than 115 years ago. There have been a lot of players with chances to push him out of the top 100 on records' lists in over a century of trying.[49]

Hoy has consistently made numerous best-of lists through the years. Bill James, the father of sabermetrics, ranks Hoy as one of the top 10 rookie centerfielders (at number five) and as one of the top 10 best old centerfielders (at number six), a player who held his value and remained productive through the years. For instance, he remained in the top five players in the American League towards the end of his career in 1901 for fielding percentage (fourth, with .958) and for doubles (fifth, with 28). Interestingly, the only other players to appear with him on both of James's lists are Tris Speaker and Earl Averill, both Hall of Famers.[50] James also counts Hoy as a noteworthy leadoff man, putting him in the company of players like Mookie Wilson, Pee Wee Reese, Paul Molitor, Dom DiMaggio, and Phil Rizzuto.[51]

In 2011, Frederick Taylor ranked him at number 37 on a list of top leadoff batters of all time.[52] In 1989, the Society for American Baseball Research counted him as one of the great 19th-century stars of baseball; in 1974, Mac Davis listed Hoy as one of baseball's 100 greatest heroes; in 1954, Ira Smith called him one of baseball's most famous outfielders; and in 1911, W.W. Aulick deemed Hoy number 46 on his list of 100 notable figures in baseball, because he carried "a concealed weapon up his right sleeve in the shape of an arm which was capable of shooting the pill from deep centre field to the plate without a relay."[53]

Due in part to his longevity and consistency as a player, Hoy remains the best-known deaf player in baseball history. Despite the fact that no deaf fan living today ever saw him play, his name still commands near instant recognition in deaf circles, more than one hundred years after his playing career ended. Though Hoy has become an iconic figure within the deaf community, he is not as well remembered in the hearing world. Deaf fans are dismayed by this lack of recognition because to them, as Hoy fan and deaf professor Robert Panara has explained, Hoy is the deaf community's Jackie Robinson: "Jackie broke the color barrier; Hoy broke the communication barrier."[54]

Given his level of play, it becomes a bit clearer why he would be, at least among deaf people, mentioned side by side with Jackie Robinson. He did not just play in the majors, like Dundon. Hoy announced his arrival with a spectacular rookie year and kept going from there. He is on top 10 lists for performances in his rookie year of 1888 and he was still appearing on them in his final year in 1901. To him, then, falls the title of first, in spite of Dundon's earlier appearance. Hoy is the deaf community's first deaf baseball star in a hearing league.

Seeing Hoy as a figure like Jackie Robinson also depends, to a large extent, on seeing deaf Americans as a minority group, like African Americans. Hoy can only be a "deaf Jackie Robinson" if there is a larger community that he represents, just as Jackie represented his community on the field. In this case, greater recognition for Hoy, as a ball player, would also mean greater recognition of and respect for his community, the larger American deaf community.

But there is a way in which this label of "the deaf Jackie Robinson" also misleads. Jackie Robinson is known to all baseball fans, black, white, and brown alike. His number is retired for all clubs. He is regarded as a first in African American history and a first in American history. Jackie Robinson is universally acknowledged as an American hero. By contrast, William Ellsworth Hoy, for all his similarity in blazing a trail into unknown territory, for being a first, is largely forgotten in the hearing world, an obscure figure, so unlike Jackie.

Deaf fans have wondered why this should be the case. From their point of view, their Jackie Robinson has been unfairly overlooked. Deaf fans have been actively trying to get Hoy into the National Baseball Hall of Fame, in Cooperstown, New York, since 1952. That year, the National Association of the Deaf (NAD) launched a campaign on Hoy's behalf that was supported by major hearing sportswriters, including Shirley Povich and Vincent Flaherty.

Povich, sportswriter for *The Washington Post*, reported on the NAD's campaign, writing, "The National Association for the Deaf is backing William E. (Dummy) Hoy for election to baseball's Hall of Fame. It points out that the Hall of Fame lists seven players whose lifetime batting averages are lower than the .288 of Hoy, the only deaf mute ever to play in the majors."[55]

Flaherty, sports columnist of the *Los Angeles Examiner*, wrote, "Hoy's all-time record and the place he won in the hearts of the fans long ago, entitle him to a place in the baseball Hall of Fame…. Unfortunately, and for some inexplicable reason, the Cooperstown wheel grinds slowly."[56]

Hoy received another burst of public attention in the late 1950s, as he neared his 100th birthday. The Reds invited him to a game to celebrate his 96th birthday in 1958. Ray Bressler, a former Cincinnati player himself, was by then serving as president of the Ballplayers of Yesteryear Association, a Cincinnati based group of former major leaguers who sought "to promote baseball among the youth of Cincinnati, especially the underprivileged."[57] Bressler sent a telegram to the White House, saying, "We hope you will favor this grand old man by sending him a telegram. While Mr. Hoy was handicapped by lack of speech and hearing, he played the game well. One of the pioneers of the game that did so much to make this great country sportminded."[58]

An internal discussion followed at the White House. Associate Special Counsel to the President Edward McCabe wrote to Eisenhower's staff assistant Fred Fox, arguing that the president should send along birthday wishes. "Because of the President's concern for the physically handicapped, I think a telegram here would be appropriate," McCabe suggested. "As you know, there are many 'old timers' days—generally involving a couple of innings of active play. I doubt if every gathering like that should call for a message. However, this one is different, since Hoy made such a mark despite his handicaps."[59]

McCabe did not want to see the president pressured to send messages to all old-timers, but he knew that Hoy was a player who connected with the President's politics. In 1953, Eisenhower had sent a congratulatory note to the New England Gallaudet Association of the Deaf, the first organization for deaf people in the United States, founded in 1854. In 1953, they were raising a memorial to the founders of the American School for the Deaf. Eisenhower commended the organization for honoring those men "who first undertook to make available to the deaf the richness and solace of learning," adding, "I take this opportunity to send my best wishes to the school, to the New England Gallaudet Association for the Deaf, and to all who have contributed to this occasion."[60]

Two years later, in 1955, Eisenhower issued Executive Order 10640, making the President's Committee on the Employment of the Physically Handicapped a permanent organization. On May 23, 1955, Eisenhower had addressed the Committee as follows: "We have a country dedicated to equality of opportunity. We make much in many Fourth of July speeches that this equality of opportunity goes to all, regardless of race, color, religion, and so on…. Indeed, this word 'opportunity' seems to me to contain much that means happiness for the human—opportunity to expand and to be useful, to know that he is contributing his share to the advancement of that great society of which he is a part…. So it seems to me we cannot afford for one moment to neglect placing opportunity in front of all that are capable of doing anything whatsoever with it. And the mere fact that a person may be minus a limb or one of his senses, or anything else, has nothing to do with it, any more than do the other differences among humans that we conclude should not be allowed to sway us in the government that is applied to all. I could think of no greater service that this Committee over the years has contributed to the United States than to bring to each—not only the handicapped people themselves but to all of us—the fact that opportunity does truly belong to all."[61]

Given his straightforward support for equal opportunity for all Americans, it is not surprising to see that Eisenhower did send a telegram on game night. He noted Hoy's deafness, but he did not dwell on it, writing, "Despite the handicaps of speech and hearing, Mr. Hoy established a fine record in major league baseball. As a pioneer of this great American game, he is a living example of the benefits of keen and vigorous sportsmanship. It is a pleasure to add my congratulations to Mr. Hoy, and best wishes to all assembled in his honor."[62]

Another organized national push for the Hall came in the 1990s. The deaf community mounted a letter writing campaign in 1992, coordinated by the Committee for William "Dummy" Hoy, a committee under the auspices of the American Athletic Association of the Deaf. Deaf organizations from across the ideological spectrum united behind Hoy. Manualist organizations, like the National Association of the Deaf (NAD) and the National Fraternal Society of the Deaf, wrote in his favor. So did oralist organizations, like Self Help for Hard of Hearing People (SHHH) and the Alexander Graham Bell Association for the Deaf. Both American deaf universities, the National Technical Institute for the Deaf at the Rochester Institute of Technology and Gallaudet University, wrote letters. The National Theatre of the Deaf, the first deaf theater troupe dedicated to bringing American Sign Language to the stage and promoting the artistic talents of deaf actors, wrote a letter, as did the hearing playwright Allen Meyer, author of a Broadway play about Hoy called *The Signal Season of Dummy Hoy*. For interested readers, copies of all of these letters are on file at the Giamatti Research Center at the National Baseball Hall of Fame.

It is truly remarkable to see the entire cross-section of the deaf community represented here. By the late 20th century, the deaf community was rarely as publicly united as this. The years of pedagogical battles, of oralist control of the schools, and of the suppression of the sign language, had taken their toll on the larger deaf community. Where early 20th century members of the deaf community had managed to stay united across the oralist-manualist divide, as we shall see in later chapters, such unity had long faded by the 1990s. Signers and speakers were increasingly pitted against one another and the organizations which represented each group more often than not found themselves taking opposing positions on public issues related to the deaf community.

The Alexander Graham Bell Association, for instance, most typically wrote public letters of opposition against any positive public display of signing deaf people, which by rights should include Hoy, a figure known for his public use and support of the sign language. The Bell Association has a very long tradition of resisting any positive depiction of sign language in American popular culture.

In 1967, they threatened a boycott of NBC for broadcasting a performance of the National Theatre of the Deaf, specifically "to counteract this effort to make the sign language of the deaf to be an artistic form to be encouraged in the theater" because "continuing to display sign language on nationwide TV destroys the efforts of thousands of parents of deaf children and teachers of the deaf who are trying to teach deaf children to speak." They added, "We are opposed to any programming which indicates that the use of the language of signs is inevitable for deaf children or it is anything more than an artificial language, and a foreign one at that, for the deaf of this country." NBC was caught off guard, but to their credit, brought the matter to the director of NTD, David Hays, who argued instead that the broadcast would "show highly gifted deaf people working in a developed art form of great beauty." NBC agreed and aired the program.[63]

In 2008, the Bell Association was back, this time protesting a sign language Super Bowl Pepsi commercial. The commercial, which can still be viewed online, features a riff on an oft told joke in the deaf community. In this 2008 version, two deaf men are driving to a Super Bowl party. They enter a dark suburban cul de sac and soon realize that neither of them can remember the house number that they are looking for. Worried that they will miss the kickoff, they hit upon a solution. The driver lays on the horn. All the lights come on, up and down the cul de sac, in the hearing houses, as neighbors flick the lights and open their doors to see where all the noise is coming from. One house remains dark. "That's it!" the driver signs, excitedly. They pull into the driveway, and arrive on time for the Super Bowl, Pepsi and chips in hand.

It really is a classic, and there are many variations. Another common version is that a deaf couple arrives at a hotel and check into their room. The husband goes back out to the car, to retrieve an item they forgot, and realizes he cannot remember the room number. He lays on the horn and the only dark room remaining must be the one where his wife is. Most deaf people watching this Pepsi commercial, in other words, would have been deeply familiar with this basic set up, which becomes part of the pleasure of watching it. It is funny because the joke is on hearing people. It is a joke about how deaf people can use hearing people's hearingness against them.[64]

The Alexander Graham Bell Association was not amused, suggesting that the company, instead of promoting sign language, could use the budget for the proposed signing Super Bowl commercial instead to "help an untold number of families obtain hearing aids and other professional services that are costly and in many cases not covered by medical insurance."

Most recently, in 2016, the Bell Association took aim at Nyle DiMarco, the deaf winner of the popular television show *Dancing with the Stars*, and at his foundation, the Nyle DiMarco Foundation, which promotes access to ASL for deaf infants. Sign language use, the Association pointedly informed DiMarco, is declining: "deaf children can hear and talk."[65]

This is an organization, in other words, with a terrible track record for supporting signing deaf adults. But here they were in 1992, lining up, side by side, with organizations that support the use of sign language, to promote William "Dummy" Hoy. It is an indication of how powerful a symbol of inclusion and success Hoy remained for the deaf community that he could bring the entire range of the community together, organizations both of the deaf and for the deaf, manualists and oralists, united behind him. As historian Susan

Burch argues, "In particular, Hoy's successes countered mainstream medical perspectives that defined Deaf people strictly by their physical deficiencies."[66] Both signers and speakers could comfortably unite together, to fight back against that perspective.

It also demonstrates the longevity of Hoy's fame within the deaf community. By 1992, none of the deaf people involved in this campaign had ever seen Hoy play baseball. His last year in the majors was 90 years before this Hall of Fame campaign was launched. Hoy died in December 1961, five months shy of his 100th birthday. And still, the power of his name could bring deaf people, in all their diversity, together. Hoy still enjoys a level of name recognition and fame within the deaf world that is simply remarkable for a man who was a 19th-century baseball player.

Hoy has, in fact, been honored by many organizations, both deaf and hearing. In 1951, he became the first deaf athlete to be elected to the Hall of Fame of the Athletic Association of the Deaf. In 1961, the Reds invited the then-99-year-old Hoy back to Crosley Field to throw out the first pitch of game three of the World Series, between Hoy's Cincinnati Reds and the New York Yankees. He died on December 15, 1961.

Several posthumous honors followed. In 2001, the baseball field at Gallaudet University was named in his honor. In 2003, Hoy was inducted into the Cincinnati Reds Hall of Fame. In 2004, he was inducted into the Shrine of the Eternals in the Baseball Reliquary. The Reliquary is a Los Angeles–based educational organization that works toward "fostering an appreciation of American art and culture through the context of baseball history," as their website puts it. The Reliquary offers its Shrine as a response to Cooperstown's Hall of Fame. Candidates are inducted into the Shrine more on the basis of their uniqueness of character and imprint upon the game. The Shrine cited Hoy as a "progenitor of the signaling system used today by managers, coaches, baserunners, and hitters."[67]

Hoy has been memorialized in popular culture as well. Allen Myer and Michael Nowak wrote the play *The Signal Season of Dummy Hoy* in 1986. It was first staged in Chicago in 1987 and premiered off-Broadway that same year. Two children's picture books about Hoy have appeared, Bill Wise's *Silent Star: The Story of Deaf Major Leaguer William Hoy* (2012) and Nancy Churnin's *The William Hoy Story: How a Deaf Baseball Player Changed the Game* (2016). Movies have also appeared: the documentary *I See the Crowd Roar: The Story of William "Dummy" Hoy* (2007) and the feature, *The Silent Natural* (2019). Both are projects of filmmaker David Risotto, with support from Hoy researcher Steve Sandy.

But the deaf community still wants to see Hoy inducted into the National Baseball Hall of Fame at Cooperstown. Brian Malzkuhn argued Hoy's case in an article in 2010, calling Hoy's exclusion from the Hall "an unjust oversight," and urging deaf fans to write to the Hall on Hoy's behalf.[68] Some think they know what has been holding Hoy back. Dick Sipek, a deaf man who briefly played for the Cincinnati Reds in 1945, and about whom more later, asserted in a 1992 interview that Hoy has been deliberately slighted on account of his deafness. "People don't want to talk about the deaf," Sipek said. "They want to keep them down."[69]

It is not clear that such blatant prejudice is the reason. But Stephen Jay Gould argues in *Triumph and Tragedy in Mudville* that Hoy's deafness has limited his legacy in the hearing community, perhaps not in the way that Dick Sipek baldly implies, but Gould does similarly point to a deep deaf-hearing divide.[70] A player's reputation is still burnished by journalistic attention and here Hoy was not well served by the mainstream hearing press. Few hearing reporters tried to interview him, on account of his deafness. The few that did manage to interview Hoy did so with a sense of clear unease. Hoy supporter Robert Panara loved to tell this story about Hoy and a hearing reporter: "Using a pad and pencil to communicate with a reporter during an interview, [Hoy] wrote, 'What is your name?' The reporter, taken aback, voiced to those standing nearby, 'Oh I didn't know he could write.' Proving he could lipread too, Hoy snatched back the pad and wrote, 'Yes but I can't read.'"[71]

Perhaps opinions are beginning to shift. In 2010, Peter Morris was asked to comment on the question of whether or not Hoy contributed to the invention of umpire's signs, as the documentary film treatment of that very issue, *Signs of the Time*, was receiving increased press attention. Morris offered that "Hoy's efforts might have influenced umpires but that the use of hand signals was inevitable, needed for players and the fans as the stadiums became bigger and bigger." As to Hoy's case for Cooperstown, Morris said that "even without credit for umpiring signals, Hoy might deserve a place in Cooperstown." As he put it, "When you look at the obstacles he overcame and the fact that he had more than 2,000 career hits, there's an argument to be made for him."[72]

The emergence of an "overcoming obstacles" narrative is troubling. In *Triumph and Tragedy in Mudville*, Stephen Jay Gould put it plainly: "Dummy Hoy belongs in the Hall of Fame by sole virtue of his excellent, sustained play over a long career. His case seems undeniable to me."[73] Gould rejected the idea of rewarding Hoy for "overcoming obstacles" out of hand, rightly pointing out that it is to unfairly diminish Hoy, an argument that serves only to distract attention from his achievements as a ballplayer.

Further, as disability studies scholar Simi Linton notes, "One interpretation of the phrase [overcoming disability] might be that the individuals' disability no longer limits her or him, that sheer strength or willpower has brought the person to the point where the disability is no longer a hindrance. Another implication of the phrase may be that the person has risen above society's expectation for someone with those characteristics ... these phrases are often said with the intention of complimenting someone. The compliment has a double edge. To accept it, one must accept the implication that the group is inferior and that the individual is unlike others in that group."[74] Too often, disabled people are invited, she argues, to "overcome" a disability, rather than "demand social change."[75]

And, of course, Hoy himself would reject the idea that he had overcome his disability. Hoy made it very clear, with his own words, that he did not experience his deafness as a trait that he had to overcome personally. Neither was it a characteristic that he regarded as an obstacle for him to overcome as a player. Instead, Hoy asserted that being deaf made him a better baseball player. Hoy, of all people, would not want us to look back on his career and conclude that he played so well in spite of the fact that he was deaf. Rather, he would want us to understand that he played so well because he was deaf.

Hoy was a proud member of the deaf community. He believed his game benefited from his deafness and he was honored to represent his community in a largely hearing major league. Hoy wanted to be seen by all fans, deaf and hearing alike, as a deaf baseball player. If he wanted to overcome anything, it was hearing prejudice against the deaf. Hoy demanded social change and sought social acceptance for deaf people on deaf terms, starting on the ballfield, where he expected accommodation to succeed as a deaf player, by having hearing colleagues communicate with him in his preferred method, of signs, gestures, and fingerspelling. Those signs stayed on the field long after he retired, as Hoy's signs became adopted by hearing umpires in major league baseball, as we shall see in the next chapter.

Through the quality and consistency of his play, William Ellsworth Hoy became a hero for deaf and hearing fans alike. Within the deaf community, Hoy was regarded as both a hero and a cultural icon. The deaf community wanted to see others follow in his footsteps, but *The Silent Worker* admitted in 1903, as Hoy left the field, that "baseball players are born, not made." The paper assured readers, however, that "there will always be room enough in professional ranks for the Hoys" of the world.[76]

Hearing fans too appreciated this deaf player. They found a new way, a deaf way, to show their appreciation for him. Adopting deaf ways as their own, when Hoy made a great play, the home crowd liked to make sure that he knew they loved it. And so "the crowd would not only cheer but also stand up, waving their arms and hats wildly."[77] Deaf applause, by hearing people, for a deaf player—a real sign that the communication barrier was being broken, and from all sides.

Parts of this chapter appeared as "No Dummies: Deafness, Baseball, and American Culture," in *The Cooperstown Symposium on Baseball and American Culture, 2007–2008*, ed. William Simons (McFarland, 2009). This volume is a juried selection of the best papers presented at the Cooperstown Symposium from the years 2007 and 2008. "No Dummies" was originally presented at the 2008 conference.

3

A Tale of Two Umpires

Today, when we go to a baseball game, all fans, whether hearing or deaf, rely on the sign language of baseball to follow a game. While 19th-century fans expected to hear a game called and umpires bellowed out their decisions, nowadays fans expect to see umpires call a game. Fans know what these gestures mean. We hold our breath, waiting for the call on a close play at second base. Was the runner safe? We see the sign—yes, stolen base! The sign language of baseball makes the game understandable to fans in the stands. We also expect to see the umpire gesture behind home plate. We delight in seeing a more vigorous call, with extra English on it, on a called third strike.

The story of how umpires started to gesture in the first place is one largely shrouded in myth and mystery. The safe and out signals are especially murky. One thing is clear: they definitely predate the signs for balls and strikes. Baseball researcher Peter Morris concludes in his comprehensive study, *A Game of Inches: The Story Behind the Innovations that Shaped Baseball*, that "somewhat surprisingly, umpires appear to have been signaling out and safe before it became customary to have signs for balls and strikes."[1] Indeed, the *Chicago Tribune* noted in 1907, "There is no rule compelling an umpire to motion 'safe' or 'out' on the bases, but nearly all of them do by force of habit on plays which are not close."[2]

There are reports of isolated instances of experimentation with gestures at various points in major league baseball in the late 19th and early 20th centuries. Baseball researchers have pointed to a handful of stories that detailed such novelties appearing in the 1880s.[3] There were increasing calls for gestures from fans around this same time. As baseball increased in popularity, ballparks drew bigger crowds and got noisier. Fans complained of not being able to follow the game, since they could no longer hear the umpire's calls. In 1889, baseball cranks in New York wrote to the *New York Sun*, debating various solutions to the problem, offering ideas both aural, using bells or gongs, and visual, using hand gestures, to signal the calls.[4] There is no indication that any of these proposals were put into action by umpires at that time.

3. A Tale of Two Umpires

Umpires have typically been given the credit for originating their various signs among themselves by baseball historians. Bill Klem is typically cited as one originator among many in these narratives. Klem served as an umpire in the National League from 1905 to 1941 and umpired in 18 World Series. Klem is credited for first indicating "fair" and "foul" with arm gestures. Fellow umpires like Cy Rigler, who worked alongside Klem in the National League from 1906 to 1935 and officiated in 10 World Series, and Hank O'Day, who worked as a National League

Umpire Bill Klem. Seen here in 1914, Klem has frequently been given credit as one of the umpires who introduced the use of gestures behind home plate. Library of Congress.

umpire from 1895 to 1927 and umpired in 10 World Series, are also frequently mentioned in many historical accounts for their work in experimenting with gestures for strikes and balls.

The quest to determine where the specific gestures for strikes and balls came from has received cinematic treatment as well. The award-winning documentary *Signs of the Times: The Myth, the Mystery, the Legend of Baseball's Greatest Innovation* (2008) explored the roles of the hearing umpire Bill Klem and the deaf ballplayer, William "Dummy" Hoy, in the creation of such signs. The film brought renewed attention to the contested role of baseball's first deaf star in their creation.

While baseball historians have largely credited umpires with creating the distinctive signs of their profession, there is a competing creation story. The deaf community has always credited William Hoy with inventing the signs for balls and strikes. As the *New York Times* noted in 2010, "The case for Hoy has been made largely by advocates for the deaf lobbying to get him in the Hall of Fame."[5] Deaf fans view recognition for Hoy's contribution to the game as a major part of the case for his induction into the Hall of Fame. If Hoy's link to the signs of baseball can be proven, his path to Cooperstown seems straighter.

Baseball researchers, however, have largely rejected the idea that Hoy had any influence on the development of such signs. They have been consistent in their rejection of Hoy for nearly 30 years now. Researcher Bill Deane first rejected the case for Hoy in 1990, when he served as the senior research associate for the National Baseball Hall of Fame, a position he held from 1986 to 1994. He became involved in a correspondence with Hoy advocate and deaf baseball researcher Steven Sandy. Sandy's work on Hoy culminated in 2007, when Sandy served as producer on a documentary film on Hoy, *Dummy Hoy: A Deaf Hero.*

Sandy wrote to the Hall in 1990, regarding his view that Hoy had helped to develop umpire's signals. Deane replied at length, in a letter dated July 17, 1990.

> We do not mean to discredit Hoy or anyone else, but merely maintain an accurate historical record of baseball. Our records indicate that hand signals came into usage a few years after Hoy's retirement as a player, and were designed for the benefit of spectators. Enclosed is a copy from the 1909 edition of Spalding's Official Base Ball guide, indicating that hand signals were first suggested in 1906 or 1907, and adopted soon thereafter. It would seem very curious that, had Hoy had any role in the development of these signals, no mention would be made of him in such an article written just five years after his retirement. Furthermore, we can find no contemporary articles about Hoy … that claim a connection between Hoy and the umpire's hand signals…. It is our impression that stories crediting Hoy with the innovation of hand signals began circulating after his death in 1961. Some writer probably made an assumption that, since hand signals were introduced around the same time as Hoy was finishing his career, there must have been a connection. Once an inaccuracy reaches print, it spreads like wildfire.[6]

Deane assumed in 1990 that the claim that Hoy played a role in creating the signs was "an inaccuracy." To reach this conclusion in 1990, he had to reject the published claims of one of Hoy's peers to the contrary. That peer is Sam Crawford, who played with Hoy in Cincinnati in 1902. In 1966, Lawrence Ritter published *The Glory of Their Times*, an oral history of early baseball. Crawford was one of the subjects interviewed for that project. In his interview, Crawford stated, "Did you know that he was the one responsible for the umpire giving hand signals for a ball and a strike? Raising his right hand for a strike, you know, and stuff like that…. That's a fact."[7] Deane rejected Crawford's account again in 2010, telling *The New York Times*, "Their case is based on the memory of one guy 60 years after the fact. I'm not saying it's not possible that there's a vague connection."[8]

Here, Deane reiterates what has become a widespread position among hearing baseball chroniclers and researchers. Admittedly, they do not agree exactly as to who brought the signs to baseball. Peter Morris argues that Bill Klem is "erroneously credited with pioneering umpires signals," admitting only that "Klem was among the first to give added emphasis to his signals." Morris mentions a proposed experiment in a minor league game in 1901, where an umpire was to have worn a red sleeve on his right arm and a white one on his left, to color code the calls of strikes and balls, respectively. It is not clear whether or not the experiment was ever conducted. Morris goes on to note that Hank O'Day reportedly experimented with using arm gestures in 1907. He writes that O'Day called a season opener in April 1907 and experimented with gestures, raising his left hand for a ball, and "in case he raises neither hand, it is a strike."[9]

Others give the credit to Cy Rigler. Baseball researcher Jonathan Fraser Light calls Rigler "the first Major League umpires to use his right hand to signify strikes." Likewise, researcher Dan Krueckeberg indicates that Rigler's gestures were covered in the press for his work in the minors, in the Central League in Evansville in 1905, when he "used his right hand when calling strikes in order that friends, sitting in the outfield, could distinguish his calls." But Krueckeberg notes that when Rigler "entered the National League a year later, he found that his raised arm call had preceded him and was in wide use."[10] Bill Deane concludes that "umpires' hand signals were in mass usage by 1907, though standardization was lacking."[11]

While they do not agree on who brought the signs to baseball, they all agree as to who did not: William Ellsworth Hoy. Jonathan Fraser Light writes that "the deaf mute outfielder Dummy Hoy" in some accounts is held "responsible for the use of hand signals by umpires to call balls and strikes…. This is probably a myth, however." Similarly, Peter Morris concludes of the Hoy story that "the evidence does not support this version of events." Bill Deane published his views on the matter in his book *Baseball Myths: Debating, Debunking, and Disproving Tales from the Diamond* (2012), arguing that the deaf community's version of events amounts to the promulgation of a "Hoy myth." Deane concluded, "The consensus is that standardized umpires' hand signals first appeared in the big leagues about 1906, give or take a year. And Dummy Hoy, who last played in the majors in 1902, had nothing to do with them."[12]

In truth, William "Dummy" Hoy had everything to do with them. Hoy's signs did make it into baseball, with the help of a hearing umpire, one unmentioned in all these accounts until now, Francis "Silk" O'Loughlin.

Untangling the mystery requires separating the fiction from the facts. Next, we must consider how the story got so tangled in the first place. How was the truth lost? Why was Hoy written out of the story entirely? How was O'Loughlin's role completely forgotten?

Deaf Players in Major League Baseball

Let's start with the most concrete fact we have. There is widespread agreement among baseball researchers that there was a period of loose experimentation with gestures of various sorts. How do we go from that to an organized codified system of discrete gestures required for use by all umpires? If baseball historians disagree as to where the signs came from, how the signs got to baseball, and who brought them there, we can agree as to when they officially arrived. We know exactly when umpires were required to gesture when they called a game in the major leagues. The *Spalding's Official Baseball Guide* for 1909, for the first time, provided baseball fans with images of umpire's gestures, with their associated meanings. Illustrations for "safe," "out," and "strike" all appeared. Umpires in both major leagues were required in the 1909 season to add gestures to their verbal calls, and they have been doing so ever since.

This narrows down our window. How did the signs arrive in baseball in 1909? It turns out that Bill Klem himself provided an answer to that very question. In April 1951, Klem sat down for a series of interviews with William Slocum of *Collier's* magazine. By sitting down with Slocum, Klem was burnishing his record for Cooperstown. He would, in fact, be voted into the National Baseball Hall of Fame as an umpire in 1953. This was a break-through moment for the Hall, as Klem, together with his American League counterpart Tom Connolly, became the first umpires to be inducted into the Hall of Fame.

In this 1951 interview, Klem took credit for transforming baseball in the early 20th century. "When next you go out to the ballpark, you will see many things that are commonplace today, but which came about only after 20 year feuds or—at least—bitter arguments among reasonable men," he told Slocum. "Many of these innovations are mine. And all of them helped baseball to grow from a country fair attraction to the great, beloved spectacle it is today."[13]

One of the innovations Klem directly took credit for was inventing the umpire's gestures behind home plate. As he put it, "Today, when an umpire calls a strike, his right hand shoots above his head so that everybody in the ball park knows it. If his hand remains at his side, it is a ball. I originated that system in 1906, when my voice went bad and I could no longer follow the custom of bellowing each decision."[14]

Klem's version of events would suggest that the journey to 1909 began in 1906. If Klem is right, this is how the signs came to baseball. Major league officials adopted the system that he originated when his voice went bad in 1906. According to Klem, officials brought his system into baseball in 1909 and, at that point, required its use of all major league umpires. Klem went even further, arguing, "The rank and file of my profession fought these innovations. But the sportswriters finally approved to a man and eventually shoved the new tactics down the throats of the reluctant umps."[15]

Klem had part of the story straight, in this account. Umpires did prove reluctant to adopt these gestures and many sportswriters were early supporters of a gestural system, as Klem correctly stated. We will explore the resistance of umpires and the support of sportswriters in more detail later, but first things first. Has Klem provided us with an accurate timeline of events? Is this when the signs started their journey into baseball? And, finally, was there an innovative umpire gesturing behind home plate in 1906? The answers are yes, yes, and yes. There was such an innovator working behind home plate in 1906. He was, in fact, having trouble with his voice. It was not, however, Bill Klem. It was his childhood friend, Francis "Silk" O'Loughlin.

Both men were born in Rochester, New York, O'Loughlin in 1870 and Klem in 1874.[16] O'Loughlin was brought into baseball as a player in the Rochester area in 1895, but soon moved into the role of umpire. O'Loughlin worked as an umpire in the New York, Atlantic, and Eastern Leagues, respectively, from 1898 to 1901. American League president Ban Johnson tapped him to work as an umpire for the junior circuit in 1902.[17] O'Loughlin would establish himself as one of the finest umpires in the early years of the league's existence, working in the American League until his sudden death in the flu epidemic of 1918.

Bill Klem turned to his friend Silk when he wanted to break into baseball. Klem played semi-pro baseball in New York and Pennsylvania in the mid–1890s, but his weak arm soon proved a liability and he finally left baseball to work construction for his brother George. As Klem remembered, "One day in Berwick, Pennsylvania, where I was working as a foreman on a construction job, and playing first base for the Berwick team on Saturdays, I saw an eight-column newspaper headline: 'The Great Silk O'Loughlin Umpired in Cleveland Yesterday.' I looked at the huge print and thought: umpiring is now a business."[18] He decided to try to break into that business and he reached out to Silk for advice.

Silk warned him against it. "Umpiring does something to you," Silk told Klem. "The abuse you get from players, the insults from the crowds, and the awful things they write about you in the newspapers. Klemmy, I wouldn't be an umpire if I knew anything else."[19] Nevertheless, Klem was determined to make a career of it and started out in the Connecticut League in 1902. He did not lack for self-confidence. "I knew even in 1904," Klem said, "that I was a great umpire and I knew baseball was a great profession."[20] Silk helped to arrange introductions for Klem that allowed him to advance into the ranks of the National League in 1905.[21]

In 1905, Klem was a rookie, but O'Loughlin had already developed a reputation as a strong umpire. One paper asserted, as the 1906 season opened, that "he is one of the greatest umpires that ever stepped on the field."[22] In 1906, O'Loughlin was chosen to work in the World Series for the first time, together with National League umpire Jim Johnstone. The 1906 World Series pitted the Chicago Cubs against the Chicago White Sox.[23]

It was a World Series of firsts. It was the first modern "Subway Series." It was the first appearance in the World Series for both franchises. It was the first World Series appearance for the Cubs' famous infield of Tinker, Evers, and Chance. And it ended in a huge upset, as the heavily favored Cubs, with the best record in baseball at 116–36, were defeated by the "Hitless Wonders," the White Sox, who had the worst team batting average in the American League (.230) in the regular season. Holding true to that performance, they batted only .198 as a team in the Series, on the way to their unlikely victory.

It was also the first World Series in which the umpires called the games with gestures. As the *Chicago Tribune* reported, "Fans who were fortunate enough to see the world's series in this city last fall will recall that the din of rooting was so great it was impossible to hear an umpire's decision. Umpire Johnstone, who worked behind the plate in the first game, had difficulty in making even the batteries understand his decisions. Next day, 'Silk' O'Loughlin supplemented his clarion voice with his characteristic gestures and his decisions were apparent to all…. [Before] the third game, both umpires were instructed to raise their right arms for strikes and their left arm for balls."[24]

"*With his characteristic gestures*"? Which gestures were these and how long had O'Loughlin been using them? Obviously long enough so that the *Tribune* thought them characteristic of the way O'Loughlin called a game, but clearly so idiosyncratic that they were not commonly in use by most umpires in major league baseball. After all, it had not occurred to his partner in the game, Johnstone, to use them, even as he struggled to make himself understood verbally.

So why did "Silk" O'Loughlin suddenly start gesturing behind home plate at the World Series in 1906? Further, where had these gestures come from? Did he invent them? Is that why the *Tribune* thought they were characteristic of O'Loughlin? And how long had he been using these gestures? He had come into the American League in 1902. Had he been gesturing all that time? In most newspaper coverage of O'Loughlin's career, he is depicted as an umpire revered for his strong voice, and not his gestures, characteristic or otherwise. O'Loughlin's idiosyncratic pronunciation of "tuh" for "two" made his call of "Strike TUH" famous in major league baseball in the early years of the American League. (Incidentally, it was not his clarion voice that earned him the nickname "Silk." It was a childhood nickname, a reference to his silky hair, and it followed him into adulthood.)

Now, Klem himself pointed to 1906, not 1902, as the critical year that had brought gestures to baseball. He said, "I originated that system in 1906, when my voice went bad and I could no longer follow the custom of bellowing each decision." Assuming that Klem was right about the year and knowing definitively that O'Loughlin used gestures at the 1906 World Series, it seemed logical to start looking for answers in the press coverage of baseball during the 1906 season. And there, in 1906, one story leaps out.

Just as the season was getting underway, in April 1906, *The Washington Post* reported that "O'Loughlin sprained his larynx Tuesday ... and had no voice today. Instead of calling the decisions, he employed 'Dummy' Hoy's mute signal code, which certainly was a novelty for Silk."[25] Over the course of the season, the use of Hoy's signal code went from a novelty to a standard feature of O'Loughlin's work as an umpire. In October 1906, the *Meriden Daily Journal* reported that O'Loughlin's gestures were an important part of his style. While arguing that both his "utterances and gestures" were "peculiar," the paper nonetheless found that O'Loughlin's "umpiring is clean cut, intelligent, and conscientious," which, the paper argued, is why he was selected for duty in the World Series.[26]

By the time the World Series rolled around, using gestures to make himself understood in Chicago would have appeared as an obvious solution to him. Faced with an inability to make his calls heard in Chicago, O'Loughlin pioneered the way forward. He knew that he could make his calls understandable by making them visible. His calls could be seen by both players and spectators alike.

As it happened, O'Loughlin was not the only umpire who lost his voice in 1906. In June 1906, *The Sporting Life* reported, "Hank O'Day umpired with his fingers. He lost his voice and gave a Dummy Hoy exhibition behind the pitcher."[27] Unlike O'Loughlin, however, there is no indication that O'Day continued to gesture. This appears to have been a one-time act of improvisation. The reporter for this story was Ren Mulford, Jr., a long-time sports reporter who had been with the paper since 1888, the same year that Hoy broke into major league baseball. He would have recognized a Dummy Hoy exhibition when he saw one. In Mulford's case, his wording was ambiguous. Was O'Day using Hoy's system itself or was he umpiring with his fingers like a deaf person might? In either case, Mulford saw Hoy's influence at work.

The reporters for both the *Washington Post* and the *Chicago Tribune* acknowledged that the credit for the gesturing system itself should go to "Dummy" Hoy. The *Post* stated directly that O'Loughlin "employed Dummy Hoy's mute signal code." The *Tribune* indirectly credited Hoy. After informing readers that the umpires were required to raise a right arm for a strike and a left arm for a ball for the remainder of the 1906 World Series, the *Tribune* reminding its readers that this was a system that had already been used in major league baseball. The *Tribune* explained, "When Dummy Hoy was playing in the big leagues, his only method of ascertaining decisions on pitched balls was by watching the coach at third base, who held up his right hand

Pictured here is the crew for the 1915 World Series. Smith, the man with the bullhorn, was the announcer. The rest were umpires. From left to right: Cy Rigler, Bill Klem, Francis "Silk" O'Loughlin, and Billy Evans. The men had also worked together in the 1912 World Series. O'Loughlin was the umpire who pioneered the use of gestures behind home plate. He was the first umpire in major league baseball history to use gestures behind home plate during a World Series, in the World Series of 1906. Library of Congress.

when a strike was called on Hoy and his left hand for a ball."[28] The *Tribune* knew that we had seen this system before and it was not original to hearing umpires.

It had arrived in baseball with "Dummy" Hoy in 1888, the year that he joined the National League's Washington Nationals. The Nationals played in the heart of the District, in the shadow of the Capitol, at Swampoodle Grounds. Swampoodle was the name of the neighborhood, then home to mostly Irish immigrants who had fled the potato famine. Swampoodle was then a largely undeveloped, mostly rural area, and its Irish immigrant residents kept goats and cows in the alleys that surrounded the modest housing stocks. The area flooded regularly, as the Tiber Creek ran through the neigh-

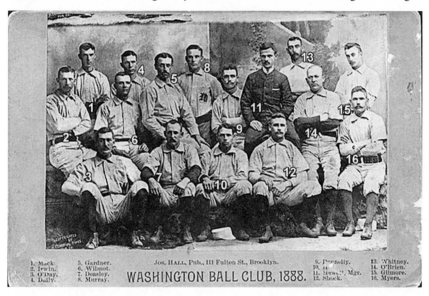

The 1888 Washington team, Hoy's first major league baseball team. Each player is numbered. Hoy is labelled as number 10 here, seated in the bottom row, with a white cap on the ground in front of him. The most prominent team members were Hank O'Day, number 3, seated in the front row, all the way to the left. O'Day broke into the majors as a pitcher and went on to have a long career as an umpire. In the back row, all the way to the left, is number 1, Connie Mack. Mack spent ten years as a catcher in the National League before going on to be the manager of the Philadelphia A's for 50 years. The rest of the players are: Ed Daily (4), Miah Murray (8), John Irwin (2), Waly Wilmot (6), and Gid Gardner (5). Jim Donnelly (9) is seated behind Hoy, next to Walter Hewett (11), the manager in the suit. Jim Whitney (13), Billy O'Brien (14), and Frank Gilmore (15). Pat Deasley (7) is between Hoy and O'Day. George Shoch (12) is seated beside Hoy, in front of the manager, all the way to the right. Courtesy Robert Edward Auctions.

borhood and was prone to overflowing its banks. The neighborhood's name of Swampoodle is said to be a mash-up of "swamp" and "puddle." Those Irish workers who called it home took jobs in the construction trades and helped build the city, as the District transformed into a capital city. The Tiber Creek, the source of all those puddles, was itself channeled underground, in a massive sewer project during the 1870s.

Suddenly, the neighborhood had attractive, dry land on which to build. Swampoodle Grounds was built for the Nationals, who played there from 1886 to 1889. It was a small park, 325 feet in right, 375 in center, and 275 in left. The Nationals did not find a happy home there. They finished last in the National League in 1889, with a record of 41–83, 42 games out of first place. Swampoodle Grounds's seating capacity of 6,000 was too frequently empty of paying fans. Soon after Hoy's departure from Washington, the park was abandoned. It was razed in 1907, along with more than 100 homes in the Swampoodle neighborhood, to make way for Union Station.

While he was only there for two years, before leaving for the Buffalo Bisons in the short-lived Players' League in 1890, Hoy's time in Washington meant that he came into major league baseball as a deaf player in the deafest city in the United States. Washington was home to Gallaudet College (now, Gallaudet University), the world's first college for deaf people, founded in 1864. Deaf students would undoubtedly have known of Hoy's arrival in major league baseball.

Unfortunately, the campus student paper, *The Buff and Blue*, did not begin publication until 1892, so there is no campus record to draw on to track student interest in Hoy's career in Washington. Given that Hoy gained a following of deaf fans wherever he went over the course of his long career, it seems likely that Gallaudet students were excited to see a deaf player in the majors. Coincidently, 1892 also marked another deaf contribution to an American sport. During the 1892 season, the Gallaudet College football team was playing another deaf football team. Not wanting his opponents to steal their signs, Gallaudet quarterback Paul Hubbard called for his team to huddle around him, so he could sign the details of the next play away from spying eyes. The football huddle was born, a distinctively deaf contribution to sport.

Signs for baseball were another deaf contribution to sport. Wherever Hoy went, whatever team he played for, whenever he was at bat, he relied on a signal system so that he would know what the umpire had called. Because he could not hear the umpire's call, Hoy's third base coach signaled the call to him. The *Washington Evening Star* reported in April 1888 that "when Hoy bats, a man stands in the captain's box near third base and signals to him decisions of the umpire on balls and strikes."[29] When he played for the Browns in St. Louis, Charles Comiskey was the one who stood on the third base line and used Hoy's sign system to communicate the decisions on balls and strikes into Hoy when he was at bat.[30]

So well-known was this system that the Cincinnati Reds even referred to it in their team ceremony as they dedicated a new ballpark in 1902. The program for that ceremony asked fans to imagine a game in progress, and invited them to look to the field to "see the speechless determination in [Hoy's] wizened face, as he stands at the bat and turns to see Heiney Peitz elevate his right hand or his left, signaling that the umpire has called a strike or a ball."[31]

It is entirely likely that this system originated at the Ohio School for the Deaf, where Hoy had attended the school and played on their baseball team.[32] In 1879, when the travelling version of the team, called the Independents, went on a tour, their use of signs on the field noted in the press. The *New York Clipper* remarked, "Of the twelve that travel with the Independent nine of Columbus, Ohio, better known as the Deaf Mutes, only one player speaks, he acting as captain, giving them signs for strikes, called balls, etc. It is amazing to see how closely they are obliged to watch him while receiving their orders in the field."[33] It seems likely that Hoy simply imported the system he had used at Ohio into the majors with him in 1888.

O'Loughlin would have been a rookie umpire in the American League in 1902. Hoy would just have finished playing in Chicago. He then departed for Cincinnati, taking his signal system with him. But it had left an indelible impression by this point, on both major leagues. The sports reporter for the *Washington Post* would instantly have recognized the thrust right hand for strikes and the upraised left for balls when O'Loughlin tried it out in 1906 as "Dummy Hoy's mute signal code," now resurrected on the hands of a hearing umpire, for hearing players.

The *Chicago Tribune* too knew exactly from whom O'Loughlin had drawn his sudden inspiration as he employed his gesture system during the World Series. Once again, a newspaper credited Dummy Hoy. Hoy's example inspired a hearing umpire to appropriate a deaf system for himself. When the voice of one umpire was silenced by the cacophony of sound produced by all of Chicago in its hometown series, O'Loughlin knew that Hoy's gestures would be understood above the din.

Though O'Loughlin had apparently been gesturing all season long, the use of the signs during the World Series took the question of gestures in baseball to the next level. The *Chicago Tribune* essentially launched a one-paper crusade to see them adopted into baseball on a permanent basis. After the

World Series ended, a fan contacted American League president Ban Johnson, requesting him "to direct the American League umpires next season to adopt some simple code for signaling decisions on 'balls' and 'strikes' so as to make them instantly intelligible to spectators in all parts of the stands," and recommending "the most simple method known and … which occasionally has been used already, that of having the umpire raise his right hand above his shoulder to indicate a 'strike' and his left hand similarly to indicate a 'ball.'"[34]

It is important to note here that the *Tribune* was finally picking up on an idea that Warren Lynch had made back in January of 1900. Warren Lynch was an assistant general passenger agent of the so-called "Big Four." The Big Four were a group of four American merchants who created the Central Pacific Railroad company in 1861. They were responsible for building part of the first transcontinental line. But Lynch was not only a railroad man—he was also a huge baseball fan.

He brought this idea to *The Sporting News*. Lynch complained that fans could not understand what the umpires were calling behind the plate. "If every time an umpire called a ball he would raise his right hand and every time he pronounced a strike he would lift up his left hand there would be no trouble to follow the game," Lynch argued. "If the League would make a rule to this effect, it would help the sport." *The Sporting News* agreed, adding, "This is a splendid suggestion. It does not involve the expenditure of any money and would help the game a great deal."[35]

It seems quite relevant that *The Sporting News* asked Billy Hoy, as they referred to him, to comment on this idea. They could have asked any ballplayer, particularly as this suggestion was framed as a system created to benefit hearing people, that is, to allow hearing fans to better understand the game when they could not hear the umpire's calls. But they asked Hoy, the only player in major league baseball who already enjoyed the advantage of such a signal system. Hoy seized the opportunity to lay claim to the gesture system already in use in major league baseball. He first agreed that it was, indeed, a very good idea. "I think Mr. Lynch's idea a splendid one," he began. "Such a rule, if established, will please not only the patrons of the game, but also the players. By reason of the distance, the outfielders do not always hear the ruling of the umpire. The same thing applies to the occupants in the distant parts of the stands."

Hoy went on to describe his system in this way. "The act of lifting up the right hand by the coacher while I am at bat to denote that the umpire has called a strike on me and the raising of the left hand to denote that a ball has been called has come to be well understood by all the League players. The reason the right hand was originally selected by me to denote a strike and the left hand to denote a ball was because 'the pitcher was all right' when he got the ball over the plate and because 'he got left' when he sent the ball wide of the plate. I have often been told by frequenters of the game that they take considerable delight in watching the coacher signal balls and strikes to me, as by these signals they can know to a certainty what the umpire with a not too overstrong voice is saying."[36]

Other papers picked up on this idea of requiring umpires to gesture. The *Bangor Daily Whig and Courier* reported in February of 1900 that "it has been suggested that the extending of the umpire's right arm above his head shall indicate that he has called a strike and that the raising of his left arm shall mean that a ball has been called." Of course, Lynch had suggested the opposite. But here, the *Bangor Daily Whig and Courier* reported that the idea was for hearing umpires to adopt Hoy's signs directly. And they too asked Hoy what he thought of such an idea. The paper reported: "Billy Hoy, who is at Cincinnati, in speaking of this scheme a day or two ago said, 'I think the idea is a splendid one.'" Again, he described his system and concluded, "I can't see any reason why the rule should not be adopted. It will cost nothing.... I hope it will be adopted. A simpler or more effective rule has never been recommended to the League."[37]

Now, having at last seen the idea in action during the 1906 World Series, the *Tribune* returned to the possibility of making its implementation permanent. Ban Johnson signaled his support for the idea, "unless," he told the paper, "it is found plausible for the American League clubs to go even farther than that in the matter of keeping spectators informed of everything that happens," namely, by installing electronic scoreboards in every ball park.[38] The *Tribune* commended the plan immediately, as one that would "increase the joy of the baseball fan."[39]

By the end of January 1907, the *Tribune* felt confident that signs were coming to major league baseball. "The movement for a system of signals to indicate an umpire's decisions during a baseball game ... seems to be spreading," the paper told readers, "and the indications are all the important leagues will adopt some such system before another playing season arrives. Announcement of the willingness of the American league to adopt the suggestion already has been made. Several club owners of the National league have urged the adoption of a similar policy by its umpires next season."[40]

The Sporting Life was similarly enthusiastic about the idea. In January 1907, it reported to readers that "President Johnson will probably instruct his umpires next season to follow the method of announcing strikes as during the world's championship series. Whenever a strike is declared, the umpire raises an arm high in the air; when he makes no move, of course, a ball is called."[41] *The Sporting Life* reported on the possible move again, quite positively, in February 1907. "The umpire arm-signal plan, so well demonstrated during the world's championship series," *The Sporting Life* commented, "is growing in favor, and, from appearances, will be in general use next season."[42]

As it happened, the American League suddenly changed course and veered back in the direction of Johnson's other communication scheme, electronic scoreboards. Just as *The Sporting Life* thought the matter settled, the *Tribune* broke a story in February 1907 that Ban Johnson had announced that "electrical score boards operated from near the home plates probably will be adopted by the American league clubs to indicate to spectators every decision made during a game instead of the signal system by umpires' gestures, which has been under consideration."

The Sporting Life soon picked up the same report, saying that "the scoreboard idea results from the protest of Hank O'Day and other knights of the indicator on the making of themselves human windmills trying to interpret balls and strikes to the fans in the bleachers. It has been proposed to have the umpire raise his arms for strikes and balls as was done in the world's base ball series."[43] The scoreboard would replace the gesture idea.

Such boards were considered "simple," "practical," and "reliable." One was already in use in St. Louis, and Johnson was sure it could be replicated in other ballparks.[44] The *Tribune* was not so sure. As the paper pointed out, there was an obvious weakness to the scheme—namely, the operator of the system would still need to know what the call was in order to post it on the scoreboard. Without implementing a gesture system for the umpires, the scoreboard operator would have to guess at the call along with the rest of the fans. Besides, the paper went on, "the real fan does not like to take his eyes off the play long enough even to glance at a scoreboard except between innings.... From the patron's standpoint, therefore, no scoreboard can replace an umpire's gestures."[45]

In this way, the *Tribune* essentially argued that all baseball fans are deaf. They all rely on vision to understand the game unfolding on the field before them. So intent are they on the action, they are loathe to take their eyes away from it, even for a moment, to glance at a scoreboard. Like the deaf players on Ohio's Independents, "it is amazing to see how closely [fans] are obliged to watch" to follow the game. Hearing baseball fans enter what cultural theorist Lennard Davis would call "a deafened moment or modality," where they are "defined by a process that does not require hearing or speaking." In a ballpark, even hearing fans are deaf and need signs to understand the calls on the field.[46]

But such signs were not universally welcomed. It seems that Ban Johnson was pushing the scoreboard solution because, aside from "Silk" O'Loughlin, umpires were largely opposed to using gestures behind home plate. Klem's comment that "the rank and file of my profession opposed these innovations" proved accurate. As the *Tribune* itself acknowledged in 1907, "The gesture system met considerable opposition from umpires, and there is a disposition to sidetrack it on that account."[47] Others argued that such a requirement would be a "hardship" on umpires.[48] Hank O'Day, one of the most prominent umpires of the National League, was said to be particularly opposed.[49]

His own day of signs apparently notwithstanding, O'Day now argued against the move, saying:

> If such a change in the rules is made it will not only be a hardship on the umpire by adding greater burdens to his lot than he now has, but he will not think of it half the time, for his mind will be getting down to first base when there is play coming off there or to some other base when there is a play there. Such a rule will work all right when there are two umpires in a game. One of the umpires could stand back of the pitcher and easily raise his arm for every ball pitched, for he would have nothing else to take up his mind, but when there is only one man officiating in a game, such a thing as raising an arm will not occur to an umpire when there is play on the bases.[50]

Spalding's Official Base Ball Guide summarized the opposition of the umpires, explaining that "[a]t first, the judges of play did not want to signal. They thought it detracted from their dignity to go through a dumb show resembling the waving of the arms of a semaphore."[51] Or, as *The Sporting Life* put it, act like "human windmills." In 1907, the umpires presented a united front to the league presidents, coming out "against the proposed rule to have umpires wave their arms to designate balls and strikes."[52]

It becomes clearer that "Silk" O'Loughlin was not simply an innovator. He was very much a risk taker. What seems an obvious solution to us, gesturing to make a call perfectly clear in a noisy ballpark, was not obvious to the majority of umpires. They were largely opposed to it. This explains why there had been only sporadic experimentation with such systems in the past and why none of them had really taken. Umpires, as a group, resisted them. "Silk" had gone out on a limb, alone. His gestures were, indeed, "peculiar."

But, at the turn of the century, it should come as no surprise to learn that umpires were opposed to gesturing, nor to find that they believed to do so would have somehow "detracted from their dignity." Given that the system of gesturing originated with a deaf ball player, the system would have been directly associated with deafness and with sign language, both of which were stigmatized at the turn of the century. Gesturing occasionally, to indicate "safe" or "out," was one thing. But to gesture all the time, with every pitch, consistently, over the course of an entire game—this was much closer to actual signing. Umpires dismissed it as "a dumb show" or wind milling.

American Sign Language, the language of the deaf community, had been under attack in the United States for decades, by this point. And deaf people, and their sign language, had come to be seen as increasingly abnormal.[53] As oralist Samuel Gridley Howe had argued back in 1867, "Certain effects grow out of these infirmities which are undesirable and the main object of the education of these children, taken as a class, should be to counteract the effect of this infirmity; to prevent it from having any influence on the character; to make them just as much as possible like other children."[54] Speech was needed to make deaf children "as much as possible like other children," that is, like hearing children.

By the time Hoy entered major league baseball in 1888, the oralist quest to make deaf people over in a hearing image had taken on a eugenic cast. Alexander Graham Bell argued in his *Memoir Upon the Formation of Deaf Variety of the Human Race* (1884) that the intermarriage of deaf people would lead to a "deaf variety of the human race." He concluded that "the production of a defective race of human beings would be a great calamity to the world." Ideally, to prevent such a calamity, states would pursue legislative action. "The first thought that occurs in this connection," Bell wrote, "is that the intermarriage of deaf-mutes might be forbidden by legislative enactment."

In the event that such legal actions failed to materialize, Bell sought other methods to transform deaf people into culturally hearing people. He argued that deaf children should attend their local public school, with hearing students; that deaf children should be educated exclusively with the oral method; and, finally, that deaf adults should be barred from serving as teachers of the deaf, to eliminate adult deaf role models from the lives of deaf children.[55] Bell scoffed at the idea that deaf people might value their signed language. To "ask the value of speech," he believed, "is like asking the value of life."[56]

In 1882, two years before Bell's *Memoir* appeared, only 7.5 percent of deaf schoolchildren were taught by the oral method. By 1900, however, that percentage had jumped to 47 percent, and by 1905, for the first time, the majority of deaf children were taught in the United States without sign language. The oralist grip on deaf education would reach its peak by 1919, when nearly 80 percent of deaf children were educated with the oral method, and oralism's hold on the field of deaf education would remain essentially unchallenged until the 1960s.[57]

By 1900, it was clear that the tide was turning in favor of oral education and against both sign language and its users. By 1907, as umpires resisted adopting the gestures of a deaf ballplayer to call a baseball game, the federal government had updated the Immigration of Act of 1882 to bar entry to persons with "a physical defect being of a nature which may affect the ability of such an alien to earn a living." As historian Douglas C. Baynton has demonstrated, deaf immigrants were turned away at Ellis Island as a result by hearing immigration officials who simply assumed that deafness would render such workers unemployable.[58]

By 1907, hostility toward disabled people more generally was increasing as well. The broader eugenics movement gained influence and promoted the adaptation of involuntary forced sterilization laws, to prevent so-called defectives from passing on their genes. In 1907, Indiana became the first state in the country to pass an involuntary sterilization law. Such laws were upheld by the U.S. Supreme Court in 1927, in the decision *Buck v. Bell*. Writing for the majority, Justice Oliver Wendell Holmes declared, "It is better for all the world if, instead of waiting to execute degenerate offspring for crime or to let them starve for their imbecility, society can prevent those who are manifestly unfit from continuing their kind." Thirty more states had followed Indiana's lead by 1937.[59]

By 1907, oralist teachers were arguing that "our first and foremost aim has been the development of the deaf child into as nearly a normal individual as possible."[60] Only by speaking, and never signing, would a deaf child become normal. A new ideal was being articulated for deaf people, the ideal of "passing" as a hearing person.[61] With the pressure to pass increasing, students who failed to do so were frequently condemned. As historian Susan Burch notes, "Students who could not achieve advanced levels ... often found themselves labeled as 'oral failures' and ridiculed as 'born idiots.'"[62] Those who could not or would not speak were clearly under attack. The deaf community had few defenders in American society, of its members or their language. Communicating by sign language was seen as inappropriate even for deaf people by 1907. It is not surprising that hearing umpires resisted doing so.

William Ellsworth Hoy emerged as a hero at this crucial cultural moment. He quickly became a symbol of deaf success in a hearing world. "As a non-college graduate who communicated only in signs and writing," Susan Burch argues, "he displayed the abilities of common Deaf people."[63]

While oralists preached that the best way for deaf people to succeed was to pass as hearing, Hoy demonstrated instead that deaf people succeeded in life by embracing, not hiding, their deafness. Hoy could not turn around and read the umpire's lips to get the call. He had to be focused on the next pitch. A quick glance to third and a clear gesture told him all he needed to know. By his example, Hoy firmly rejected the idea that passing was the only way for a deaf person to succeed in a so-called hearing world. Hoy made it clear that a truly deaf way, relying on visual communication, was the best way to succeed.

Hoy's performance in major league baseball also suggested that signing deaf people were already perfectly ordinary people. They did not have to pass as hearing to be ordinary Americans. Hoy did not pass. But what could be more mainstream, more patriotic, more American, than a baseball player? Deaf sport was a powerful way to lay claim to ordinariness and perhaps even acceptance by the hearing majority. A deaf body performing to the same athletic standard as hearing bodies made a powerful case that the deaf body was in fact just as capable as a hearing body. As Susan Burch suggests, the deaf community hoped that hearing fans would, by rooting for Hoy, come to see "Deafness in a more positive way. In turn, Deaf people could celebrate heroes of their own community, represented in a mainstream spotlight."[64]

Hoy's success as a deaf ballplayer in a hearing league not only made a powerful argument for the benefits of signed communication for deaf people but also suggested how useful such forms of communication could be for hearing people. Hoy's hearing teammates on the Reds all learned at least some sign language in the four years he played there. There were, one sportswriter noted, "times when the players would be having dinner and would communicate exclusively by sign language to avoid being interrupted by autograph seeking fans."[65] Chicago White Sox manager Clark Griffith quickly found his own uses for Hoy's manual alphabet. And "Silk" O'Loughlin proved willing to adopt the power of signs for himself. These hearing people recognized the benefits and contributions of deafness to society. In a noisy ballpark, the deaf way to communicate, by gestures, was ahead of the hearing way of doing things, by trying to scream louder. O'Loughlin's use of the Dummy Hoy mute signal code was, in its own way, a recognition of and appreciation for deaf gain.

Still, given how denigrated the sign language was by the turn of the century, and by professionals involved in deaf education no less, given how disabled people were seen as burdens in an able-bodied society that increasingly favored eugenics, it is not surprising that a growing number of hearing people viewed the gestures of the deaf with suspicion. Given that deaf people were labeled "oral failures" and "born idiots" for signing, one can more easily understand why most hearing umpires resisted using gestures to make their calls behind home plate. They were risking their dignity as hearing people. Even deaf people were not supposed to use signs and gestures! Why would hearing people voluntarily choose to do so?

But there was a further difficulty, from the umpire's point of view. The deaf origins of the signs of baseball they were being asked to adopt had been widely reported by this point. It was too late to claim that this was "Silk" O'Loughlin's idea, the innovation of one of their own. The press had already acknowledged that the system under consideration was "Dummy Hoy's mute signal code." This system was clearly not something that hearing umpires had come up with independently. It was a deaf innovation that hearing umpires were being asked to embrace as their own, in a time that was deeply anti-deaf. It made the work of getting them into baseball that much harder.

It is why it took two years of wrangling. The umpires were worried about their public image, fearful of appearing to be performing "a dumb show." After the umpires presented the leagues with their opposition to the idea, the *Tribune* complained in 1907 that there was "too much consideration for the umpires."[66] *The Sporting Life* thought the umpires' opposition to the gesture idea baseless:

> The umpire who cannot use the arm signal system without confusion or trouble is not fit even for amateur umpiring. All that is required of him is to raise his right arm every time he calls a "strike." No signal is necessary to indicate a "called ball," as the fact that he does not raise his arm denotes that no strike has been called and therefore necessarily the decision must be a "called ball." Furthermore, vocal announcement will not be abandoned, but will be used simultaneously with the arm signal. The system was tried in the world's championship series and worked to a charm—so well, in fact, that everybody wondered why it has not been thought of, or tried, in the regular championship games long ago. As Umpire O'Day witnessed the world's series, and therefore the arm-signal system also, his belated objection is rather singular, to say the least.[67]

They hoped that umpires would voluntarily agree at least to experiment with it, in order to get used to it.

It would seem that this is what in fact happened over the course of the 1907 and 1908 seasons. As Bill Deane correctly asserts, "umpires' hand signals were in mass usage by 1907, though standardization was lacking."[68] By the 1907 season, O'Loughlin had been experimenting in the American League with gestures for an entire season. Hoy's system had already been required for use by umpires during the 1906 World Series. Sportswriters were urging its permanent adoption in major league baseball. Though umpires, as an organized body, resisted, some of their number reluctantly tried their hand at it. Hand signals were indeed in "mass usage" in 1907, as public pressure on the umpires to gesture increased.

In February 1907, the *Sporting Life* ran a story with the headline "Arm Signal System Endorsed." They predicted that the adaptation of the system would "popularize the sport and may make the umpire himself less unpopular."[69] While umpires seemed to resist based on how the use of such gestures would make them look in the public eye, sportswriters focused more on the benefits of the proposed gestural system for hearing fans. One side seemed to frame the gestures as signs, and therefore as too deaf, while the other posited that these signs were different because they were for the benefit of hearing people, even if they came to the sport by way of a deaf player.

In May 1907, the *Sporting Life* went into more detail about the coming change. The paper noted, "President Ban Johnson has finally instructed all American League umpires to always indicate strikes by raising the right arm." But the paper went further. "President Pulliam should similarly instruct his National League umpires," the paper announced. And it could not help but take one more shot at the resisting umpires. "It is a reflection on the intelligence of umpires that they should require command to uniformly employ so simple a method of pleasing the patrons of the sport."[70]

O'Loughlin, for his part, carried on with his gesturing behind the plate throughout the 1907 season. The *Sporting Life* noted his work as an umpire, writing, "'Silk' O'Loughlin … is also in a class by himself. Silk yells 'Stri-i-ike' with particular emphasis on the 'I' and draws his right hand back over his shoulder and points his thumb at the grandstand. When he calls a ball, he makes no movement with his hands. Silk calls two 'tuh,' which never fails to raise a laugh."[71]

While "Silk" was quick to continue with his use of gestures, the National League continued to reject them. In a surprise move, President Harry Pulliam rejected both the gesture system *and* the scoreboard in 1907. The *Sporting Life* concluded that the umpires were simply a hopeless lot, after the Joint Rules Committee rejected the idea of requiring the signal system. "Umpires are naturally conservative, always fearful of added work or responsibility, and very few real improvements in the rules or practice of the game have emanated from them."[72]

Having dispensed with the signs, at the annual meeting of the board of directors of the National League in 1907, the question was raised as to whether or not the league should require all teams to adopt a scoreboard to provide "a convenient method for the patrons to follow the game." Most team owners were opposed to the idea, on financial grounds. As John Brush remarked, "The space that they asked at the Polo Grounds would displace two thousand dollars' worth of advertising that we now have."[73] After more discussion, the motion to adopt uniform scoreboards in stadiums across the league was rejected.[74] Perhaps as a result, according to Rob Edelman, "electric scoreboards did not become mainstays in professional parks until the 1930s."[75]

The signs did not have to wait quite so long. In 1909, the signs were made mandatory in both leagues. A majority of umpires had apparently concluded by that point that such a system would not render them undignified in the public imagination, nor would it be too difficult to use. Perhaps O'Loughlin's continued use of the system himself had helped to move his peers along. Or perhaps umpires had finally been persuaded that baseball was indeed a business. Catering to the needs of fans, that is, to the demands of paying customers, was a serious concern for baseball owners and executives. By the time the signs were made mandatory in 1909, "[e]ven the older umpires who were more loath to give their consent to the new system on the field are now frank enough to admit that it has been of invaluable assistance to them in making their decisions understood when the size of the crowd is such that it is impossible to make the human voice carry distinctly to all parts of the field."[76]

Spalding's Official Base Ball Guide for 1909 included photographic illustrations of the mandatory signs for fans. There is "Silk" O'Loughlin, pictured making gestures for strike, safe, and out. And there is Hank O'Day, pictured for the same.

Now we know how the signs for balls and strikes got into baseball. Yet, visitors to the Hall of Fame can read Bill Klem's brass plaque, where it states, in part, "Known as 'The Old Arbitrator.' Umpired in 18 World Series. Credited with introducing arm signals indicating strikes and fair or foul balls." Klem gets the credit. How and why did this happen?

"Silk" O'Loughlin's contemporaries recognized him for his characteristic gestures as an umpire. But O'Loughlin's career was cut short by his untimely death at the age of 48 in the flu epidemic in 1918. Upon his death, sportswriters praised the veteran umpire and mourned his passing. Several singled him out for his innovative work with the signs of baseball. No more will fans "hear 'Ball tuh!' shouted from behind the plate ... this summer. Nor ... enjoy the sweeping gestures of one of the most picturesque figures in baseball," mourned *The Washington Post*. "Silk O'Loughlin is dead."[77]

The *Chicago Tribune* recognized his leadership on the issue of bringing signs to baseball. "The rules committee of the game passed up the gesture idea when many baseball followers were urging the adoption of a uniform system of making clear the decisions of an umpire," the paper noted, "but O'Loughlin continued his methods with improvements."[78] In 1918, baseball seemed to have the story straight.

Two decades later, in 1939, Hoy was still receiving credit for his role in originating the signs. That year, sportswriter Bob Ray was recalling the history of the 1903 Los Angeles Angels, who won the inaugural pennant in the new Pacific Coast League. "Another member of the 1903 squad," he wrote, "was outfielder Dummy Hoy. Hoy, deaf and dumb, was the man who started the umpires raising their right hand to indicate a strike."[79]

1—"Str-r-i-ke Tuh" ("Silk" O'Loughlin); 2—"Safe" ("Silk" O'Loughlin); 3—"Out" (Silk" O'Loughlin); 4—"Strike" (Hank O'Day); 5—"Safe" (Evans); 6—"Safe" (Tom Connolly); 7—"Out" (Hank O'Day); 8—"Safe" (Hank O'Day). Photos by Conlon.
CHARACTERISTIC ATTITUDES OF WELL KNOWN UMPIRES IN RENDERING DECISIONS.

Umpires were finally required to gesture in major league baseball beginning in the 1909 baseball season. This illustration features various major league umpires, including "Silk" O'Loughlin, demonstrating those gestures in the *Spalding's Base Ball Guide for 1909*. Courtesy National Baseball Hall of Fame Library.

3. A Tale of Two Umpires

Sportswriters still had the story straight as late as 1943. Bill Klem had retired to Florida in 1941. There was a one-year wait rule at get on the ballot for the Hall at that time. With the Hall holding elections every three years (it would return to annual balloting in 1946), sportswriters were gearing up to debate whether or not an umpire should be on the next ballot. No umpire, to this point, had ever been voted into the Hall.

Guy Butler, with the *Miami News*, weighed in on the chances of Florida's adopted son. He was supportive of the idea of electing an umpire. "Sure," Butler wrote, "and why not ONE umpire in the Hall of Fame? I suspect eventually at least a couple of others—Tim Hurst, Silk O'Loughlin, and perhaps also Billy Evans—will be admitted to the sacred niches. Which is only as it should be."[80] The *Lewiston Morning Tribune* agreed. "A sportswriter wonders why the baseball hall of fame at Cooperstown, New York, includes no umpires. The only explanation that comes to mind," the paper quipped, "is the traditional idea that umpires have no friends." The paper agreed that Bill Klem should be considered for the honor, but the reporter was quick to add another name for consideration to the list: "Silk" O'Loughlin. "Did not Silk O'Loughlin originate the custom of raising the right arm to indicate a strike?"[81]

The credit seems to have shifted to Bill Klem because he claimed it. Nothing in the early coverage of his career, in the period of 1905 to 1909, found to date, mentions his gestures. There are two articles, both of which appeared after his retirement, where Klem discusses his use of gestures. One is the 1951 interview where Klem indicated that he started using signs in 1906. This led to the discovery that it was in fact his friend "Silk" who was using gestures that season. There was also an earlier interview in 1941, where Klem explained that when he broke into the National League in 1905, he wore out his voice and "so turned to the gestures that made him famous and that most umpires since that time have followed in varying styles."[82]

But gesturing behind the plate was such a novelty that when O'Loughlin did it, it was covered in the press at the turn of the century. No such coverage has yet turned up for Klem, to independently verify his claims. There was coverage in the press of a Klem throat injury, however. In 1914, it was reported that Klem might not be ready to start the National League season. He had been hit in the throat by an errant foul ball during a winter ball tour in December 1913. He was forced to undergo "a delicate operation to his throat" as a result.[83] As it happened, Klem recovered fully and came back for the season. No other reported throat injuries have yet been uncovered.

There are, of course, many newspaper reports of a gesture that was entirely unique to Bill Klem. When Klem died in September 1951, several obituaries rightly mentioned his most characteristic gesture, the drawing of his famous line in the sand. In 1904, working in the minor league American Association, Klem "drew his line on the field with his spiked shoe, a line which later deterred such tough competitors as John McGraw, Mike Donlin, Frank Chance, and Frankie Frisch." He warned players who argued his calls that they were not to cross the line, or he would toss them out of the game. "That little trick made me an umpire," Klem later recalled. "I drew that line on a lot of great players in the National League and it always worked."[84] If there is one gesture most associated with Bill Klem, it is surely this one, made with his foot.

And what of Dummy Hoy? Within the deaf community, he has always been credited with bringing the signs to baseball. *Deaf Life* asserted in 1992, "When Hoy entered the leagues ... there were no signals. Umpires still called out strikes and balls verbally. No one had yet thought of replacing the shouts with signals, but Hoy was a trailblazer. He left the game of baseball with a legacy that remains to this day." After describing how Hoy's signals worked, the paper concluded, "Eventually umpires began to signal strikes and balls for all batters. Signaling became the standard procedure, and the practice has endured."[85]

Deaf Life complained that baseball historians refused to give Hoy his due. To them, "this story is unauthenticated or apocryphal. Or worse, hearsay or folklore. Some go as far as to say that early 20th century umpires Cy Rigler and Bill Klem were responsible for creating the signals."[86] It is fairer to say, the paper concluded, that the hearing umpires appropriated them for their own use, adding "it is a grave disservice to the truth not give credit where credit is due."[87]

Deaf baseball researcher Matthew Moore points out that baseball has faced other murky origin stories in its history. William "Candy" Cummings, a 19th-century pitcher for the Hartford Dark Blues, Moore reminds us, largely got his spot in the Hall on the "strength of his having invented the curveball. At least five other contenders have also claimed to be the inventor. It would be gratifying if Cooperstown were to likewise recognize Hoy's role in the invention of umpire's signals."[88] (And, in fact, Cummings's plaque reads in part: "Pitched first curve ball in baseball history. Invented curve as amateur ace of Brooklyn Stars in 1867." He was inducted into the Hall in 1939.)

Moore raises an important point. Baseball has attempted to wade through the conflicting stories and sparse evidence in other such similar situations, but in the case of Hoy and umpire signals, hearing researchers have never taken the case for Hoy's part in the story very seriously. For instance, in 1990, after Bill Deane concluded in his correspondence with Hoy advocate and deaf baseball researcher Steven Sandy that the Hoy connection to signs was "an inaccuracy," one that had spread, in the years since Hoy's retirement, "like wildfire,"[89] Sandy wrote again to argue Hoy's case, offering a 1952 interview Hoy gave on the subject to *The Silent Worker*, a major deaf newspaper. Deane wrote back to reject this evidence.

In a letter dated 16 October 1990, he wrote to Sandy, "While this does suggest an indirect connection between Hoy and the umpire's hand signals, it also proves that this practice was not adopted until **after** Hoy's career. Also, as far as we know, Hoy merely **assumed** that his coaches' signals gave later-day umpires the idea. He may have been correct, but there is no way to prove it."[90] In 2010, Deane reiterated his view that Hoy's role in this history is unprovable. "There are an awful lot of holes in this story. But you can't prove a negative, so the story survives."[91]

It is clear that Deane has simply never believed that this deaf man could have made this important contribution to baseball. There is a level of audism at work here. Audism is a term coined by Tom Humphries in 1977 to indicate "the notion that one is superior based on one's ability to hear or to behave in the manner of one who hears."[92] Audism is a form of discrimination against deaf people based on their inability to hear and on their use of signed communication. As Harlan Lane has argued, audism can go beyond individual discrimination against a deaf person. Structurally, it is "the hearing way of dominating, restructuring, and exercising authority over the deaf community."[93]

Here, in baseball, it has been a way of consistently marginalizing the contributions of a deaf player. Hoy is being held to a standard of proof that Klem never had to meet. As recently as 2012, Deane noted that a check of "Hoy's voluminous clipping file at the National Baseball Library turns up only one article written during Hoy's long lifetime that mentions anything about hand signals."[94] It is *The Silent Worker* article that Sandy had pointed out to Deane, an article that Sandy himself had added to the file. But one could say exactly the same thing about Klem's file. There is nothing in there about his supposed gestures, beyond his famous foot gesture, that dates from the early 20th century.

There is a double standard at work here, one that revolves around Hoy's deafness. As David A. Stewart points out in *Deaf Sport*, deaf athletes are always seen by hearing players, coaches, and fans as deaf first. He concludes that "how they judge a deaf player might still be influenced by societal and personal notions about deafness."[95] The deaf community has always known that Hoy's deafness, as well as hearing ideas about deafness more generally, have deeply influenced how Hoy has been remembered within the baseball community, by both researchers and fans alike.

In 2004, Stephen Jay Gould, in *Triumph and Tragedy in Mudville*, flatly argued that Hoy deserved election to the Hall of Fame. Gould reluctantly concluded that Hoy was being discriminated against on account of his deafness. He wrote that he had tried to avoid reaching that conclusion. "But I suspect," Gould remarked, "that Hoy's deafness did deprive him of a necessary tool for the later renown that gets men into the Hall by sustained reputation.... Hoy never received much press coverage. Journalists refrained from interviewing him, even though he was the smartest and most articulate player in baseball. So Hoy was forgotten after he left the field—and his fierce pride prevented any effort at self-promotion. His inbuilt silence abetted the unjust silence of others."[96]

Gould at last puts his finger on what has separated Hoy from Klem in this tangled history. Hearing journalists simply did not know how to interact with the deaf Hoy. They did not seek him out for interviews often, either during his career or after. Hoy therefore never enjoyed the "sustained reputation" that other players have used to mount campaigns to get into the Hall. Klem faced no such barriers, as he gave multiple interviews with the press to claim the credit for himself, and, as a hearing man, the press corps found him to be accessible and affable. He also had no qualms about stretching the truth, to cement his case for the Hall. Due to his untimely death, "Silk" O'Loughlin, too, had largely faded from hearing memory by the time Klem was building a public case for his election to Cooperstown.

For all of his contributions to baseball, Hoy deserves to be considered for a place in the Hall. In *Triumph and Tragedy in Mudville*, Stephen Jay Gould put it most plainly: "Dummy Hoy belongs in the Hall of Fame by sole virtue of his excellent, sustained play over a long career. His case seems undeniable to me. A dozen players from Hoy's time have been elected with records no better than the exemplary statistics—particularly the great fielding and savvy baserunning, not to mention the more than adequate hitting—of Dummy Hoy."[97]

But this undeniable case has been continually overshadowed by the legend of his role in the development of the signs of baseball. It is why solving this mystery is so important. Gould observed that the legend has, ironically, derailed, rather than advanced, Hoy's case. He hinted at the dynamic between deaf supporters and hearing baseball researchers. The deaf community emphasized "his role in inspiring the use of umpire's hand signals," such that the story of Hoy's supposed role has become a piece of information "that now occupies a space in the cultural knowledge of millions of Americans," yet the story is still regarded by many baseball researchers only as a legend, a myth, an inaccuracy.[98]

The focus on the signs in some ways hinders Hoy's case for Cooperstown. Historians too are caught up in examining the truth or falsity of the signals story, usually to demonstrate that the deaf community has it wrong. Then, having determined that his legend is merely that, a fiction, they are free to reject Hoy entirely. The rest of his case, built on his career stats, never receives any sustained attention at all. His legend is allowed to overshadow his legacy and both are in turn dismissed.

It is past time to do as Gould has suggested and "break the circle of silence that still surrounds this intelligent, savvy, wonderfully skilled, and exemplary man."[99] Breaking that silence starts with settling the question of Hoy's contributions to his sport. Those contributions certainly include his career statistics as well as his pioneering role in the development of a gesture system in baseball. Breaking the silence starts with challenging the standard consensus around Hoy that allows his contributions to baseball to be dismissed. "The consensus is that standardized umpires' hand signals first appeared in the big leagues about 1906, give or take a year," Bill Deane writes. "And Dummy Hoy, who last played in the majors in 1902, had nothing to do with them."[100]

In fact, William Ellsworth Hoy had everything to do with them. "Dummy" Hoy and "Silk" O'Loughlin. Both men, it seems to me, are long overdue to get credit for their enduring legacy to the national pastime.

An earlier version of this essay appeared as "A Tale of Two Umpires; Or, Restoring the Legacy of Dummy Hoy" in *NINE: A Journal of Baseball History and Culture* 23, 2 (Spring 2015), 1–32. Preliminary thoughts on this topic were first presented as "Whose Sign Is It, Anyway? A Fresh Look at the Hoy-Klem Controversy" at the 22nd Cooperstown Symposium on Baseball and American Culture, held in Cooperstown, New York, in 2010. I would like to thank the audience at that presentation for their questions, suggestions, and feedback. I would especially like to thank the late Dorothy Seymour Mills, who was in attendance that day, for her support for this work.

4

Three Deaf Men and Eighteen Dummies: Luther Taylor's New York Giants

In the 1902 season, baseball fans witnessed a piece of baseball history that had never been seen before and has never been seen since. On May 16, 1902, William Hoy's Cincinnati Reds played Luther Taylor's New York Giants in Cincinnati. As Randy Fisher and James Goodwin reported, "A diverse crowd of 5,000 deaf and hearing people witnessed this once-in-a-lifetime event."[1] Taylor was pitching for the Giants, and even here, at the end of his career, Hoy batted leadoff for Cincinnati. As Hoy came to the plate, he signed to Taylor "I'm glad to see you" and promptly drove a hit into center field. Taylor quickly fell behind, but the Giants staged a late rally to win the game, 5–3. This 1902 contest remains the first and only time a deaf pitcher and a deaf batter have faced each other in a major league game.[2]

"Dummy" Hoy has long been the most celebrated baseball hero of the deaf community. "Dummy" Taylor, however, has been less well remembered. Yet, to this day, Luther Haden Taylor remains the only deaf pitcher of note to have played major league baseball. Taylor was an above average pitcher for most of his career, playing for the New York Giants. He was a key pitcher on their staff on their National League championship teams of 1904 and 1905. Taylor won 21 games for the Giants in 1904 and his 1906 ERA of 2.20 was the lowest of a pitching staff that included the legendary Christy Mathewson. He was a top 10 leader for strikeouts among National League pitchers twice, once in 1901 and again in 1904. He finished in the top 10 for shutouts in 1901, 1904, and 1905, and he pitched 21 shutouts over the course of his career. That puts him in the 230th spot among pitchers of all-time; baseball-reference. com runs the list out to number 915, so his 21 shutouts have aged pretty well. He still ranks in the top 100 pitchers in major league history (89th out of 999) for lowest career ERA at 2.747, which, again, is a solid mark for a man whose major league pitching career ended in 1908.

Taylor was born deaf to hearing parents in 1875 in Oskaloosa, Kansas. Where Hoy grew up as the only deaf child in his hearing family, Taylor had a deaf older sister, Fannie. Though his hearing parents most likely did not know it, the deaf community was already well established by then. The decade of the 1850s had seen deaf people hold public events and raise monuments to their heroes; saw the birth of a flourishing deaf press, with newspapers and journals catering to concerns of deaf readers; and witnessed the creation of the first deaf founded and led organizations. As Deaf Studies scholar Christopher Krentz has concluded, the events of the decade "marked the emergence of deaf Americans' collective consciousness." By the late 1850s, deaf people seemed well on their way to claiming a Deaf-American identity.[3]

Residential schools for the deaf were where most deaf children were first exposed to this community. The Kansas School for the Deaf, in nearby Olathe, had been established in 1861, as a manual school. But the decade of the 1860s saw the emergence of a competing educational system for the deaf, called oralism. It taught deaf children exclusively by speech and lipreading and forbid the use of any kind of signed language. In this way, oralism's proponents hoped that deaf children would come to see themselves as hearing impaired members of the larger hearing community, identity with that community, and communicate like them, eschewing sign language and the deaf community altogether.[4]

As more and more deaf children were brought into the orbit of oralism, the wider deaf community increasingly worried about its future. How would the sign language survive? How would deaf people gain access to this visual language, if not at school? How would deaf children grow successfully into adulthood, without deaf adult role models in schools to mentor them? Could the deaf community survive, if the schools became enemies instead of allies?

Luther Taylor attended the Kansas School for the Deaf in the midst of this critical period of deaf history. As oralism grew in popularity among instructors, the manual Kansas School introduced limited instruction in articulation and lipreading for students in 1879 "to those who were found profited thereby."[5] Taylor arrived at the school in 1884, one of 157 pupils.[6] Fannie also attended the Kansas School. Apparently, athletic talent ran in the family; Fannie had served as the secretary of the girls' athletic club, the Amazonia Athletic Club.[7] Taylor was described as "bright and active" at school, "quick to learn, always busy."[8] The school grew over his time there. By 1893, there were 261 pupils. Taylor graduated as valedictorian in 1895.

Luther Taylor as a student at the Kansas School for the Deaf. He is shown here in printing class. The class instructor, Walter Mundell, is the man in the suit, holding a newspaper. Taylor is the third boy from the left, standing with his left hand on Mundell's shoulder. Mundell worked as the printing instructor at the school from 1888 to 1891; this photo must have been taken in this period. Taylor recalled KSD as the place where he was first introduced to baseball. Courtesy Kansas School for the Deaf.

As the school grew in numbers and more students graduated, the alumni in Kansas became more organized. The Southern Kansas Deaf-Mute Association was organized in 1889 by "former pupils of this school ... the object being social enjoyment and religious privileges." The Kansas City Deaf-Mute Club was founded in 1892, and "though strictly speaking the Club is a Missouri organization," it was also serving deaf Kansans, as "nearly one-half the present membership were formerly pupils here."[9] Taylor, in other words, would have witnessed the steady growth of the deaf community within his own state during his lifetime.

Always interested in athletics, Taylor originally wanted to be a boxer, but his parents discouraged that choice and pushed him toward baseball instead.[10] Taylor, like Hoy, had been exposed to baseball at school. As he later remembered his years at the Kansas School for the Deaf, he wrote, "This is where I was educated and graduated and learned the baseball game."[11] After

94

he graduated from Kansas, he played minor league ball in the west for a few years before signing as a pitcher with the New York Giants. He pitched for them from 1900 to 1908. When he started in 1900, the 25-year-old Taylor only pitched seven games. In the 1900 U.S. Census, his occupation was listed not as ballplayer but as printer, undoubtedly the trade that he had been taught at the Kansas School. Printing was finally abandoned as his major league career took off. That same census confirmed that he could read and write English but did not speak it.[12]

Like Hoy, Taylor was quickly nicknamed "Dummy" and was referred to as "Dummy" in the press. While the word "dumb" had signified "mute" throughout most of the 19th century, including when Hoy had entered the majors in 1888, by the early 20th century and Taylor's arrival in the sport, the term was starting to connote "stupid" as well. As a result, the deaf press expressed increasing dissatisfaction with the term.

Unsurprisingly, much of this conversation was framed around Luther Taylor. Hoy's long career was coming to an end just as this discussion around the nickname was heating up. With Hoy's impending retirement, Taylor increasingly moved into the public eye, serving as the face of deafness in baseball and as the most prominent deaf player to endure the nickname of "dummy." As *The Silent Worker* editorialized in June 1903, "Dummy with reference to the deaf seems to be a favorite word with the common people. We read Dummy Hoy and Dummy Taylor.... Oh, the idea of a 'dummy' playing good ball! Be fair—give these abused players the respect they deserve. Certainly it is not flattering to be called a dummy."[13]

The *Deaf-Mutes' Journal* took a slightly different tack on the question. "When we read in the papers about 'Dummy Hoy' or 'Dummy Taylor,' our two most noted baseball players, we know no insult is conveyed in the term, though we wish very much the word was left out. One of the school papers of recent date remarked that deaf-mutes will be called 'dummies' whether they like it or not when they play professional baseball. The open season for baseball is not here yet, but memories of things we have heard in the bleachers in past seasons warrant us in saying that the deaf-mute gets off easy when he is called nothing worse than 'dummy.' The advantage is on his side, too, in that he cannot hear it. Hearing players are not so lucky, nor does a little, gentle, mild-mannered word like 'dummy' sound bad at all compared to some the leather-lunged and frenzied bleacherites yell when things happen to be going the wrong way."[14]

The *Silent Worker* was unconvinced. Columnist Alexander Pach commented in May 1905, "The highest salaried deaf man in the United States is the much heralded Dummy Taylor—I say Dummy only to serve to show how contemptible the epithet looks." While lamenting that one could expect no better from the hearing press, the deaf press was quite another. "And do the papers supposedly published in the interests of the deaf protest? Do they? Well, notice next time and see with what avidity and without comment or protest they clip and reprint every item about Dummy Taylor that they come across."[15] He urged his readers to remember, instead, that Luther Taylor is "an intelligent, self-respecting citizen who happens to be a deaf mute." In other words, they were all Luther Taylor. That is, all deaf people wanted to be seen as proud American citizens and not as dummies. It is not hard to see why Pach and *The Silent Worker* refused to let this issue drop.

And, finally, this came in June 1908: "Now that baseball season has opened we may expect to see that offensive term dummy brought into frequent use again in the sporting columns of the daily papers, in referring to numerous deaf professional players in baseball. There seems to be no way to secure a cessation in the use of the objectionable term so the deaf will have to accept the situation philosophically.... One thing that the editors of the l.p.f. can and should do—discountenance the word and never admit it to their columns.... Every paper has some influence and should use it all and at all times in the interest of the Deaf." L.P.F. stands for "little paper family," a collective term for the various papers that constituted the deaf press. Another author suggested that hearing people "are not aware that the deaf object to its use." He argued that "when the term is used in the case of the deaf it does not imply what is meant when the same word is used for a hearing person."[16]

Perhaps that was the case. Perhaps, when used for a deaf player, the term was still meant to signal merely their physical and not mental condition. But Alexander Pach doubted it, writing plainly in 1910, "Mr. Hoy is no dummy. Mr. Taylor is no dummy, either."[17] Luther Taylor himself made it clear that he agreed with Pach. To him, the term was an insult. As Taylor remembered, looking back, "In the old days, Hoy and I were called Dummy. It didn't hurt us. It made us fight harder."[18] The "us" here referred to the two ballplayers, but it is clear that, to Taylor, the wider "us" was the deaf community. Taylor identified as a deaf man, and as a non-speaking deaf man. He was proud to be a member of the larger signing deaf community, and he was committed to fighting for it.

But if he was going to be known as "Dummy" while he played ball, Taylor was going to wear the label as a deaf man and fight harder, for himself and for his community. Taylor insisted on being included on his team, on his terms, that is, on deaf terms. "I never heard a sound or spoke a word in my life," Taylor once noted.[19] He expected his teammates to sign with him. As Sean Lehman put it for the SABR Biography Project, "The Giants didn't just add Taylor to their roster; they embraced him as a member of their family. Player-manager George Davis learned sign language and encouraged his players to do the same. John McGraw did likewise when he took over as Giants manager in July 1902."

In fact, when McGraw came to the team, the Giants had just come off a season where they had three deaf men on their roster, all pitchers: William Deegan, George Leitner, and Luther Taylor. Or, as McGraw remembered it, he had "three deaf men and 18 dummies on the Giants."[20]

William Deegan played only in the 1901 season, for the Giants. He appeared in only two games, pitching all of 17 innings. Deegan was born in 1874 to Irish Catholic immigrant parents, who settled in the Bronx. When they discovered that their son was deaf, they enrolled him in a school for the deaf in the Bronx, St. Joseph's Institute for the Improved Instruction of Deaf Mutes.

Founded in 1869, St. Joseph's was an oral school, run by the nuns of the Society of the Daughters of the Heart of Mary. Since baseball was clearly not a full-time profession for Deegan, his other day job was at the school, where he worked as a supervisor of boys. Later, Deegan also worked for the school as an "instructor of physical culture."[21] He continued to try his hand at baseball, playing for several minor league teams, in Connecticut in 1902, in Massachusetts in 1905, in New Jersey in 1907, and in Pennsylvania in 1909.[22] According to the census records of the school, Deegan could read, write, and speak English. Press coverage of his minor league career called him "an excellent pitcher" who was "hard of hearing" with "a slight impediment of speech."[23] The nickname

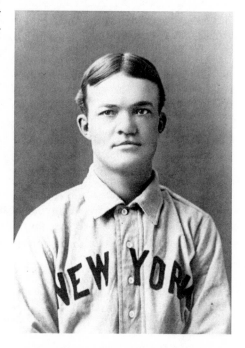

Luther Taylor in 1903. Taylor pitched for the New York Giants, helping them win two pennants, first in 1904 and again in 1905. Library of Congress.

"Dummy" apparently should not have applied to him. Deegan died in the Bronx in 1957.[24]

George Leitner played two seasons in major league baseball, pitching for the Philadelphia A's and the New York Giants in 1901 and the Cleveland Indians and Chicago White Sox in 1902. Of course, Hoy had played for the White Sox in 1901, so the club would have had experience with a deaf player. Like Deegan, Leitner appeared in two games for the Giants, pitching 18 innings. Unlike Deegan, Leitner had attended a signing school. Born in Parkton, Maryland, in 1871, he attended the Columbia Institution for the Deaf and Dumb and Blind, with his deaf siblings Lydia and Frank.[25] The school was opened in Washington, D.C., in 1857. It later expanded its educational reach when it was granted the right to confer college degrees in 1864. The school still exists today and is called the Kendall Demonstration School. It continues to serve deaf students from pre-school to eighth grade on the campus of what is now known as Gallaudet University.

Leitner went on to attend Gallaudet College and he played for their baseball team in 1889. He also pitched for the Baltimore Athletic Club, before he joined the Giants. After his major league career ended, the then-35-year-old Leitner pitched for one more season, for the Baton Rouge Cajuns in the Class D Cotton States League in 1906.[26]

Deaf history chronicler Kathleen Brockway demonstrates that Leitner was an important community leader within the Baltimore deaf community, where the family settled. In 1897, George Leitner married Helen D. Wells. Wells was Deaf of Deaf. Her father was James Sullivan Wells. He was born deaf in 1832 in New York City and he attended the New York School for the Deaf. Wells moved to Texas, where he became one of the first teachers at the Texas School for the Deaf. The Wells family moved to Baltimore in 1879. James Wells then became an important figure in the Baltimore deaf community. He helped to organize annual deaf events at Druid Hill Park and was seen as a community leader until his death in 1891. His daughter Helen followed in his footsteps. Her marriage to George Leitner produced her family's third generation of deaf members with the birth of their deaf daughter, Helen. The family were members of Christ Deaf Church, an important deaf community organization in the city. Leitner also coached deaf baseball teams in Baltimore after his playing days ended.[27] He worked as a printer in the composing room of *The Baltimore Sun* for roughly 30 years before he retired. Leitner died in 1960. His obituary in *The Sun* broke the news to the greater Baltimore community with the headline "George Leitner, Ex-Athlete, Dies."[28]

With Deegan and Leitner having but brief major league careers, Taylor was soon left as the only deaf player in major league baseball. Yet, even among all hearing teammates, he signed to communicate all the time. When the press referred to the Giants as having hearing players who "learned the sign language," these accounts seem mostly to indicate that they learned how to fingerspell, or, to use McGraw's phrase, "wigwagged."[29] McGraw, incidentally, got so good at reading fingerspelling, no easy achievement, he once reported that, in a heated moment with Taylor, "in sign language, Dummy consigned me to the hottest place he could think of—and he didn't mean St. Louis."[30]

McGraw, just like Clark Griffith, took to using fingerspelling to send in signs, rattling off S-T-E-A-L, "so plain," Giant Fred Snodgrass once said, "that anyone in the park who could read the deaf and dumb language would know what was happening."[31] McGraw remarked that he used fingerspelling due to the fact that his baserunners would sometimes forget what the agreed upon team signs for "steal" or "bunt" were. They knew he could just spell it to them instead.[32]

McGraw was known to get himself into trouble with umpires. His knowledge of fingerspelling helped when he found himself suspended and barred from the dugout. In one case, during the 1908 season, he found himself facing a suspension that one sports reporter called "purely technical." McGraw "can keep out of sight of umpires here and still be where he can put his hand on any player on the Giants' bench. That and the language of Luther Taylor will do the rest."[33] As a manager, McGraw clearly recognized deaf advantages for himself, especially deaf communication, and he did not hesitate to claim them.

Snodgrass recalled that the whole team learned to fingerspell, as Taylor "took it as an affront if you didn't learn to converse with him. He wanted to be one of us, to be a full-fledged member of the team." So, as Snodgrass explained, "we all learned. We practiced all the time. We'd go by elevated train from the hotel to the Polo Grounds and all during the ride, we'd be spelling out the advertising signs. Not talking to one another, but sitting there spelling out the advertising messages."[34]

Taylor too remembered the Giants as always willing to sign with him. As he explained to a reporter in 1942, "Most of them learned to talk with their fingers so as to help me. All were great."[35] And again in 1945, Taylor asserted, "Being mute wasn't much of a handicap. John McGraw learned the sign language well and then made the whole New York team take it up. I always carried a pad and pencil but never had to on the ball field. During my eight years with the Giants, every player learned to sign. Some of them were all thumbs, and Joe McGinnity was very careless with his spelling."[36]

Many newspapers, in both the hearing and deaf presses, confirmed the overwhelming presence of sign among the Giants during Taylor's playing days. *The Atlanta Constitution* reported in 1907, "Among the players, Taylor is a great favorite. They all love him and every man on the club can talk to him in the language of fingers."[37] *The Silent Worker* reported the same, as in this instance in 1905: "All the Giants can talk the sign language and sometimes in dining rooms and hotels Taylor will talk to two or three of the players and persons seated nearby look on but are unable to tell which man is the mute."

Taylor also advocated for his inclusion. It was widely reported in the deaf press that he used to hand out manual alphabet cards to newly arrived Giants, to encourage them to learn how to fingerspell as well.[38] When Irishman Tom Needham came to the team in 1908, Taylor took one look at Needham's "knotted digits" and joked, "I'll bet he has a brogue."[39] Again, learning fingerspelling might seem like an obvious choice here, but its use is striking in the context of the times. By the turn of the century, nearly 40 percent of deaf Americans were taught without the use of any sign language, including fingerspelling.[40] In other words, while some 40 percent of school-age deaf children in the United States at this time were denied access to any form of signed language, hearing ball players were signing alongside their deaf teammate. Not only were they learning the language, over time, some of the Giants proved curious about the larger deaf community that Taylor belonged to. Once, while the Giants were on a road trip in Philadelphia, it happened that a deaf convention was being held there. Taylor, unsurprisingly, took the chance to attend. Somewhat more surprisingly, some of his hearing teammates did too. "Several of the players, out of curiosity, went with Taylor to the convention and all they could see was a sea of wiggling fingers."[41]

Taylor had come to the Giants in 1900. In his sophomore season in 1901, Taylor led all National League pitchers in appearances, making 45 in total, while compiling an 18–27 record.[42] He left for the new American League in 1902, heading for Cleveland, with a chance to negotiate a more lucrative contract. John McGraw had other ideas; he wanted Taylor back. Losing record aside, McGraw firmly believed that Taylor was developing into a great pitcher. McGraw told Taylor's favorite catcher on the Giants, Frank Bowerman, to go after him. "Give him what he wants," McGraw told Bowerman. "Don't come back without him."[43] Bowerman had become very good at fingerspelling, and he and Taylor shared a friendship off the field.

Sending Bowerman proved a stroke of genius. Taylor was unhappy in Cleveland. The team was not using him; he had pitched only four games in two months. And, unlike the Giants, his Cleveland teammates proved uninterested in learning any sign language, including the manual alphabet. This would seem to suggest that the signing of the Giants was an active choice that the franchise made to cultivate inclusion. Most hearing people, like the Cleveland players, did not take up any form of sign language. After all, most hearing people did not assume it was their responsibility to help break down the communication barrier between deaf and hearing people. They put all of the burden of communication on deaf people. The Cleveland players stuck with their hearing privilege and spoke. Taylor felt very isolated on his new team.[44]

And then, at one game, Taylor spotted Bowerman in the stands. "Frank sat in the grandstand," Taylor recounted, "and every time I walked to the pitching mound and back to the bench he kept talking to me with his fingers. I kept shaking my head 'no' and Frank kept boosting the money. Soon, I nodded my head 'yes' and that night I was back on my way to New York with Frank."[45]

Taylor roomed with Charlie Hemphill. Hemphill came back to their hotel room, having forgotten his room key. He was most worried about getting into the room, "me with no key and a deaf and dumb man to wake up before I could get in the room and go to bed." He began his effort to gain access to the room by stopping at the front desk and was surprised to find a key there. "When I opened the door and struck a light, the first thing I noticed was the Dummy's two uniforms spread out on the bed. A closer search revealed that he had taken his other belongings with him. I picked up the uniforms and shook out a note which read: 'Good-by, Charlie—I am back with New York.'"[46]

McGraw wanted him back for good reason. Taylor had established himself as a pitcher. Taylor's drop ball was considered the best in baseball. As Ned Hanlon, the father of the hit and run, watched Taylor warm up once, he blurted out, "I don't see how that man can continue pitching that ball. I couldn't imagine a harder delivery and I don't think another pitcher would have the strength."[47] As David W. Anderson puts it, "On the mound, Taylor had an unorthodox corkscrew delivery. He had a good fastball, curve, and a devastating drop ball. But he had another edge. He was adept at stealing other team's signs because of his eyesight, and he could read a base runner's intentions by studying his facial expressions."[48]

Taylor had, in fact, put his skills at reading baserunners to use immediately, in his major league debut. In his very first game for the Giants, hearing baserunners had challenged him. As Taylor recalled, "It was against Frank Selee's Boston club, one of the best. It had … fast men. Those fellows thought they would take advantage of me because of my deafness. Five of them tried to steal third base and I nailed each one. I walked over to [Herman] Long, the last man caught, and let him know by signs I could hear him stealing."[49]

Taylor's joking aside, and he was known as a man with a terrific sense of humor, it was his eyes that he relied on to pick off base runners, though some did not believe it. Joe Tinker, the famous shortstop for the Cubs, was one. "I'm convinced he can hear," Tinker said in 1905. The reason? Watching Taylor pick off Cubs who were trying to steal. Tinker reportedly argued: "Look what happened to Harry Steinfeldt today when he tried to steal third, breaking for the bag

Luther Taylor. Manager John McGraw recalled the Giants as a team featuring "three deaf men and 18 dummies." Courtesy Johnson County Museum.

while Taylor was standing on the mound and facing the plate. Taylor stepped off the slab as soon as Harry started running, turned around, and threw the ball to third, getting him by several feet. Larry Doyle, down there at second for the Giants, yelled when he saw Steinfeldt start for third. Nobody can make me believe Taylor didn't hear that yell. How else could he have caught on to what was happening, with his back turned toward Steinfeldt when the play started?" Taylor had his own explanation. He explained that he saw the sudden change of expression in the face of his catcher, Frank Bowerman, and figured out quickly from that what was happening.[50]

"Players throughout the league assert that it is more difficult to steal third base off Taylor, even when his back is turned," *The Atlanta Constitution* reported, "than any pitcher in either league." The paper stressed that Taylor "depends entirely upon the facial expression of his team mates for direction in a close play.... This in some respects is an advantage because Taylor is never confused by the yelling of three or four men at the same time."[51] The

4. Three Deaf Men and Eighteen Dummies

New York Clipper explained the advantages of Taylor's deafness to fans in this way. "After all, Taylor's deaf-mute misfortune is really an asset on the baseball diamond. He is never confused, as others are, by the mass of sounds that comes up when a play starts. Under such a condition, he simply gets accurate information with utmost speed through use of his extremely alert and well-trained eyes."[52]

Just as we saw with Hoy, Taylor too saw advantages to his deafness. It made him a better player. Playing professional baseball as a deaf man allowed Taylor to reinforce the idea that Hoy had also stressed. Deafness could be an advantage, and not an obstacle, in life. This early version of deaf gain would have been revolutionary to hearing players and fans, most of whom were unfamiliar with deaf people. Many were skeptical that deaf people could perform athletically at the same level as hearing people. And sometimes, when they did, they faced the rumor that they were really more hearing than they let on. After all, even Tinker believed that Taylor's success on the diamond indicated that he could not possibly really be deaf. He was such a good player that he had to be hearing. No disabled player could be that good. It was just that sort of prejudice that Taylor's presence in the majors was challenging.

Taylor was able to make his greatest contribution to promoting this wider cause of deaf capability by being successful on a pitching staff crowded with talent. After he rejoined the Giants, Taylor posted an ERA of 2.29. Unfortunately, the Giants' hitters squandered his strong pitching, as he compiled a 7–15 record.[53] Taylor pitched besides future Hall of Famers Christy Mathewson and Joe "Iron Man" McGinnity. As the *Deaf-Mutes' Journal* noted with obvious pride, "In the New York Club, Taylor is in fast company, but he is equal to the pace."[54]

In 1904, the pitching of the trio led the Giants to the pennant easily, as they finished 13 games ahead of the second place Cubs, posting a record of 106–47 in the process. Mathewson went 33–12 and McGinnity went 35–8. Taylor had his best season, going 21–15, pitching 296 innings in total, including 29 complete games.[55] They would have to be content with the pennant. McGraw refused to play the American League champion Boston Pilgrims, calling the new league inferior.[56]

The three were back to pitch together in the 1905 season and they delivered McGraw another pennant. Mathewson went 31–9, McGinnity went 21–15, and Taylor went 16–9. Additionally, pitcher Red Ames hurled his way to a career-best 22–8, peaking at the right moment. As Tol Broome remarks, "Not surprisingly, the 1905 Giants' pitching staff is considered by baseball historians to be one of the most dominant staffs on one of the most dominant teams in the annals of the national pastime."[57] The team posted a record of 105–48.

This time, the Giants agreed to play the A.L. champs, the Philadelphia A's, in the World Series. Taylor was scheduled to start for the Giants in Game 3. In the first game, Mathewson blanked the A's, 3–0. The A's returned the favor in Game 2, 3–0, with McGinnity taking the loss. Then, nature intervened. Game 3 was postponed due to rain. With an additional day of rest, McGraw went back to Mathewson, instead of Taylor, for Game 3, and Matty pitched his second shutout of the series, winning 9–0. Taylor never got his chance to pitch in the World Series. If McGraw had stuck with him, he would have been the first deaf player to appear in a World Series game. The Giants won Game 4, 1–0, behind McGinnity. Mathewson wrapped up the series for the Giants in Game 5 with his third win, 2–0, a win which was also his third shutout and his third complete game of the Series, a Series in which he gave up only 13 hits, a performance which established his legend as a pitcher for the ages. The 1905 World Series remains the only one where each game was a shutout.[58]

Rings for World Series champions did not come into vogue until the 1920s. The members of the 1905 Giants all received quarter-sized gold pins. In "brilliant gold lettering" at the top of the pin was the inscription "World's Champions 1905." Then came "a white baseball at the top, just under the inscription." Beneath the baseball, "crisscrossing the pin, were two baseball bats with a star in the middle, centered by a diamond. But the most spectacular feature was the 22 diamonds that framed the circular pin."[59] Though he undoubtedly would have preferred to have pitched, Taylor would have to be satisfied with becoming the first (and so far only) deaf man to play for a World Series champion and with earning this World Series pin.

Looking back, Taylor believed that the team's willingness to use sign language was the key to its success. As he wrote in a November 9, 1942, letter, "The reason why we beat Phil. Athletics in the Series in 1905, every one on our team gave out signals and worked altogether. When Mack heard of it, he ordered his men to learn the sign language the next time they met the Giants and his men could read and that is how they beat McGraw."[60]

The prominent use of signed communication by the Giants over the course of Taylor's career led to several memorable incidents. Taylor was accustomed to communicating with his catchers by fingerspelling. Frequently, that was Roger Bresnahan, his usual battery mate. Bresnahan is widely considered to be the deadball era's most famous catcher and an innovator in his own right; he pioneered the development and use of catcher's protective

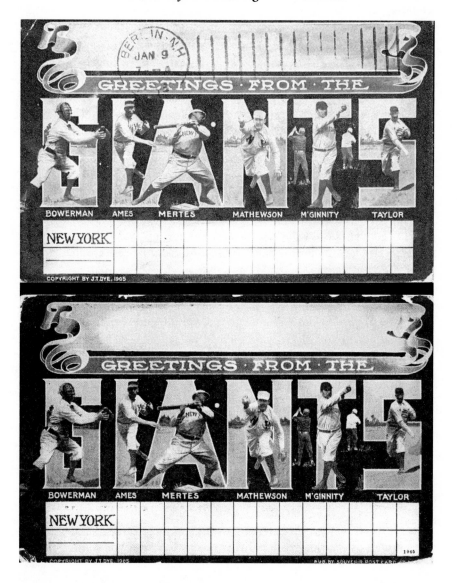

A 1905 postcard for fans, offering "Greetings from the Giants," featuring, from left to right, catcher Frank Bowerman, pitcher Leon "Red" Ames, outfielder Sam Mertes, pitcher Christy Mathewson, pitcher Joe McGinnity, and pitcher Luther Taylor. Courtesy Robert Edward Auctions.

equipment, including helmets and shin guards.[61] As one news report put it, "The old Giants all learned the sign language from Dummy Taylor. Roger Bresnahan, next to the Dummy, was the fastest with his fingers."[62] Spelling quickly with one another, Taylor and Bresnahan were confident no one could follow their conversation.

But in one particular game, when the Giants met up with the Chicago Cubs, they were facing Del Howard. Given that it been 1899 when last they had played together, Taylor can be forgiven for having forgotten. But Del Howard and Taylor had spent a season together playing for Kokomo/Mattoon in the Indiana-Illinois League. As a result, "Howard mastered the sign language and became extremely fluent with his fingers. He could talk a blue streak with his hands." He took full advantage at the plate. "Del interpreted Taylor's conversation with the catcher and knew just what was coming up. They are still looking for the ball."[63] The pair took more care around Howard after that.

This was apparently not the only time Bresnahan and Taylor were taken by surprise in this way. McGraw told a story of spending a night out with the pair. "We all liked Taylor well enough to learn the mute language, so that we could talk with him," McGraw recalled. "One day we were riding on a street car when a remarkably handsome woman came in and sat opposite us. We watched her with considerable admiration for a minute, then Roger signed to the 'Dummy' on his fingers, 'Doesn't she look good to you?' Before either of us could sign back, the woman flashed over in the sign language, 'Yes, and you also look good to me.' And she got off the car without even glancing back at us."[64]

Taylor is sometimes credited with having invented the signs that pitchers and catchers use to indicate the next pitch.[65] This does not seem entirely likely and no evidence from the period has emerged so far that makes any note of Taylor's work with catcher's signs. Having said that, the practice of the pitcher and the catcher using signals was in flux for decades. As Peter Morris explains, at first, during the pre-curve ball era, there were no signals whatsoever. Then, as the curve emerged as an option, the pitchers gave the signals to the catcher, when they chose to give them at all. They were the ones throwing the ball, so they believed it was their right to determine what pitch they were going to throw. The catcher was just there to catch and not to dictate to the pitcher how to do his job.

Catchers seem to have seized control over the signals in the 1880s, as sign stealing became more widespread. Even so, many pitchers resisted the change, even into the 1890s. Christy Mathewson said that he gave the signs himself in the 1911 World Series, to thwart sign stealing.[66] It is not impossible that Taylor experienced, and perhaps even influenced, some of this ongoing back and forth between pitchers and catchers.

Still, Taylor typically signed at the ballpark without imagining that many onlookers there could understand his conversations. He was known to take pleasure in hurling insults at the umpires, to the happiness of fans who "were delighted by his finger-talk arguments with umpires," all the while assuming that he would be safe from punishment since the umpires had no idea what he was saying.[67] Taylor was especially known to complain about umpire Hank O'Day. Many accounts of the following story survive in the press. As one put it, "Hank knew that Taylor and his pals were calling him uncomplimentary names, but he could not prove it. So O'Day spent one whole winter mastering the sign language. The following spring he suddenly jumped on Taylor like a ton of bricks, and talking back at Dummy, fired him out of the game and fined him $50."

According to another, "He gave Hank O'Day many arguments, using his hands rapidly. Hank realized that something was being said to him, and became curious what it was. That caused Hank to learn the language of the fingers. After he mastered it, he rendered a decision against Taylor one afternoon. Dummy immediately began telling O'Day how ignorant he was. O'Day read it all and finally began talking back to Taylor in the same language. This is what Mr. O'Day made his fingers say; 'You go to the clubhouse. Pay $25.' Taylor didn't care to talk back to O'Day after that day."[68]

Taylor's sign language was not his only contribution to his team. His good nature and sense of humor made him a team leader. "Luther Taylor is a natural born humorist as well as a natural born athlete," one account recalled. "When things are looking gloomy for the club, he always comes to the front and puts them in good humor by springing some practical joke. McGraw says that he is a most valuable man to a club for that reason alone." McGraw offered Taylor this praise, saying, "Many a time have I seen him turn a lot of sour faces into smiles and so revive the spirit of the players that they would go out and win."[69]

And McGraw liked to win. Known as a man willing to push the envelope in the pursuit of victory, he proved willing to exploit even Taylor's voice to his advantage. Taylor was called a "dummy" insofar as he did not speak. But he nonetheless had a distinctive voice all his own. Mike Donlin, outfielder for the Giants, was Taylor's roommate on Giants' road trips.[70] He described Taylor's use of his voice as the sound of a "crazed shrieking jackass."[71] McGraw liked to keep Taylor on the bench with him, even when he was not scheduled to pitch, in order to use his voice to rattle opposing pitchers. He would set Taylor to work from the dugout, emitting an annoying, distracting racket.[72]

Taylor also used his unusual voice along the lines. He sometimes served as a coach at first base. "Taylor would put on a show when he coached first base," baseball chronicler David Anderson writes. "Not only did he give signs to his teammates, but he also showed approval and disapproval of the umpire's calls."[73] Additionally, Taylor had a two-word vocabulary, "ma-ma" and "pa-pa." When he coached, he would repeat the phrases over and over again, a monotone stream of sound that "could crack the concentration even of the steadiest hurlers."[74] This signing deaf man proved willing to raise his voice in the cause of his team. And his hearing teammates were willing to accept this unorthodox use of sound as well.[75] What Taylor was unwilling to do was modify his use of sound to conform to hearing norms. He never learned to speak.

Like Hoy, Taylor stood as a powerful example of both what deaf people could accomplish in and what they would contribute to the hearing world. Taylor demonstrated that a deaf person could be successful in life precisely by acting like a deaf person. He insisted on using his language to communicate. He insisted on signs and on fingerspelling. By adopting them, the team truly came together. The Giants became a signing team, the only one in major league history. They found success by coming together, winning pennants and the World Series, with Taylor as a full-fledged, well-respected member of the team. For the deaf community of these years, it was precisely Taylor's lack of speech and his insistence on sign language that made him a powerful deaf role model. Arguably, neither Taylor nor Hoy would have achieved the same respect within the deaf community of those years if they had been oralists, attempting to pass as hearing.

Taylor earned widespread respect within the deaf community. The *Saturday Evening Post* reported that "wherever Taylor goes he will always be visited by scores of the silent fraternity among whom he is regarded as a prodigy." An account in the *Deaf-Mutes' Journal* called Taylor "the idol of the deaf fans."[76] *The Buffalo Commercial* reported that Taylor's fellow deaf Americans "looked upon him as a hero."[77] Everywhere, deaf people came forward to support him. In an exhibition in West Virginia, it was noted that "Dummy Taylor found a friend or two in town and was able to converse with ease. There seems to be a fraternity of fellowship existing between mutes and as soon as Taylor hits a town he finds some one he knows."[78]

At Newark, in 1909, when Taylor was pitching in the minors, he "was presented with a pair of diamond cuff links by his deaf-mute admirers. John

Shea made the presentation, in the presence of several thousand rooters and fans, who applauded with might and main. The contributors represented the League of Elect Surds, the Deaf-Mutes' Union League, the Brooklyn Frats, and individuals whose names were not given to the writer. There were nearly a hundred deaf-mutes at the game."[79]

The *Deaf-Mutes' Journal* would not have needed to introduce or explain these organizations to its readers. But hearing audiences should be aware that the presence of these groups indicates how deeply Taylor was tied to the early 20th-century deaf community. The Deaf-Mutes' Union League was the oldest deaf organization in New York City. It served an urban elite population, charging a dollar as a membership fee, with an additional monthly fee of 50 cents.[80] It was founded in 1886. It was a rather unusual organization, as it limited its membership to male alumni of the Institution for the Improved Instruction of Deaf-Mutes, typically referred to as the Lexington School, after its location in New York. The Lexington School had opened in 1867 as one of the very first oral schools in the country. Deaf children educated there were taught using only speech and lipreading, as both sign language and fingerspelling were forbidden.[81]

As historians John Vickrey Van Cleve and Barry Crouch note, "The irony was that the league's members were all orally educated. The great virtue of oral education, according to its proponents then and now, is that is supposedly prepares deaf people for social intercourse with hearing persons. Armed with the ability to articulate clearly and to read speech from the lips, graduates of oral schools … were supposed to venture out into hearing society and function as though they were hearing themselves. They were supposed to choose their friends and spouses from among the larger society of hearing people; they were not supposed to be inclined to seek the society of other deaf persons."[82]

These Union League members, however, demonstrated that even orally trained deaf people preferred the company of other deaf people. Further, these deaf men supported causes traditionally associated with the signing deaf community. In 1888, for example, the league held a formal ball, its first ever, which served as a fundraiser for the recently established Gallaudet Home for Aged and Infirm Deaf-Mutes. As the name suggests, the home was established near Poughkeepsie, New York, in 1886, to create an environment where elderly deaf people would be cared for, by, and with people who could understand their sign language.[83] In 1889, the league helped to raise money for the erection of a statue of Thomas Hopkins Gallaudet and Alice Cogswell on the grounds of Gallaudet University. Gallaudet was the hearing co-founder of the American School for the Deaf, the first school for the deaf in the United States, and Alice was its first student. It was a signing school, as was Gallaudet University.

The oralist Union League members supported the causes of the larger, and largely signing, deaf community. They acted as members of that community, regardless of their own communication preferences. And they came out to support the most public deaf figure of their time, Dummy Taylor, a non-speaking, signing deaf man. They were there with their signing brethren from the League of Elect Surds. The League was founded around 1893. As honorary member Henri Gaillard explained, "The objectives are the League of Elect Surds are to contribute to the well-being of its members and to the deaf in general, and in particular to raise the moral level of its members; to cultivate feelings of friendship among them; to assist those who might be in need as well as their families; to create ties among them; and to create an organization within which each can act for the common good. Its motto is 'Faith and confidence in God everywhere. Good will and love to all our brothers.'"[84] The League was non-sectarian and non-political, open for membership to any deaf man over the age of 21 with "an honest means of support and a respectable education."[85] The League was thought to be somewhat modeled on a Masonic Lodge.

In the early 20th century, its leadership ranks were full of prominent men in the national deaf community. Its grand ruler was Edwin A. Hodgson, the editor of the *Deaf-Mutes' Journal* who served as president of the National Association of the Deaf from 1883 to 1889. Hodgson, in fact, had been the driving force behind founding a national organization for deaf people. The NAD was his dream. He had pushed for a civil rights organization for deaf people in the pages of the *Deaf-Mutes' Journal*. The deputy grand ruler was Issac N. Soper, who had been educated at the American School, moved to New York City, and was active in the deaf community there. The grand secretary and treasurer was Thomas F. Fox, an 1883 graduate of then Gallaudet College, and the associate principal of the New York School for the Deaf. Fox served as president of the National Association of the Deaf from 1893 to 1899. Under Fox's presidency, the NAD passed a resolution opposing the use of the pure oral method as a universal method to instruct all deaf children. The grand tyler (the door keeper) was none other than the journalist Alexander Pach.

The League demonstrated the diversity of the early 20th-century deaf community. Hodgson had lost his hearing around age 18 and retained his speech as an adult. Pach had lost his hearing when he was around 16 and by his own admittance was a terrible lipreader. Fox had been deafened around the age of 10. Soper had been born deaf and was a fluent signer. All of these men embraced their deafness and the deaf community. Pach made his loyalties plain for all; his column in *The Silent Worker* was called "With the Silent Workers." For all of them, whether their deafness was born or acquired, it was a characteristic that each embraced. They rose to positions of leadership and influence in a community that they cherished and advocated for passionately.

Finally, the Brooklyn Frats represented the Brooklyn chapter of the National Fraternal Society of the Deaf. The NFSD was founded in 1901 by a group of Michigan School for the deaf alumni who were working-class deaf men. Henri Gaillard noted that the Frat worked "to establish a fund to assist sick or temporarily incapacitated members; to pay varying sums of money on the death of a member to persons whom the deceased has designated in accord with the bylaws. The society also seeks to advance honor, fraternity, public-spiritedness in its members; to encourage industry, ambition, honesty, and perseverance; to avoid, if possible, that they be blamed, cheated, or imposed on, that they be maltreated in any fashion that would appear malicious or disgraceful."[86]

As historian Susan Burch explains, "Insurance companies commonly believed that Deaf people had shorter life spans. Moreover, they considered them too risky and too accident prone to cover. The NFSD sought to redress these wrongs. At the outset it offered only burial benefits and meager assistance in cases of illness or accident. Still, it provided another important asset: fellowship for the numerous working-class Deaf people."[87] Besides insurance policies, the NFSD, at both the national level and through its local affiliates, sponsored numerous public events, including picnics, banquets, and balls.[88] Burch concludes, "Such affairs reinforced notions of normality, cultural pride, and success among members. The very public display also aimed to show hearing society that Deaf people were normal and able citizens."[89]

Over time, the NAD and the NFSD worked in tandem, even across class lines. Burch argues that "the NAD sought to protect Deaf people's rights in a competitive world by defending their livelihoods, educational opportunities, and citizenship. The NFSD ... limited itself to protecting members' economic well-being in general and their insurability in particular.... [The NFSD] catered more to rank-and-file workers, whereas the NAD, while claiming to represent the entire community, spoke to and for the educated urban elite."[90]

As these groups came together to honor Luther Taylor, they made it clear that the whole of the deaf community stood behind him: the elite, the working class, the oralists, the signers, the residential school graduates, the college graduates, the NAD, the Frat. The deaf community, in all its diversity, offered its united support for its most prominent public figure. Deaf community leaders realized that they needed to present deaf role models for hearing people—that is, they needed hearing people to see that deaf people were good citizens who made valuable contributions to American society, as deaf people. Oralists pictured nonspeaking deaf people as "defective, deviant, even un–American."[91] The deaf community wanted to fight back against that oralist image in public life, to fight for acceptance in a hearing world. Most importantly, they wanted to do so on deaf terms. Demonstrating the positive power of sign language in public life was a service that Taylor performed not only for his team, which came together by signing together, but for the larger deaf community as well.[92]

Baseball gave the deaf community an important platform to prove their worth. As historian Susan Burch puts it, "Having Deaf athletes compete on the national scene—particularly in baseball, 'America's pastime'—challenged important stereotypes." Their success on the field "countered mainstream medical perspectives that defined Deaf people strictly by their physical deficiencies."[93] Pushing back against this medical perspective gained new urgency in the early 20th century. New immigrations laws, supported by eugenicists, targeted so-called defectives at the nation's borders, including deaf people. As historian Douglas C. Baynton writes, "Deaf people were among the thousands of disabled immigrants turned back at American ports as defective and undesirable. They were excluded in large part because they were thought likely to be bearers of a defective heredity.... The official justification for their exclusion was that deaf people were social dependents rather than contributors."[94]

Taylor was well aware of the need to fight for greater acceptance of the deaf community and against such stereotypes. He was known as the clubhouse clown for the Giants and he could take and make a good joke among his peers. But, *The Silent Worker* related, "when a stranger in Chicago on the last western trip told him he was wanted on the telephone, they had a hard time keeping Taylor from knocking the man down."[95] Here is where the greater meaning of sport in American life becomes clear. Taylor had been accepted and welcomed as an equal member of the team by his hearing peers, but he still endured insults about his deafness, disparaged for his physical difference, on the road, from hearing strangers. It was all the more reason to continue to fight harder.

A belief in the power of sport to promote the cause of deaf acceptance was still apparent years after both Taylor and Hoy had retired, as when J.

4. Three Deaf Men and Eighteen Dummies

Frederick Meagher noted in *The Silent Worker* in 1919, "A few more successes like Hoy [and] Taylor … and the general public will be immensely more respectful to the average deaf mute."[96] Meagher's words would have carried a lot of weight to his deaf readers. He had become a towering figure in the deaf community in his own right, by the first half of the 20th century. Born in 1886 in Rochester, New York, he attended the Rochester School for the Deaf. He was a well-known deaf athlete himself, excelling as a wrestler and a football player. Later, he became a sportswriter and a columnist, writing in both *The Silent Worker* and *The Frat*. He was a tremendous advocate for the deaf community, active in both the Frat and the NAD. With Art Kruger, Meagher co-founded the American Athletic Association of the Deaf in 1945. Meagher died in 1951.[97]

Similarly, James F. Brady offered in 1924, "In industrial life and social periods we deaf people are reminded consciously or otherwise of our handicap and we are 'different' from others, but in sports—well, that is another matter. There we are all right. It has been commented upon that when one player of the team is a deaf-mute—be it baseball, football, or basketball—he is invariably the star. Why should it cause wonder and surprise? We are built the same as any member of the [human] family and the loss of the sense of hearing in no way deprives us of the ability to shine anywhere and it does not make us helpless."[98]

Like Meagher, Brady saw the advantage of using sports as a vehicle to showcase what deaf people were capable of and it combat common stereotypes about deafness. Brady was an alumni of the Pennsylvania School for the Deaf and an oralist. He was a good lipreader. However, he also knew the sign language. He and his deaf wife regularly signed with each other to communicate. Brady, like Meagher, was a strong supporter of the deaf community. While Brady appreciated his own speech skills, he wanted more deaf children to be exposed to sign language, arguing against the oralists of his day that "the greatest good for the greatest number should be the aim of the schools and the greatest good can be accomplished with and by properly supervised signs."[99]

The deaf community hoped that deaf sport would lead to greater acceptance by the hearing majority, as it demonstrated the deaf community's embrace of mainstream norms of athletic competition and "presented the deaf body as a model of the whole masculine physical body," one that was in no way deficient.[100] The later proved a difficult goal to achieve at that time, given the prejudices against disabled bodies that prevailed in the early 20th century. As historian Robert E. Bionaz reminds us, "Although not suffering the kind of oppression many turn-of-the-century disabled persons experienced, these two men [Hoy and Taylor] felt the disdain of men who, reflecting the cultural norms of the period, had no compunctions about including narrow-minded commentary in their sports reports."[101]

Deaf sport also provided deaf people with the chance to celebrate their own community's heroes in public, which was a way, as historian Susan Burch argues, to portray "Deafness in a more positive way."[102] The career of Luther Taylor represented a specifically deaf claim to the mainstream of American life, as he played as a recognizably deaf athlete in a hearing league. Still, the deaf press well knew that claiming a space in the mainstream was not easy for deaf people. Deaf men in sports were treated differently than their hearing counterparts.

Beyond being saddled with the nickname "dummy," the deaf press also noted bias in the coverage of Taylor. Too frequently, the fact of his deafness was brought up in reporting on his defeats. "Isn't it funny the way some of the baseball reporters chronicle the playing of Luther Taylor," the *Deaf-Mutes' Journal* noted. According to the *Journal*, more often than not, "if Mr. Taylor wins for his team, the reporters praise him, but his deafness is seldom mentioned, but if he should lose, which he sometimes must, as all of the best pitchers must get their bumps, once in a while … well, then it is 'Dummy Taylor.'" The *Journal* concluded, "Some day, perhaps, there will be a baseball team composed all of deaf-mutes, who will be world beaters at the National sport—then perhaps the baseball reporters will say something really nice about the deaf—until then, the same state of affairs are likely to continue."[103]

As loyal as the deaf community was to Taylor, Taylor's commitment to the deaf community in return was equally unwavering. After he was let go by the Giants in 1908, in what one news outlet called "probably the hardest official order that McGraw has ever been compelled to issue," on account of their "more than ordinary friendship,"[104] Taylor at first continued to pitch in the minors, in Buffalo, in Montreal, and in New Orleans. Eventually, he went back to his home state of Kansas, where he played minor league ball in Topeka, before finally retiring as a player in 1915. From 1915 to 1923, he worked at the Kansas School for the Deaf as a coach in five sports: football, boys' baseball, girls' baseball, boys' basketball, and girls' basketball. At Kansas, he worked beside fellow Kansas School for the Deaf alumni Paul Hubbard, who had invented the football huddle at Gallaudet.[105]

From 1915 to 1920, he also worked as an umpire in the Midwest, calling games in Kansas, Iowa, Nebraska, and Illinois. He gestured behind the plate, but also used a whistle to provide an aural call as well. He would whistle once for a strike and twice for a ball. Earlier, in 1908, Taylor had guest umpired in New York City for the New York public schools' baseball championships. There, he used "one hand for balls and the other for strikes. A wave of his arm indicated that the ... runner was out, while a patting hand meant safe." The hearing kids understood his gestures quite well, and only once did he have to resort to writing, when one team tried to bring a pitcher, whom they had already removed during an earlier inning, back into the game. "He shook his head and then resorted to his pad and pencil and wrote 'No' many times, each time larger than the previous time."[106]

Additionally, Taylor teamed up with Hoy, after the professional baseball careers of both men had ended, in Akron, Ohio. Home to the Goodyear and Firestone corporations, the companies faced a labor shortage during World War I. To take advantage of wartime contracts, the companies mounted an aggressive hiring campaign targeting the deaf community, as deaf men were ineligible for military service. The companies literally "recruited hundreds of young deaf men and women to work on their production lines. Both companies put together teams of deaf employees to work in the same areas on the same shifts and provided sign language interpreters so that deaf people could work throughout the two companies."[107] The use of sign language interpreters proved crucial, allowing the companies to hire more deaf workers and a broader range of those workers, in turn. "Consequently, deaf workers apparently held a broader range of positions at Goodyear than at any other single company in the nation," historian Robert Buchanan asserts. "They were successfully integrated into skilled technical and professional positions—including management and office work, as well as work in the rubber, chemical research, and mechanical departments."[108]

Goodyear referred to its employees as its Silent workers. They acknowledged that their deaf employees relied upon the sign language, and not their voices, to communicate. Similarly, local press coverage referred to the new arrivals either as "Silents" or as "Mutes." The large community of deaf people attracted to Akron came to be known as "The Silent Colony." The experience of hiring such large numbers of deaf employees in such a compressed period of time at Goodyear helped to successfully challenge hearing stereotypes about deaf people. As the company's newsletter, *The Wingfoot Clan*, explained, "It has always been a requisite in placing Silent workers that they be given work where they will not be handicapped. But experience is showing that there are few such jobs. The field has broadened continually, until now there are but few operations that they cannot perform. In fact, their keenness of sight and touch, and ability to concentrate, has made better workers on delicate jobs than their fellow workers possessed of all five senses."[109]

W.P. Souder, a prominent member of the National Association of the Deaf, declared, "Akron is the first city in the union to give the deaf full rec-ognition—equal pay for equal work, and no apparent limits to the height an individual may climb."[110] As a result, Akron's deaf population exploded, liter-ally overnight. About 1,000 deaf people from across the country flocked to Akron in the war years.[111] Goodyear reported that it had 450 deaf men and 50 deaf women working for the company by 1918.[112] Most of the earliest arrivals were young single white deaf men, in their 20s and 30s, though as the war progressed, both companies recruited deaf woman as well.[113]

Most deaf people lived within a one-square-mile of the city. Addition-ally, Goodyear offered its employees access to a program to purchase homes in what was called Goodyear Heights. This was a development located about a quarter of a mile away from the factory. As the local press explained, "[Here] Goodyear workers are sold or build homes on a payment plan that makes it possible for every man to purchase a thoroughly modern and attractive home on a large lot. Eighteen of the Silents now own homes there, while about fifteen more own lots and will build in the near future."[114] A Silents Grocery opened in 1920 in Goodyear Heights as well. It was a co-op, founded by five deaf men in Akron. Local deaf people from Akron, Cleveland, and Detroit owned it, buying in at 25 cents per share.[115] By 1920, there were 180 stock-holders in the co-op, 75 percent of who were deaf. The *Akron Evening Times* told readers that "there will be both silent and hearing clerks to wait on the customers."[116]

Historians frequently remark on Akron's singular place in 20th-cen-tury deaf history. As Douglas C. Baynton notes, "More so than any other city in the country, the deaf people of Akron had all the advantages of urban life available to them: Deaf churches, silent films, signed lecturers, Deaf theater, Deaf dances, Deaf literary clubs, and all manner of events designed by and for people who signed."[117] There were many social activities, from picnics and outings to a debate society and public lectures to dancing class-es.[118] The company's social hall for employees, called Goodyear Hall, in-cluded a club room for "members of the Goodyear Silent Colony."[119] An Akron chapter of the National Fraternal Society of the Deaf was established in 1915.[120] But because Goodyear understood that traditional life insurance companies frequently refused to cover deaf people, Goodyear also offered a $1,000 life insurance policy to all its workers through the Goodyear Relief Association.[121]

4. Three Deaf Men and Eighteen Dummies

The Silent Colony also enjoyed their own semiprofessional sports teams to root for, as both companies sponsored sports programs for their employees, both deaf and hearing alike. These were company sponsored teams that competed in larger industrial and independent leagues in the area. A semiprofessional deaf football team, the Goodyear Silents, played from 1917 to 1922, quickly becoming "among the best loved teams in the city, if not the region."[122] They built a record over those years of 54–6, with three ties.[123]

There was a semiprofessional baseball team, also called the Goodyear Silents. Luther Taylor played for them. He also was worked as an athletic instructor in 1918.[124] As one local paper noted as the 1918 season got underway, "Dummy Taylor, the old New York Giant pitcher, is ready to do his bit for Goodyear at all times. This veteran of many big league games ... is doing quite a lot to help the Goodyear boys. He shows them the way they hit the ball in

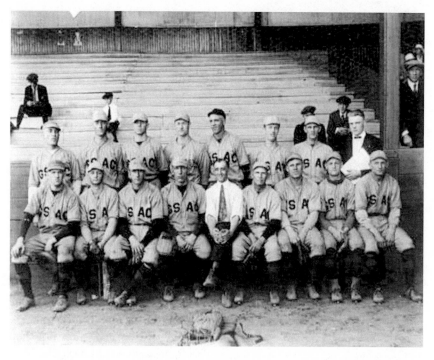

Akron, Ohio, became known as "The Silent Colony" during World War I, as corporations recruited deaf employees for a wide variety of positions, as production needs expanded during the war. These same corporations offered recreation for employees, including baseball. Pictured here are the Goodyear Silents. Hoy was hired as the baseball coach and Taylor was hired as an athletic instructor. Courtesy Gallaudet University Archives.

the big leagues, and aids them many other countless ways."[125] William Hoy was hired as the baseball coach of the Silents in 1919. As historian Susan Burch notes, "Hoy's influence clearly improved the Silents' style and teamwork. He also won the respect and attention of both Ohio's Deaf society and the national community."[126] The Silents played in Midwestern independent baseball leagues, frequently facing hearing teams. Their "prowess in sports held considerable symbolic power for the Deaf community, supplying hard evidence in the form of winning scores that deaf people could compete with anyone."[127]

In spite of all their successes—economic, sporting, social, and cultural—the Silent Colony that attracted both Taylor and Hoy did not last. When the war ended, layoffs, not unexpected, swept Akron, as the companies scaled back to peacetime production. Deaf workers hoped to be rehired. But, Robert Buchanan writes, "company policies favored long-standing Akron residents. By the winter of 1921, the majority of Akron's deaf community had been forced to leave the city."[128] Some deaf people remained, however, even if the majority of the Silent Colony departed. The 1930 census found 276 deaf people, 153 men and 123 women, were still living in Akron, enough to maintain a comfortable deaf community life among them, but not enough to support all of the previous era's larger social events and sporting teams.[129] The economy of Akron could support this smaller number of workers. Goodyear and Firestone both invested in technology in the interwar period that reduced the sizes of their workforces across the board.[130]

TAYLOR, BUFFALO

A Luther Taylor baseball card, created sometime between 1909 and 1911, picturing him from his time on the Buffalo Bisons of the Eastern League. Taylor played for them in 1909 and 1910. Library of Congress.

Taylor moved away from Akron in 1920. By 1923, Taylor had a new job in Iowa, at the Iowa School for the Deaf, where he coached both football and baseball. He remained there until

1933, when he went to the Illinois School for the Deaf where he worked until 1949. There too he worked as a teacher, coach, and house father. While Taylor took up his new position in Illinois, deaf baseball fans were wondering where the next deaf player would come from. The *Deaf-Mutes' Journal* lamented in 1935, "As this has been printed and on its way to subscribers, the baseball season will have been inaugurated by the professional leagues, but so far in glancing at the league organizations, we fail to see a single name of a deaf player. Will we ever have another Hoy or a 'Dummy' Taylor?"[131]

It was at the Illinois School that Taylor himself would discover the next deaf player who would make it to the majors: Dick Sipek. (Sipek's story is taken up in more detail in the next chapter.) For his part, Luther Taylor returned to place that had nurtured him, to the residential schools of the deaf, in support of his community. He well understood that, even in the middle of the 20th century, the deaf community needed to continue to fight to make progress. In mentoring Sipek, Taylor made it clear that he wanted to see more deaf players in the game, accepted as deaf, to be sure, but also accepted as good ballplayers, as peers, and as equals.

It was exactly what Taylor had sought and achieved for himself over the course of his career with Giants. In recognition of those achievements, Luther Taylor became the second deaf sportsman, after William Hoy, inducted into the Hall of Fame of the American Athletic Association for the Deaf in 1952.[132] Taylor died of a heart attack at the age of 82, in 1958.

He has been the subject of multiple posthumous honors. A proud son of Kansas, the Kansas School for the Deaf renamed its gym for Taylor in 1961. Taylor was the subject of a Darryl Brock novel, *Havana Heat* (2000). In 2006, Taylor was inducted into the Kansas Sports Hall of Fame and into the Kansas Baseball Hall of Fame. A monument, honoring his baseball career, was erected at his grave in the Prairie City Cemetery in Baldwin City, Kansas, in 2008, with the help of the Baldwin City Rotary, the Olathe Santa Fe Trail Rotary, and the Society for American Baseball Research. A Taylor relative, Pat Copeland, spoke for many when she praised the new monument, saying, "It means a lot to us that he's finally recognized."[133]

The forgotten dummy, forgotten no more.

Early thoughts on the career of Luther Taylor were presented as "An Unbroken Circle: From the Residential Schools to the Major Leagues and Back Again," at the 23rd *Cooperstown Symposium on Baseball and American Culture*, Cooperstown, New York, in 2011.

5

No Dummy: The Brief
Career of Dick Sipek

Dick Sipek found himself a singular player in the 1940s, the only deaf player in all of organized baseball. In 1945, Sipek arrived in major league baseball, playing for one precious season for the Cincinnati Reds. His appearance on a major league roster demonstrated the existence of what might be called a deaf baseball pipeline, for Sipek owed his major league chance not to himself alone but to the larger deaf community, and, specifically, to the efforts of the former big-league deaf pitcher Luther Taylor, who had pitched for John McGraw's New York Giants from 1900 to 1908.

At first, after the Giants let him go, Taylor continued to pitch in the minors, in Buffalo, in Montreal, and in New Orleans. Eventually, he went back to his home state of Kansas, where he played minor league ball in Topeka, before retiring as player in 1915. Taylor then returned to work within the deaf community, seeking jobs at residential schools for the deaf. From 1915 to 1923, he worked at the Kansas School for the Deaf, as a coach in five sports: football, boys' baseball, girls' baseball, boys' basketball, and girls' basketball. In 1923, Taylor went to the Iowa School for the Deaf, where he coached both football and baseball. He remained there until 1933, when he went to the Illinois School for the Deaf, where he worked until 1949. There too he worked as a teacher, coach, and house father.

It was at the Illinois School that he discovered a young Dick Sipek. Sipek became a student at Illinois in 1932.[1] Accounts of the reasons for his deafness vary; while many sources claim that he lost his hearing in an accident at the age of five, it is also possible that his deafness was genetic. Two out of three of his children would be deaf, as would three grandchildren. Whatever the cause, his deafness caused his hearing parents to enroll him at the Illinois School for the Deaf when he was nine years old.[2] There, he soon met Luther Taylor. Taylor recalled that Sipek attracted his attention because the young boy carried a baseball around with him at all times.[3] Taylor wrote in an undated letter, "Sipek will be heard from some day. Hard hitter. Good all around player. He is hard of hearing."[4]

Taylor initially reached out to his old club, the Giants, about Sipek, but they failed to take an interest. In 1943, Taylor contacted Bill McKechnie, an acquaintance of his over in Cincinnati. McKechnie had been in baseball from 1907 to 1920 as a player and then began a career as a coach and manager. From 1938 to 1946, he was the manager of the Cincinnati Reds. He managed them to the NL pennant in 1939 and finally to World Series victory in 1940. Perhaps not coincidently, another deaf ballplayer, William Ellsworth Hoy, had spent many successful years in Cincinnati, where he was beloved by fans. Hoy

Luther Taylor, the pride of the Kansas School for the Deaf. Taylor also discovered the next deaf major league player, Dick Sipek, at the Illinois School for the Deaf. Image courtesy Kansas School for the Deaf.

played in Cincinnati from 1894 to 1897 and then joined the Reds for one last season in 1902. The strength of Taylor's word was enough to convince McKechnie to send over a scout to see Sipek. He was immediately signed and went into the Reds farm system in 1943 to the Birmingham Barons.[5]

Sipek's classmates at the Illinois School for the Deaf were excited to see one of their own advance into professional baseball. The students followed his progress avidly. The school's March 1943 newspaper headline blared "SIPEK IS GIVEN CONTRACT" when Sipek was extended a contract to join the Barons. The article explained, "Everyone at I.S.D. was very happy and surprised when Dick Sipek, our outstanding all-around athlete from Chicago, was given a contract by the Birmingham Baseball Club of the Southern League and ordered to report for spring training April 1." The reporter noted that Warren Giles, the manager of the Reds, was willing to bring Sipek into their organization and that Giles "accepted him for trial because he knew

Dummy Taylor was an experienced scout." The reporter concluded that the school's best wishes would follow him to Birmingham, where "we know he will try hard and that inexperience will be his greatest handicap."[6]

Sipek himself understood as he embarked on a career in baseball that "there was more at stake than the career of one player. Back in Jacksonville, Illinois, the eyes and hopes of a large school of similarly handicapped hang on Sipek's every move in organized baseball. He is their proudest symbol of triumph.... For twelve years he was one of them at the Illinois School for the Deaf. He reached there at the age of ten, unable to say, hear, or read a word.... His accelerating success in baseball is a shining beacon for nearly a thousand students."[7] Sipek made a point to include his schoolmates in his baseball journey. The school newspaper reported in April 1943 that "many students, especially boys, have received letters from Dick Sipek. We have heard much good news from him. He told us that he likes his training with the Birmingham club.... He is one of the best liked members of the squad."[8]

Sipek spent two seasons in Birmingham, playing in 1943 and 1944. In 1943, the *Birmingham Post* introduced the new Baron. "Dick Sipek, the Baron's rookie outfielder ... is almost stone deaf, but can speak pretty well," the paper explained. The school had three educational units when Sipek was there. Unit I educated students by the oral method exclusively. Unit II offered what were called "auricular classes," in rooms "equipped with the latest models in the way of electrical hearing appliances, every effort is made to conserve and develop any residual hearing the children may have." Unit III offered manual, that is, sign language–based, classes. It seemed that children moved around the units "according to individual needs and ability."[9] Dick learned sign language there, but apparently, he also received speech lessons.

The paper told fans that Sipek also learned baseball at school. "[He] learned most of his baseball from old Luther [Dummy] Taylor, famous pitcher of the New York Giants nearly 40 years ago.... Sipek will enter his senior year this fall at the Illinois School for the Deaf.... Dummy Taylor is coach there, and has done wonders in athletics for boys handicapped like himself. [Sipek] has been a three-letter man at the school for three years. Last year, he was chosen all-state half back in football and led the central conference in scoring. In basketball, he was awarded a gold trophy for all around play and scoring. An outfielder on Taylor's baseball nine, Sipek hit over .400 in each of his three seasons. He played softball on a deaf team in Chicago for four years."[10] Beyond Taylor's word, Sipek's own play in Chicago had also attracted attention. *The Birmingham Post* reported, "The Barons picked Sipek off the Chicago sandlots, where he was rated one of the finest players in the Windy City's amateur circles."[11] Sipek had been doing all he could to promote his own cause in baseball.

In Birmingham, Sipek thrived as a player. In 1943, he played in 74 games and was at bat 253 times, where he garnered 85 hits, including 12 doubles, seven triples, and two home runs, for a batting average of .336 and a slugging percentage of .462. Sipek's fellow Illinois classmates were pleased to know that he had made good in his first year. As student reporter John Neal told his school, "Definitely sold on Sipek's ability … is Paul Florence [the Barons president]." The paper quoted Florence as saying: "I don't think the kid can miss."[12]

Sipek returned to Birmingham for the 1944 season, which saw him maintain his level of performance. In 134 games with 508 plate appearances, he had 162 hits, with 17 doubles, nine triples, and four home runs, for a batting average of .319 and a slugging percentage of .411. *The Birmingham Post* considered him "one of the best defensive outfielders in the league."[13]

Much of the press coverage of his time in Birmingham focused not on his deafness but on his personality and his ability as a player. One writer dubbed him "The Personality Kid," calling attention to his "engaging personality that he advertises with a winning smile and sparkling eyes." On the field he is "agile, cool, and alert."[14] His deafness was noted as a factor in his play, but most commentators mentioned Sipek's keen use of vision as the key to his fielding. As one put it, "He has overcome the obstacle of telling the power of a hit ball by substituting an almost uncanny sight judgment for the sound made by the crack of the bat."[15] Manager Johnny Riddle also noted Sipek's remarkable powers of attention and the way that he played the outfield by "using his eyes to compensate for his poor hearing."[16] Others noted his skill at the mental side of the sport. "An honor student," one sportswriter noted, "he is brilliant in sizing up opposing pitchers, stealing signals, and accomplishing the headwork tasks of the diamond that some players never learn."[17]

Sipek quickly gained a following in Birmingham, as Baron fans voted him their "most popular player" in both 1943 and 1944. Indeed, the fans' love for Sipek would become part of the team's lore. Rickwood Field, where the Barons played, was the first concrete and steel park in the minor leagues, when it opened on August 18, 1910. Until it was abandoned in the 1980s, there was a sign with pictures of important players who had worn the Barons' uniform, "an old sign," as one writer said, that included a picture of "Dick Sipek, the first deaf mute to play for the Barons and the most popular player in 1943."[18]

In the 1940s, Barons fans "loved his hustle, his cheerful attitude, and his willingness to sign countless autographs for admiring children."[19] Reporting approvingly, one sportswriter noted, "Outfielder Dick Sipek, a deaf mute, has been selected by baseball fans here as the most popular member of the Birmingham's Southern Association club for the second straight year. He was given a $25 War Bond last night in ceremonies at the Atlanta-Birmingham game."[20]

Sipek was obviously a special favorite of deaf fans in Birmingham. The pride of local deaf people was clear. Henry "Zipp" Newman, the sports editor of the *Birmingham News* and the dean of southern sports writers, reported that the "Birmingham deaf mute paper carries a day-by-day account of Dick's play with the Barons. He is the idol of the deaf in Birmingham and not so long ago they pitched a party for Dick."[21] Other residential schools for the deaf, beyond Sipek's own alma mater, broadcasted Sipek's achievements to their students. *The Hoosier*, the school newspaper for the Indiana School for the Deaf, for instance, reprinted "Zipp" Newman's article on its first page in November 1944.

African American fans too gravitated to Sipek. The white press in Birmingham took note. "Last year fans voted him their favorite, and out in right field—close by the bleachers—Negro rooters passed the hat to get him a handsome gift."[22] Another reported, "Well-liked by all his mates, Sipek was voted by fans the most popular Baron last year, and only recently a group of Negro spectators gave him $7.50 in nickels and dimes."[23] Sipek played in right field, which would have brought him into close contact with black fans. "Over there in right field," former Black Baron William H. Greason recalled, "they had stands. When the whites played, that's where the blacks sat, and when the blacks played, that's where the whites sat."[24]

African Americans may well have been responding to something more than simple physical proximity. Sipek's own educational background likely contributed to his friendly relationship with the black baseball fans of Birmingham. The Illinois School for the Deaf was racially integrated. Sipek, in fact, had played beside African American teammates, both on the school's baseball team, with Loveless Weaver, and on the basketball team, with Richard Durham and Jesse W. Fisher. To be clear, these were not the only African American students in the school; they were the students that Sipek called his teammates.

Loveless Weaver was the catcher of the baseball team. Weaver attended the school from 1939 to 1942. Weaver was about two years younger than Sipek, and he came to the school when he was 13. Weaver was an all-around athlete.

5. No Dummy: The Brief Career of Dick Sipek

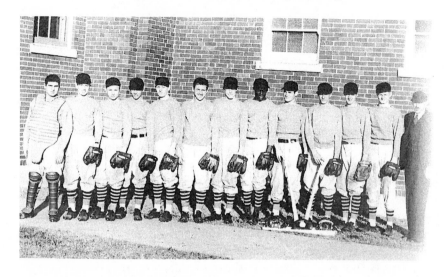

Dick Sipek's baseball team at the Illinois School for the Deaf. From left to right: Sammy Scola, C; Lloyd Judge, P; Douglas Burris, 2B; Verle Hall, P; Bryan, C; Richard "Dick" Sipek, P; Edward Wohlrab, F; Loveless Weaver, F; White, 3B; Floyd Neal, F; Kelling, 1B; A. Baga, SS; Coach Bill Milligan. Image from *The Illinois Advance* (May 1943), 21. Courtesy Illinois School for the Deaf Alumni Association Museum.

In addition to baseball, Weaver also played on the school's basketball and football teams. While the Illinois School for the Deaf was racially integrated, not all of the schools that their teams faced were. Weaver did play football against I.S.D.'s rivals within the state. However, when the team travelled out of state to play against other school rivals, Weaver was sometimes left behind. When the team took a road trip to the Texas, to face the Texas School for the Deaf, for instance, Weaver remained in Illinois. Integrated games were illegal in Texas.[25]

Richard Durham was at the school from 1936 to 1942. Sipek and Durham had been teammates on the school's basketball team. In 1941, the school hosted the National Deaf Basketball Tournament, which pitted basketball teams from deaf schools across the country against one another. The tournament was created in 1935 by J. Frederick Meagher. Meagher was a famous figure within the deaf community. He was a prolific writer in deaf publications, contributing columns in *The Silent Worker, The Deaf-Mutes' Journal,* and *American Deaf Citizen.* He was an activist on behalf of the deaf community and an active member of the National Association of the Deaf. Meagher was also a passionate promoter of deaf sports, which had led him to create the National Deaf Basketball Tournament.[26] The Illinois School was proud to serve as the tourney's host in 1941, and even found success in early rounds. The Illinois Tigers had scored an upset win over Pennsylvania, the champions out of the East, to make the tournament finals. There, Illinois lost to the Arkansas Leopards.

Durham, playing at center, had figured prominently in that tournament victory. Though they did not claim the national title, Durham could take some consolation in the fact that he was named to the all-tournament team. As the school paper reported, "Richard Durham is the big, tall, good natured colored boy who specialized in recovering rebounds defensively and in tipping in shots under his own goal. Assisting a teammate's shot through the hoop was becoming an art with Richard. He will reach the age limit before the 1941–42 season and his place at center will be a hard one to fill." Sipek was at forward, and the school paper called him "another good rebound man. He is not a tall lad but he seems to have springs in his legs that enable him to outjump his taller opponents. He plays an excellent floor game, either at guard or down court.... He was the spark plug of the team."[27] Sipek was named to the all-tournament second five.

Two more African American boys attended the Illinois School at this time, as both students and athletes, Jesse W. Fisher (1933–1942) and Wilford Purcell (1934–1943).[28] Fisher, in fact, had just come up from grade school to the high school level and was the newest addition to the basketball team in the 1940–41 season. The 1941 tournament was his first. The school paper noted, "He is fast and breaks like lightning on offense. I.S.D. will be expecting big things from Jesse next season."[29]

Without knowing the precise composition of all of the student bodies at every school for the deaf across the country in the middle of the 20th century, it is hard to know whether Illinois's integration was typical or unusual. At least two northern schools, the American School for the Deaf and the New York School for the Deaf, had been racially integrated since the early 19th century. The American School welcomed its first student of color in 1825, the New York School in 1818.[30]

The Arkansas School, which won the tournament, was racially segregated. Arkansas first tried to open a school for the deaf in 1850, but it closed for lack of funding. After the Civil War, an effort was made to revive deaf education in the state, and the Arkansas Deaf-Mute Institute opened in Little Rock in 1868, for white deaf students. In 1887, a separate building was erected to educate black deaf students. The two units remained separated until 1965, when the Arkansas School for the Deaf was at last integrated.[31]

5. No Dummy: The Brief Career of Dick Sipek

The school paper included photographs of the first, second, and third place teams in the 1941 tournament. Only the Illinois Tigers were racially integrated. All that can be stated with certainty is that Sipek was accustomed to interacting with black deaf peers, both as classmates and as athletes at his school. One wonders what he thought of Rickwood's segregated seating, and of racially segregated Birmingham.

By the end of his time in Birmingham, many observers assumed that Sipek would get called up to the majors, on the strength of his playing. As Baron general manager Paul Florence remarked, "I have never seen a more accurate arm anywhere." In fact, Sipek topped the Southern Association in 1944 in throwing out men at first, second, and third.[32] In his second season, a sportswriter commented that Sipek was "rapidly developing into one of the top outfielders both offensively and defensively in the Southern Association."[33] Team manager Johnny Riddle considered Sipek "one of the best outfielders in the Southern League" and expected him to get called to the majors.[34]

Baseball Digest summed it up well in 1945, "Sipek is no sensational player. But he is steady, he has better than average speed, and he gets a good break on the ball, and covers plenty of territory."[35] And as he advanced to play with the Reds, it was clear that to his Illinois classmates, "Sipek is something special, one of their own, pitted against competitors who have everything."[36] When they learned that Sipek would join the Reds, the school paper wrote, "We are all thrilled with the idea of having another famous baseball player from our Alma Mater. I.S.D. Dummy Taylor was the first."[37]

In all of this reporting, Sipek's deafness was never hidden from fans or readers, but it was not inordinately dwelled upon either. Surprisingly perhaps, hearing sportswriters demonstrated their knowledge of the deaf history of the sport. *The Evening Independent*, out of St. Petersburg, Florida, reprinted an editorial from the *Sanford Herald*, of North Carolina, in 1945. They were offering to their readers a sense of "what other editors think." *The Herald* opined, "Being a deaf mute is not always a handicap, Dick Sipek finds. A hard hitting outfielder with Birmingham, he has just been signed by Cincinnati. While it has been years since the major leagues have had a deaf mute player, there have been some successful ones.... Hoy, an outfielder, was a star of the '90s. Luther Taylor ... was for years a valuable pitcher on the first New York championship teams managed by John McGraw." Having established the relevant historical precedents, the paper concluded confidently. "Deaf mutes should make good ballplayers. They attend strictly to their work, and are not distracted by yells from opposing coaches or the crowd. If Sipek lives up to his advance notices, Cincinnati has a prize."[38]

Sipek was only rarely linked in the press to Hoy, as he was in this article, but he was frequently and correctly connected to Taylor in most mainstream press coverage. The story of how Taylor brought the young player to the attention of major league baseball was widely and accurately reported. As one headline announced, "Sipek, Dummy Taylor's Mute Protégé, Big Noise for Birmingham at the Plate." The *Saturday Evening Post* reported, "This has been a happy year for Dummy Taylor, the great deaf mute pitcher for the old New York Giants. Dick Sipek, a protégé of Dummy's from the Illinois School for the Deaf, broke into professional baseball as an outfielder with the Birmingham Barons."[39]

As Frank McGowan noted in Sipek's biographical statement for the team's official scorecard, "Richard [Dick] Sipek is one of the most popular players to show with the Barons in a long while. Despite the handicap of being a deaf boy, Sipek is a real ball player as his two great years with the Barons testifies.... [He was] voted the most popular Baron, a great honor for a first year man.... He will report to the Cincinnati Reds at the close of the Southern League season and Birmingham fans who have watched the play of the clean-living Illinois boy will wager that he becomes the first deaf boy to play in the majors since his coach, the great Dummy Taylor, was hurling for the New York Giants of John McGraw."[40]

A Birmingham newspaper article told fans, "When Dick Sipek moves up to the Cincinnati Reds from the Birmingham Barons ... the Reds will boast of the first mute player in the major leagues since Luther [Dummy] Taylor was member of the Giants, back in 1902–06. And this same Taylor is the fellow responsible for Sipek getting his start in pro ball."

The story even crossed borders. *The Buckingham Post*, in Buckingham, Quebec, told it this way.

> When his playing days were over, "Dummy" Taylor left the game of baseball with a proud ambition to find some youngster who wanted to play ball in the big time. He searched for many years until, one day, he came across an eager kid named Dick Sipek. Taylor thought he saw in the boy the makings of a major leaguer. He watched him carefully, gave him instruction, and finally got him up to the Birmingham team in the minor leagues. There, Dick Sipek made so fine a record that he was picked up by the Cincinnati Reds. Dick made good as a major league outfielder. Of course, the old timer, "Dummy" Taylor was tickled pink at the kid's success. Anyone would be happy to send an ambitious youngster to the major leagues. But "Dummy" Taylor was especially proud and happy because Dick Sipek was more than just an ordinary rookie who made good. He too was deaf and dumb.[41]

This deaf history shaped Sipek's career in other ways. Explaining this history provided a guide for hearing fans, to understand how Sipek had emerged into the sport and where he fit within the sport's larger deaf history. But the historical examples of Hoy and Taylor also provided a road map for Sipek as he entered the majors, about how to function as a deaf player on a hearing team and how to manage communication issues. Like both Hoy and Taylor before him, Sipek set about teaching his hearing teammates some sign language. He expected them to share some of the responsibility for communication between them.

It started at Birmingham. "During games, his teammates communicate with him by very rapid hand motion—especially when signaling who is to take a fly ball. But in the dugout waiting for their turn at bat, a number of Barons can be seen conversing with the silent Sipek on their fingers. He is gradually teaching them all the universal sign language of the mute."[42] Another article noted, "Although Dick and his fellows frequently have to rely on pad and pencil to expedite communication, he has taught them quite a bit of sign language. He reads lips and that helps too."

His fellow Barons clearly considered him a member of the team. Just as the Giants had rallied around Luther Taylor when he faced taunts on account of his deafness, so too did Sipek's Barons. "After a night game in Memphis in 1944," Sipek would later tell a reporter, "he was walking along with some other Birmingham players when some sailors began making fun of him. Sipek had been walking a bit ahead of his friends … by the time he turned around, his teammates were pummeling the sailors."[43]

Sipek also borrowed directly from Hoy's playbook regarding how to handle fly balls in the outfield. "Wherever he played," William Mead reported, "Sipek trained the center fielder and the second and first basemen to let him decide who was to catch a batted ball. If Sipek called for it, they had to get out of the way because he could not hear their calls. If he did not call for it, it was theirs to catch."[44] *Baseball Digest* reported on the success of the system: "He never has made a mistake in crossing up his teammates on puzzling fly balls."[45]

Sipek continued to teach sign language as he moved up to the Reds. His roommate on the team was utility infielder Kermit Wahl.[46] Sipek reported that Wahl was quite willing to learn, saying, "he learned it very fast, the alphabet and everything."[47] Other Reds also made progress, at least with a few key signs. "In one game, upset at being called out on a close play, Sipek used a sign for a vulgar word. The umpire didn't understand it, but the Reds' bench broke up with laughter."[48]

In fact, Sipek's decision to use sign language, following the lead of his predecessors, Hoy and Taylor, was very much both a deliberate choice and a political move. As was noted above, in 1943, the local press explained to readers that Sipek was "almost stone deaf, but can speak pretty well."[49] Other baseball chroniclers confirmed that Sipek was "able to speak a little."[50] He was also "an excellent lip reader."[51] Yet, Sipek chose to communicate primarily not with his voice but with sign language. He taught his teammates sign language as well.

Sipek made this communication choice precisely to make his deafness visible to teammates and fans alike. He wanted to be known in Birmingham as a deaf baseball player and the very visibility of the sign language helped to broadcast that fact. As Sipek put it, reflecting on his time in the sport, "I was motivated and I showed them that deaf can do it. No matter if I can't hear or I'm hard of hearing. It doesn't make any difference. I can do it."[52]

Hoy and Taylor too had publicly represented the deaf community as baseball players; they had chosen to stand up for deaf values. The example of their playing careers demonstrated that deaf people could find success by acting as deaf people, not by hiding their deafness. Their message was clear: deaf people could succeed without speech and deaf people could succeed with sign language. To the deaf community, the very public deafness of Hoy and of Taylor was an important part of their legacy. Though he could speak, Dick Sipek proved eager to carry on that legacy himself.

Sipek, the direct beneficiary of the baseball legacy of Hoy and Taylor, well understood that the deaf remained an all too often misunderstood minority group in the 1940s. Their language, culture, and community were all still largely unfamiliar to hearing people. There were an estimated 60,000 deaf Americans in the early 1940s; approximately 20,000 of that number were enrolled in the 312 schools for the deaf.[53] Hoy and Taylor had stood up for sign language in a time of oralism at the beginning of the 20th century. But the deaf community would face other challenges as the first decades of the 20th century unfolded. These were challenges that, in turn, deeply shaped the deaf world that Dick Sipek would enter and represent on the ballfield in the middle of the 20th century.

Oralism, of course, continued its assault throughout the first half of the 20th century on the deaf community's language, American Sign Language (ASL).[54] Eugenicists turned to popularizing their ideas to a mainstream audience. Eugenic science increasingly made its way into popular textbooks. A study of college and high school textbooks concluded that, between 1914 and 1948, eugenic ideas were commonly found in biology classes. Eugenics was included as a topic in over 87 percent of textbooks in these years, and, perhaps more troublingly, was presented to students as a legitimate science in slightly more than 70 percent.[55]

Eugenic policies were frequently recommended as well, with selective breeding mentioned by nearly all texts, either in exhortations for the superior to breed more or in calls for restrictions on the breeding of the so-called inferior stock. Nearly 20 percent of textbooks suggested immigration restriction as a way to curb the population of the inferior. In addition, 14.6 percent recommended implementation of additional public policies, such as segregation and sterilization.[56] Steven Selden concluded, "It is clear from these data that eugenics significantly penetrated the high school biology curriculum between 1914 and 1948."[57]

In fact, as late as 1941, George W. Hunter's textbook *Life Science: A Social Biology* told students that eugenics was "the science of being well born, or born well, healthy, and fit in every way" and that it required us to "make a real effort to separate those who are socially, physically, and morally fit from those who are not." Doing so would allow "only the fit to hand down their traits to their offspring."[58] Importantly, within the eugenic movement, deaf people were among those who were categorized as unfit.

Deaf people tried to fight back against these eugenic assaults on their community. Historian Susan Burch has chronicled the history of the deaf community in these years and found that "in many ways, Deaf people approached the issue of eugenics in a manner similar to that of immigrant and minority communities. Publicly, they encouraged their children to emulate American-ness.... Although some rejected even moderate eugenic measures against their community, they internalized the prevalent notions toward 'undesirables and defectives,' excluding only Deaf people—themselves—from the category."[59] Burch argues that deaf leaders pursued a course of what she calls "conservative subversion" in these challenging years. As she puts it, "Their strategy minimized differences between their members and the broader society, illustrating their ability to do what 'normal' people did."[60]

But it was precisely the ability to claim a deaf identity as a perfectly normal identity that was increasingly under attack. Even the right to drive for deaf people called into question. Again, influenced by eugenics, deaf drivers were depicted as "defective" and "dangerous." They were a "menace" on the roads. Various states, including New York, Pennsylvania, and Maryland, saw anti-deaf driver laws initiated in state legislatures. Maryland successfully passed a ban in 1925. Historian Susan Burch reports, "Between 1923 and 1941, Deaf people in various other states combated proposals to ban deaf drivers. In almost all cases, they defeated the measures before they became law."[61]

Deaf Players in Major League Baseball

The American Automobile Association (AAA) supported deaf drivers, but the deaf community founded its own distinctive organization to protect deaf driving rights, called the Protective Auto Clubs, which apprised members of possible legislation against them to encourage them to take action to fight for their rights. The last of these clubs died out after World War II, by which time the question of deaf driving rights seemed settled and secure.[62]

Sociologist Harry Best noted in his 1943 book, *Deafness and the Deaf in the United States*, that the rise of eugenics had strongly and negatively influenced the public image of the deaf, in the minds of the hearing public. Eugenic proponents had planted the notion that the deaf were members of the "defective classes" in the popular imagination. He posited that deaf people faced increasing prejudice in hearing society, "in large part due to the increasing emphasis today upon eugenics, with the desire to weed out from the population as many as possible of the 'unfit' or 'defective.'" Best warned that, in this way, "a real and measurable injury is done to the deaf as a class."[63]

Given the current climate, Best concluded that the deaf were too often misunderstood by hearing people. "The deaf are liable to be looked upon as queer or abnormal, and at times as even surly, or uncivil, or rude, or brutish; they may be regarded as morose or moody ... they are to be approached and dealt with a degree of caution; they may even be shunned or rebuffed. There may be built up toward them an attitude combined with wonder, misgiving, fear, aversion—a vague feeling that they are more or less different and distinct in their thought and actions from other people, that they are somehow 'unnatural' or 'uncanny.'"[64]

Best also pointed out that the deaf community's attempts to defend itself against such prejudices and to defend their sign language as well were often met with resistance by a skeptical hearing public. "The deaf," Best explained, "highly resent statements or implications that failure to employ speech and lip reading indicated mental backwardness, or that something is wrong with one." Instead, the deaf argue that "restrictions or prohibitions upon the use of the sign language are nothing less than forms of repression, or even acts of tyranny ... they are to be placed in the same category or on par with efforts of different nations to put down foreign languages in their territories."

Best explained that deaf people in the middle of the 20th century understood their fight for linguistic self-determination as part of a larger civil rights struggle.

> Such attempts constitute a denial of fundamental rights; they run counter to rights of self-determination. The deaf declare that the sign language is their mother tongue....
> It is stated moreover that the deaf who have to live their lives and to fight their battles

in the world about them are in the best, if not the only, position to know what is and what is not for their benefit and advantage; they are the ones who are … best fitted to judge in a matter that is so vital to them…. The deaf … almost entirely, almost as a body, strongly and vehemently demand the retention in their midst of their beloved sign language.[65]

Best's work makes it clear that a century of oralist propaganda against the sign language had made a profound impact on the hearing public's view of the sign language. To use sign language in public to communicate in the 1940s was to take a political position. It was to take a stand for deaf self-determination. It was to demonstrate that deaf people were in the best position to make language choices for themselves. And it was to indicate that deaf people, as a community, viewed the sign language as their mother tongue, as their birthright. In spite of all of the hearing prejudice against it and in spite of the fact that he could personally both speak and lipread, sign language was the language that Sipek insisted on using in major league baseball.

With this critical background in mind, Sipek's emergence into baseball in the early 1940s can now be seen as an effort to represent deaf people in mainstream society as people on a par with hearing citizens. When Sipek joined the Cincinnati Reds for the 1945 season, he became the first deaf player in major league history not to be saddled with the nickname "Dummy." He was always referred to as "Dick Sipek," "Dick," "Richard," or just "Sipek."[66] This was a point of pride to Sipek. He was glad to see "Dummy," which had long since drifted away from its earlier connotation of "mute" to one of "stupid," fall from favor. But Sipek still wanted very much to be seen as a deaf player and be recognized as a representative of the larger deaf community.

As the literary scholar

Dick Sipek. Coming up to Cincinnati in 1945, Sipek was the first deaf player in major league baseball since 1908. Courtesy National Baseball Hall of Fame Library.

Christopher Krentz has noted, "Deaf people's community, values, and language are formed by being deaf over a period of time and are socially produced. Deafness, as an identity, extends far beyond audiograms and eardrums."[67] Sipek personally embraced this deaf identity, and his career reveals how much, in fact, a deaf identity is a chosen identity. He was a man who used two languages fluently; he signed American Sign Language and he spoke English. His speech, together with his lipreading skills, could have persuaded him to act more like a hearing person in the majors. He could have opted to pass as hearing, to speak with his teammates and not to sign. But, as Krentz notes, those were not the values of Sipek's deaf community in the middle of the 20th century.

And Dick Sipek very much saw himself as a member of the deaf community, one he had entered when he was at the Illinois School for the Deaf. Those students and teachers were his people. Sipek claimed a culturally deaf identity for himself. He understood that his public position as a ballplayer gave him a platform that most deaf people lacked and he was quick to use it, to advocate for sign language and for the deaf community. In spite of his ability to speak, Sipek made a commitment to using the sign language to communicate, as a way of signaling that deaf identity to hearing fans.

Embracing an open deaf identity at work ran counter to the standard advice within the community. For example, *The Pelican*, the newspaper of the Louisiana School for the Deaf, armed its students with this advice for how best to succeed at work: "to do your work better than your co-workers if possible; to obey your superiors whether you like them or not; to refrain from talking while at work because signs are so noticeable ... and to so conduct yourself in the shop and out that people will like you, respect you and your capabilities, and be impressed with the fact that deaf workers DO make good and are reliable."[68] It was fairly typical advice to young deaf people graduating from school and heading into the work place.

Sign language use at work was discouraged, precisely because it was seen as drawing attention to deafness. Deaf people assumed that drawing attention to their difference would be detrimental to their advancement and acceptance at work. Sipek knew that he occupied a privileged position as a major league baseball player, one that would allow him to try to change the public perception of deafness for all deaf people. It was a burden that he gladly accepted.

With his passionate commitment to the sign language, Sipek also signaled that he understood that he owed his chance in the majors to the existence and support of the larger deaf community, one born and nurtured within residential schools for the deaf. Taylor had grown up in a residential school himself and had returned to work in the residential schools when he retired from baseball, to nurture the next generation of deaf people. The reach and force of the deaf culture of those years was still evident, as newspapers dubbed Sipek "Dummy Taylor's Mute Protégé."

This unbroken circle, going out from the residential school and returning back to it once again, was an important source of cultural strength for the deaf community in the first half of the 20th century. It allowed the community to weather the challenges of those years, which included full frontal assaults on the community's language, its members' right to marry and have children, and even to drive.[69] The strength and support offered within the walls of residential schools was rewarded by the loyalty of deaf alumni. It is why, in the late 20th century, as the educational tide turned toward mainstreaming, that is, the practice of integrating deaf children into their local public schools, deaf people continued to favor residential schools for the deaf as an important source of strength and pride for their community.[70]

Luther Taylor returned to the residential schools that nurtured him, in support of his community, because he understood that, even in the middle of the 20th century, the deaf community still needed to fight to make progress. While he was rightly proud of Sipek's budding career, he offered a sharp criticism of baseball nevertheless. "Instead of viewing a deaf mute's entrance into big-league baseball as a breathtaking event," as one newspaper report put it, "Taylor wonders what has prevented a wholesale invasion. And he believes that setting a mute apart in the game as something special creates an obstacle."[71]

In mentoring Sipek, Taylor sought to strike a blow against the prejudice he believed was holding talented deaf players back. Taylor made it clear that he wanted to see more deaf players in the game. He certainly wanted them to be accepted for themselves, as deaf, but Taylor also wanted them to be accepted as good ballplayers, as peers, and as equals. He wanted that chance for Sipek. He "has given Sipek a lot of coaching and the older deaf baseball star will be very much surprised, as well as disappointed, if Sipek does not make good in a big way."[72] The inclusive vision offered here—to be seen as deaf and to be welcomed into the mainstream of American life as deaf—mirrored exactly the sense of inclusion that other ethnic minorities sought when they took to the ball field.

As Lawrence Baldassaro puts it, baseball "which remained undisputed as *the* American game for much of the twentieth century, provided a passport to at least a part of mainstream American culture, making them more recognizably 'American' and less foreign."[73] Playing baseball allowed ethnic minorities to advance positive role models into public view, providing both touchstones for ethnic pride within the group and for increasing recognition of their claim to Americanness outside of it. It is little wonder that so many ethnic minorities, from the Irish to the Jewish to the Latino, have taken to the baseball diamond in their quest to become Americans. It is clear that deaf people too sought to use baseball as a means to be seen as less different and less foreign, especially at a time when eugenic forces had made deafness out to be an undesirable, even dangerous, condition, and deaf language a despised, inferior form of communication.

Sipek knew that he was standing up for his people every time he played. He remembered his time in the majors with personal excitement and pride.

"It was just overwhelming and I met so many different people," he said. But Sipek also knew that he carried a larger mission with him to the majors. As he put it, "I had to do my best when I played, to show them that the deaf can do."[74] In fact, Sipek drew a parallel between himself and a famous peer in the minor leagues with him in 1946. As he told a television reporter late in his life, Sipek felt that his baseball aspirations were mirrored and shared by his contemporary, Jackie Robinson. He recalled a meeting with Robinson. After asking Robinson how he was feeling as the game progressed, Sipek took the chance to tell him, "You're black and I'm deaf—the two of us are the same" and the men shook hands.[75]

Dick Sipek. Sipek was the first deaf man to play in the majors who was not saddled with the nickname "Dummy." He is pictured here in his uniform for Syracuse, where he played in the International League in 1946. Courtesy National Baseball Hall of Fame Library.

Sipek's path would have crossed with Robinson several times in 1946. Both men were playing in the International League that season, Robinson for the Montreal Royals and Sipek for the Syracuse Chiefs.[76] To some hearing fans, it might seem an unlikely parallel. To Sipek, it would have made perfect sense. Like Robinson, he too was trying to break barriers, to break what deaf professor and baseball fan Robert Panera called "the communication line." Like Robinson, Sipek too was attempting to represent his minority community in a more positive light for a majority audience. Like Robinson, Sipek too was aware that he carried the hopes of an embattled minority community with him, every time he took the field.[77]

Other deaf baseball fans felt a similar affinity with Robinson. In *Hands of My Father: A Hearing Boy, His Deaf Parents, and the Language of Love*, Myron Uhlberg recalls his deaf father's sudden fascination with baseball, when Jackie Robinson came to Brooklyn in 1947. This was a man who had never taken much interest in the game. "I was puzzled," Uhlberg recalls. "I simply could not fathom my father's sudden interest in Jackie Robinson."[78] But, naturally, he was not going to turn down a trip to see the Dodgers play at home! After a game at Ebbets Field, the pair, father and son, made their way home on the subway, and the explanation for his deaf father's support for Robinson became clear to his hearing son.

> On the subway ride home my father signed, "I am a deaf man in a hearing world. All the time I must show hearing people that I am a man as well. A man as good as them. Maybe even better."
> The subway car was packed. As usual, people in the car stared at my father with mixed looks of curiosity, shock, and even revulsion. I paid no attention to them as I watched his hands.
> "Jackie Robinson is a black man in the white man's baseball world. All the time he must show white people that he is a man. A man as good as them. Maybe even better. No matter that his skin is a black color. The color of his skin is not important. Only what Jackie does on the ball field is important."
> Just when I thought my father had finished speaking, his hands spoke to me sorrowfully. "Very hard for a deaf man. Very hard for a black man. Must fight all the time. No rest. Never. Sad."[79]

The experience of shared social prejudice created a bond between this deaf fan and Jackie Robinson. Perhaps the reverse was also true, and so the black fans of Birmingham were quick to see Dick Sipek as a player engaged in a struggle that they too could understand.

But in 1946, Robinson was on his way up, to the majors and on to history. Sipek was on his way down, going from AAA ball in Syracuse in 1946 to A in the South Atlantic League in 1947, finally ending his career in 1951 in the Class B Carolina League playing for the Reidsville Luckies. It is likely that his time with the Cincinnati Reds is scarcely remembered today. Sipek played as a pinch hitter in 82 games in the 1945 season, hitting .244, and finishing with 6 doubles, two triples, and 13 RBIs.

And when it is, his appearance on the Reds' roster is not usually attributed to his talent as a player. Traditionally, Sipek's appearance in the majors has been attributed to the game's rather desperate state in World War II. The notion that the war forced baseball to take anyone who showed up has also been used to explain the big league appearance of one of Sipek's fellow players in the Southern Association, the one-armed Pete Gray. Gray played for the Memphis Chicks in 1943 and 1944. In 1943, sportswriters honored him as the Most Courageous Athlete of the Game. Gray accepted the honor, but reluctantly. As he put it "Boys, I can't fight. And so there is no courage about me. Courage belongs on the battlefield, not on the baseball diamond. But if I can prove to any boy who has been physically handicapped that he, too, can compete with the best—well, then, I've done my little bit."[80]

Gray had acquired his disability in a boyhood accident. But the nation was paying more attention to the issue of acquired disability, as war veterans returned from the front as amputees. Reluctantly, Gray came to realize that he was a role model for these newly disabled men, a symbol that they, like him, could adjust to their new bodies and reclaim their lives. As Gray biographer William C. Kashatus explains, "[Gray] went on USO tours after completing the season, visiting army hospitals and rehabilitation centers. He spoke with recovering GIs, many of whom were amputees, reassuring them that they too could beat the odds and lead a healthy, happy, successful life after the war."[81]

Gray himself found increasing success on the diamond. Sportswriter Henry Vance noted in 1944 that Gray was "a great box office attraction" but argued that Gray was also "undeniably just about as great an athlete as minor league baseball boasts at the moment." As a result, Vance believed Gray "stands a chance of advancing all the way to the major leagues by the next season ... because he's a great ball player—and a money player at that."[82]

At the close of the 1944 season, Gray was voted the Southern Association's Most Valuable Player. His numbers had earned him the honor. As Kashatus points out, "His numbers were prodigious. In 129 games, he compiled a .333 batting average while collecting 119 hits for 221 total bases and drove in 60 runs. His .996 fielding percentage and .336 put-outs led all Southern Association outfielders and his 68 stolen bases tied a league record set in 1925."[83]

John Klima, in his study of wartime baseball, *The Game Must Go On: Hank Greenberg, Pete Gray, and the Great Days of Baseball on the Homefront in World War II*, concurs with Kashatus. "Pete's numbers would have been good enough for any two-armed player in the Southern Association to make the jump to the majors without any hesitation."[84] Still major league baseball resisted bringing Gray up. Disgusted by this show of prejudice, *The Birmingham Post* complained, "[The] Southern League's most valuable player will not be given a big league tryout. It's not an open and above board ban. It's just a little agreement among 'gentlemen' that taking on Gray wouldn't be the best thing for major league baseball. They're afraid that a one-armed man's appearance in a major league park would prompt someone to say, 'Look what baseball has come to!' That's why we say baseball biggies are a pretty sour lot."[85]

The so-called gentlemen's agreement, however, did not hold. St. Louis scout Jack Fournier had seen enough. He telegraphed the Browns' front office. "War or no war, Gray is a big leaguer. Advise you to buy at once."[86]

All of this suggests that Renwick Speer had it right when he wrote in defense of disabled players in baseball in SABR's *Baseball Research Journal* in 1983. Speer argued, "Handicapped players have always progressed as far as their talents would take them so we must be careful not to attribute their success to a war when they make it to the top."[87] In this way, Gray and Sipek were quite similar; as two disabled men, they broke into the majors together. They each challenged the prevailing social prejudice against disability. For both men, it was getting their talent recognized in the first instance that was generally difficult. For as much as the *Post* condemned the prejudice major league baseball displayed toward Gray, Billy Evans, the president of the Southern Association, had himself once commented of Gray, "The manpower situation was pretty serious but hardly to call for signing a crippled fellow."[88] As Gray found more success in his league, Evans eventually changed his mind. "I never tire of watching him and I think he has a chance to stay in the majors."[89]

As with Gray, Sipek's talent, and not the war time shortage of players, had taken him to the majors. After all, "Zipp" Newman had called Sipek "a natural ball player" when he went up to join the Reds. Going further, Newman wrote, "In all the history of the Southern League, there never has been a more accurate throwing outfielder—and this includes Tris Speaker and Joe Jackson. There have been many outfielders with stronger throwing arms than Sipek's good right, but none more accurate."[90]

But, just as with Gray, there are indications that he faced prejudice there on account of hearing perceptions of his deafness. As one account related, "Everyone, even manager Bill McKechnie, who wouldn't play him, liked Sipek. The only person who didn't like him was ornery coach Jimmie Wilson. When McKechnie wasn't looking during one pre-game drill, Wilson ordered Sipek to stand in right field and to chase fungoes repeatedly hit toward left field. Sipek, a good fielder, was forced to run across the outfield to snag these flies. Though winded, Sipek did not complain. However, the teammates watching this senseless drill forced Wilson to cut it out."[91]

Curiously, Gray too had faced extra fielding drills. Klima writes, "His manager, Luke Sewell, was convinced Pete needed help fielding, though it's hard to imagine he would have complaints with a two-armed outfielder who led the Southern Association in putouts and in fielding percentage." Sewell put Gray through his paces in practice in the outfield and Sewell quickly realized how wrong he had been. "I thought I could help his fielding, but he has been showing me tricks instead," Sewell admitted.[92]

Both players drew support from other disabled Americans. Sipek always had the support of his mentor, Luther Taylor, of course, and he counted on the support of the last deaf major leaguer. But the depth of support for Sipek went further than perhaps even he knew. One day in 1945, at Crosley Field, a surprised Sipek found an elderly William Hoy, by then 83 years old, waiting to greet him after a game.[93] Sipek remembered, "I was honored to meet him personally." The two men chatted about baseball, their respective time with the Reds, and Hoy's creation of umpire signs for balls and strikes.[94] Gray drew large crowds of disabled veterans to Browns' games. By June 1945, nearly 150,000 more paid customers had come out to see the Browns at home than had attended to that point in the 1944 season.[95] On the road, "amputees were there at every ballpark waiting for him."[96]

In the end, Pete Gray was not so very different from many minor leaguers. He had undeniable talent, but major league pitching proved Gray's undoing. During his one season with the Browns, pitchers figured out his weakness. At first, they had assumed a man with one arm could never keep up with a major league fastball and they tried to overpower him at the plate. Gray proved them wrong. He had tremendous strength in his left forearm and a quick wrist. He also had a good eye at the plate and a terrific sense of timing. In fact, Gray was an excellent fastball hitter.[97] What he couldn't hit was an off-speed pitch. As Kashatus explains, "Once he started his swing, he could not change his timing, and the fact that he had no second hand to check his swing made him extremely vulnerable to curve balls."[98] Gray's batting average fell to .218, his slugging percentage to .261, in 253 plate appearances across 77 games.

It can be argued that Dick Sipek was never given a real chance to demonstrate his talent. As one account puts it, "Several times, Sipek begged his manager to put him more often in the starting line-up. The manager wouldn't budge."[99] He finished his time in Cincinnati with 170 plate appearances across 82 games, with a .244 batting average and a .308 slugging percentage.

Dick Sipek was the last deaf major leaguer until 1993, when Curtis Pride debuted with the Montreal Expos, nearly 50 years after Sipek had last played. The press reached out to Sipek to get his reaction to Pride's appearance in the sport. While undeniably happy to see a deaf player back in major league baseball, Sipek expressed dismay at the fact that Pride was not easily recognizable as deaf. Unlike all of his deaf predecessors, Curtis Pride did not sign to communicate. "It hurts my feelings," Sipek said. "What's wrong with sign language? Why can't he use both spoken English and ASL?"[100]

Sipek represented the values of his deaf community, just as much as Curtis Pride stood for his, as we shall see in the next chapter. Sipek wanted hearing people to see and understand: "No matter if I can't hear or I'm hard of hearing. It doesn't make any difference. I can do it."[101] He did not believe that he needed to be more like a hearing person to make it in baseball or in life, for that matter. Sipek also understood that he owed his chance in the majors to the very existence and support of the larger deaf community, to Luther Taylor, the man who discovered him, and to William Hoy, the man in whose footsteps they both followed. Sipek wanted to be seen in their company. He wanted hearing fans to know this deaf history of the game.

After his baseball dreams ended, Sipek settled in Quincy, Illinois, the hometown of his wife, Betty Ann Schmidt. The two had been classmates together at the Illinois School for the Deaf. He went to work in Bueters Bakery in Quincy and later worked as a custodian at the St. Mary School, a local Catholic school.[102] His major league roots still had the power to inspire awe in Quincy. A local sportswriter shared the following story after Sipek's death in 2005. "The autographs make Sharon Terwelp's pieces of Chicago Cubs memorabilia valuable. The heart-felt gesture behind the gifts makes them priceless. While teaching at St. Mary School, Terwelp received an autographed picture of Ryne Sandberg and a baseball signed by the Cubs as a birthday present from the school custodian, Dick Sipek. A major league outfielder in the 1940s, Sipek called on an old friend, former Cubs general manager Dallas Green, to help secure the gift. 'No one would have known this humble, salt-of-the-earth man would have affiliations with such influential people,' Terwelp said."[103]

For the rest of his life, Sipek was an advocate for deaf athletes. At a convention for the deaf, playing in a golf tournament, another golfer pointed him out and explained to his party that Sipek was the last deaf player in professional baseball. Sipek sought the man out in the clubhouse later and told him not to identify him like that again. He did not want to be known as the last deaf player in baseball; he wanted more to follow him.[104] To that end, Sipek urged deaf children to chase their baseball dreams. Three weeks before he died, Sipek attended a baseball camp for more than 1,000 deaf children in the St. Louis area. He told them, "I don't want people to forget about the deaf. I want deaf people to come up and play."[105]

While fighting for the future of deaf players in professional baseball, Dick Sipek also wanted the history of deaf players in baseball to be remembered and appreciated, too. He especially hoped that the contributions of one of his fellow deaf players would be honored. "I have a dream that someday Dummy Hoy will be elected to the Hall of Fame."[106]

Research assistance for this chapter provided by Bob Dramin, Ralph Reese, Marene Clark-Mattern, David Brewer, and Alexandra Kyle. My thanks to all of them.

Additionally, I owe thanks to the audience that let me share my thoughts on Sipek and his career with them as the presentation "No Dummy: The Brief Career of Dick Sipek," at the 29th Cooperstown Symposium on Baseball and American Culture at Cooperstown, New York, in 2017.

6

Pride, of the Expos

Dick Sipek was the last deaf major leaguer until Curtis Pride debuted with the Montreal Expos, nearly 50 years after Sipek had last played. In 1992, Pride signed with the Expos and entered their minor league system. He was called up to the majors in 1993. On September 23, 1993, Pride recorded his first hit in a major league game. It was a moment of history, as it was the first hit that major league baseball had seen from a deaf player since 1945. It was also the first hit that major league baseball had ever seen from a black deaf player. Pride was the first, and, as of 2020, remains the only, deaf African American man to play major league baseball. The crowd gave him a standing ovation. "It was," Pride said, "the most exciting moment of my entire life."[1]

Pride, of course, could not hear the cheers of the five-minute standing ovation that the Montreal crowd poured out to him. Pinch-hitting with runners on first and second against the Phillies, Pride hit for a two-run double in only his second major league at-bat.[2] As he was standing on second base, however, the stadium was so loud that he could feel the vibrations of the ovation. As he was standing there, Pride recalls that he was thinking only of the game itself and how the crowd must be carrying on so because those two runs were signaling an Expos comeback. In fact, the Expos would go on to win the game over the first-place Phillies. "Then the third base coach walked onto the field. 'He told me to take off my helmet and I thought there was something on top of it,' Pride said. 'Then he raised my arm and turned me around. I was overwhelmed.'"[3]

The arrival of Curtis Pride signaled the arrival of a new generation of deaf player into major league baseball. Unlike his predecessors, Hoy, Taylor, and Sipek, Pride had not come out of the residential schools for the deaf. He was a product of mainstreaming, that is, the practice of sending deaf students to local, predominantly hearing public schools, with the support of interpreters, notetakers, and/or technological devices. While members of the deaf community largely continued to favor residential schools for the deaf, as a source of strength for the community and its unique culture, the wider field of deaf education, led, it should be noted, by mostly hearing educators, had moved towards mainstreaming for deaf students.[4]

The landscape of deaf education had changed profoundly since Sipek's brief time in major league baseball. Hearing parents of deaf children increasingly faced a mixed message from professionals in the field. A popular guide for hearing parents of deaf children, *Your Deaf Child: A Guide for Parents*, had appeared in 1950, authored by Helmer Myklebust, a professor of audiology at Northwestern University.

It struck an odd tone. Myklebust wanted to correct certain stereotypes of deafness, arguing that too many individuals "confuse deafness with low mental ability." He condemned the fact that too many "consider the deaf unable to fulfill their obligations as citizens." In fact, he argued, "the deaf are happy, socially capable, and self-supporting." Myklebust went further, writing that "the deaf have made a place for themselves in society. They have a heritage which is an inspiration to all who are familiar with it."[5] Myklebust may have learned about some of this deaf heritage while he earned a master's degree at Gallaudet University in 1935 in the psychology of deafness.

Curtis Pride. Pride was the first black deaf player in major league history. Courtesy National Baseball Hall of Fame Library.

For all of Myklebust's emphasis on deaf capability, however, he rejected the use of sign language with deaf children altogether. All of his advice to hearing parents was to use speech and speech reading exclusively with their deaf child, and to adopt a program of auditory training via the use of hearing aids. All the resources for parents listed at the end of the book were heavily tilted toward oralist organizations and publications. The book's index contains no entries for "fingerspelling," "manual alphabet," "sign language," or even "gestures." Parents

reading the guide might not ever know that sign language existed as an educational choice. This was by design. In a later work, in 1957, he would make
his view even more explicit, calling sign language "inferior to the verbal as a
language."[6]

As it turned out, Myklebust's hard-line position would be oralism's
high water mark. The field's relentless emphasis on oral-only approaches was
about to be challenged. The Department of Health, Education, and Welfare
organized a committee to study the state of the field in deaf education. In
1964, that advisory committee delivered its report, "Education of the Deaf:
A Report to the Secretary of Health, Education, and Welfare by his Advisory
Committee on the Education of the Deaf," to HEW Secretary Anthony Ce-
lebrezze. The report would become more commonly known as the Babbidge
Report, after its committee chair, University of Connecticut president Homer
Babbidge. And the report was damning.

The Committee did not mince words. It declared the state of deaf education in the United States to be "unsatisfactory." Its very opening sentences
provided a bleak picture of the state of the field in 1964.

> The American people have no reason to be satisfied with their limited success in edu-
> cating deaf children and preparing them for full participation in our society.... The
> average graduate of a public residential school for the deaf—the closest we have to
> generally available "high schools" for the deaf—has an eighth grade education. Seniors
> at Gallaudet College, the nation's only college for the deaf, rank close to the bottom in
> performance on the Graduate Record Examination. Five-sixths of our deaf adults work
> in manual jobs, as contrasted to only one-half of our hearing population.[7]

The Committee was comprised of both men and women, largely from edu-
cation backgrounds and oralist leanings. Edgar Lowell, the head of the John
Tracy Clinic, an oralist organization in Los Angeles, served on the commit-
tee, as did Dr. Leroy Hedgecock, an audiologist from the Mayo Clinic, and
Dr. Miriam Pauls Hardy, an associate professor of otolaryngology at the
Hearing and Speech Center at Johns Hopkins Hospital in Baltimore.

The Committee could not deny that "programs of education for the deaf,
by and large, are not succeeding. The test performance of deaf students at all
grade levels is disappointingly low. Despite sincere and determined efforts by
students and teachers alike, the achievement of most deaf students remains
markedly inferior to that of hearing students."[8] The report did not condemn
the oral method, as it called the efforts of all teachers in schools for the deaf
both sincere and determined. Yet, the Committee could not deny the reality
that oralism dominated the field of deaf education in 1964, nor could it fail to
recognize that it had done so since 1918. If, after 45 years of near total control

of deaf education, oralism's results were so poor, there was simply no way for the Committee to hide that fact from public view.

The Committee could also not disguise that oralists and manualists, even on the same committee, did not see the issues facing deaf children in the same way. What some members saw as advantages to a system, others saw as disadvantages. At points, the Committee found itself arguing both sides of a question. In a section of the report describing the advantages of residential schools for the deaf, for instance, the report concluded, "Surrounded as he is by deaf companions, the deaf child can lead a less strained life in out-of-school hours. (Some will dispute that this is an advantage, contending that it may encourage at an early age the segregation of the deaf in our society)."[9]

Likewise, in a section meant to outline the disadvantages of residential programs for the deaf, the report explained, "Many factors in residential schools operate to encourage the segregation of the deaf in our society. The children do not have opportunities to play and associate fully with hearing children or the challenge of finding ways to communicate effectively with them. The reliance on manual methods of communication at least outside of the classroom in the majority of such schools tends to fix a habit of such relatively easy communication for social purposes and thus to dull the motivation to surmount the more difficult obstacles to oral communication. (Some will point out, on the other hand, that many deaf children, who are psychologically and socially handicapped as well, suffer a greater degree of isolation in a hearing environment at home and that it is only in a segregated setting that they find the social satisfaction of communicating with their peers)."[10] What was an advantage to one side was a disadvantage to the other. Compromise seemed impossible.

Perhaps unsurprisingly, their report called in the end for more of everything.

The Committee urges that educators of the deaf continue to place emphasis on oral methods, but that manual methods be employed in individual cases where it is clear beyond a reasonable doubt that success by oral methods is unlikely. There will continue to be failures in the oral method, and facilities for teaching in the language of signs should therefore be retained. Furthermore, many deaf adults will prefer the use of the language of signs and the company of the deaf as an easier and more relaxing social experience. They have a perfect right to make that choice, and no aura of failure or opprobrium should surround it. The Committee believes, however, that the option should be kept open for deaf children to make such a choice as responsible adults. The choice should not be made for them in the schools unless it is clear after careful professional analysis on an individual basis that the choice cannot be kept open.[11]

While the Committee attempted to thread the needle, the poor educational results of the oral method, particularly that eighth-grade academic achievement level even for high school graduates, proved impossible for the public to ignore. Hearing parents increasingly demanded new educational options for their deaf children, including sign language.

Meanwhile, the sign language itself was on the verge of its own public breakthrough. Just as the educational limitations of oralism were being made clear, the sign language of the deaf community was being labeled as American Sign Language and recognized as a fully realized language. In 1965, a research team from Gallaudet University, hearing professor William Stokoe, together with deaf research assistants Carl Croneberg and Dorothy Casterline, published *A Dictionary of American Sign Language on Linguistic Principles*. Their work forcefully demonstrated that the sign language of deaf people in the United States was a bona fide language, and that signed languages, more broadly, were just as much fully developed languages as any spoken language. Their work ushered in not only the new field of sign language linguistics but also Deaf Studies, as researchers in fields like anthropology, sociology, and history began to study the community of sign language users, as well as their language.[12]

Sign language use suddenly enjoyed a public resurgence. The Babbidge Report itself had called for the language choices of deaf adults, especially a decision to use sign language, to be respected with "no aura of failure or opprobrium." With ASL now recognized as a language, sign language use became more common in American cultural life. The National Theatre of the Deaf was founded in 1965, the world's first professional deaf theater company. It not only staged works by English language playwrights translated into ASL, it also produced original theater productions in ASL.[13] Deaf actor and National Theatre of the Deaf alum Linda Bove brought signs to *Sesame Street* on PBS in 1972, in what was supposed to be a guest appearance. By 1975, she was a permanent cast member and she remained on the show until 2003.

Rainbow's End, a five-part deafcentric children's series created by deaf professionals for deaf children, using ASL, premiered on public television in 1979. It featured several deaf actors, including National Theatre of the Deaf alum Freda Norman as a kind of deaf superhero. She portrayed the character SuperSign Woman. Much like Clark Kent, the mild-mannered secretary would remove her glasses, don a cape, and rush to the side of a deaf person in linguistic distress, showing them the ASL sign they needed so that they could stop fingerspelling English words.

Sign language books, such as *A Basic Course in Manual Communication*

147

(1970), *The Joy of Signing* (1978), and *A Basic Course in American Sign Language* (1980), appeared on the mass market for the first time, providing more access to the language to a wider audience than ever before. More schools for the deaf, even schools that still put a heavy focus on speech acquisition, experimented with adding manual communication to classrooms.

Sign language interpreting also became increasingly professionalized. Interpreting had usually been a volunteer activity, most typically taken up by the hearing child of deaf parents, as a service to their family community. The founding of the Registry of Interpreters for the Deaf in 1964 began to change that. The Registry, as chronicler of deaf history Jack Gannon explains, "established criteria and classifications for interpreters, set up evaluation procedures, printed a national directory, opened a headquarters, offered workshops and training sessions, and gave interpreters a new respectability."[14] The creation of the Registry meant that deaf people could increasingly expect to have qualified professionals interpret for them in institutional settings like hospitals, courts, and schools. This was another clear indication of the deaf community's language preferences being taken seriously.

Beyond sign language, deaf people won additional victories for accessible communication during this time. The teletypewriter (TTY) was invented in 1964, finally providing the deaf community access to long distance communication over the telephone lines. The device allowed deaf people with the TTY device to call other parties, who also had to have a TTY, and they would type back and forth to communicate. The device was initially expensive and ownership was limited, but by the 1980s, TTYs were increasingly common in deaf households.[15] The ability to contact a party who did not have a TTY came to the entire nation in 1993, when a relay system finally operated in all 50 states. With relay, a deaf caller could use a TTY to contact an independent, confidential operator who would then "relay" the call to a hearing person who did not have a TTY. The operator would read the TTY feed into the phone and then type the spoken reply of the hearing person, transmitting it on to the deaf caller.

Closed captioning, which made television programming accessible to deaf people, was experimented with in 1973, most notably for the presidential inauguration. By 1976, the FCC had reserved a line for broadcasters to use for close captioning, though it did not mandate that stations provide such captions. By 1980, most major networks were experimenting with closed captioning for their programs and Sears was selling "telecaptions decoders" for the first time.[16]

Accessible communication for deaf people on deaf terms was finally happening. ASL was becoming more visible in American popular culture. Technology was finally addressing the communication needs of deaf people from a deaf point of view, emphasizing visual, rather than aural, access to information, as technological options seemed to move from the hearing aid to the TTY. Yet, the revolution in deaf lives that all of these events would seem to have indicated stopped short.

A wholesale return of ASL to schools for the deaf, for example, did not occur. Just as sign language began to make its reappearance into the national conversation, another pedagogical innovation emerged, one that would have profound consequences for the deaf community. In 1975, Congress passed the Education for All Handicapped Children Act, later renamed the Individuals with Disabilities Education Act (IDEA). The Act prioritized free and appropriate public education for all children and required school districts to educate all disabled children in what was called the "least restrictive environment."

The regulations implementing IDEA state that "to the maximum extent appropriate, children with disabilities including children in public or private institutions or care facilities, are educated with children who are *non*disabled; and special classes, separate schooling or other removals of children with disabilities from regular educational environment occurs only if the nature or severity of the disability is such that education in regular classes with the use of supplementary aids and services cannot be achieved satisfactorily."

Oralists and manualists did not agree on which kind of environment was an advantage or a disadvantage for a deaf child, as the muddier moments of the Babbidge Report had indicated. But as IDEA was implemented over the course of the 1970s, the term "the least restrictive environment" was widely interpreted to mean that all children should be able to access their local public school for an education. For deaf children, that would usher in an educational practice that would come to be called mainstreaming, which saw deaf students attend their local, predominantly hearing, public schools, with the support of interpreters, notetakers, and/or technological devices.

For the deaf community, this emerging system of mainstreaming proved a threat to the network of residential schools that had served as not only as places for deaf children to be educated, but also as spaces where they entered into the larger deaf community for the first time, by meeting large numbers of deaf peers and by interacting with deaf adults who worked at the schools. The impact of IDEA was remarkably swift, as an exodus from deaf residential schools began. By the early 21st century, "more than 80 percent of deaf children were attending public schools, and most of them had no deaf classmates."[17] The educational world that had nurtured Sipek, Taylor, and Hoy had literally vanished.

Adult members of the deaf community were largely opposed to the new trend. A *Deaf Life* reader's poll in 1992 asked if mainstreaming should be the choice for the majority of deaf schoolchildren. An overwhelming 85 percent responded no, mostly on the grounds that deaf children miss out too much educationally, socially, and emotionally in such a setting.[18] One reader commented that mainstreaming "has done more harm than good." Another labeled mainstreaming "the most restrictive environment." A third lamented that, in a mainstreamed setting, "a healthy self-identity and self-image as a deaf person is denied." Since only 10 percent of deaf children have deaf parents, however, there proved little those deaf adults could do to stop this educational transformation. Hearing parents of deaf children overwhelming opted for educating their deaf children in their local public schools.

It should be noted that, even where deaf children were in a classroom besides hearing children with the support of a sign language interpreter, one of the most important oralist goals was being realized. As far back as Hoy's day, oralist educators wanted not simply to see sign language eliminated from the lives of deaf children. They also wanted to see deaf children raised in a completely hearing world. In 1884, Alexander Graham Bell had argued that the ideal school, in his view, "would contain only one deaf child." In 1893, oralist teacher Emma Garrett had declared that the "ideal education for a deaf child was that he should never see another deaf child."[19]

As historian Douglas C. Baynton has noted, "mainstreaming is now making their dream a reality: thousands of deaf children now sit in classrooms where all the other students and every teacher is hearing." Even though a sign language interpreter might be making their inclusion in a hearing classroom possible, as Baynton concedes, the result is still that "thousands grow up with few or no deaf friends; most encounter no deaf adults to look up to. They have no access to the deaf community, with its collective knowledge, accumulated over generations, of how to live happy and productive lives in a mostly hearing world."[20]

Even the Babbidge Report, which refused to abandon the oral method completely, did not deny that the existence of the deaf community in the United States was an enormous benefit in the lives of deaf Americans. They emphasized how fortunate deaf Americans were, especially compared to their European peers.

> In looking at special services and social activities for and of the adult deaf in Europe and in the United States, one is bound to become much impressed with the fact that

the deaf in our country have done a great deal more for themselves than the deaf in Europe have been able to do. The adult deaf in the United States have managed to secure a standard of living that is unequaled by the deaf anywhere else in the world. In addition, the deaf as a group have been able to successfully develop a series of church, athletic, social, and fraternal organizations at local, state, and national levels which are designed to meet their special needs. These accomplishments have been the result of their efforts and without public or other technical or financial assistance.[21]

Even as they wanted to undo oralism's worst educational effects, in other words, the Committee that produced the Babbidge Report in 1964 did not want to see the deaf community, and its impressive network of religious, athletic, social, and fraternal organizations, undermined. In the midst of emerging educational regulations and continuing pedagogical debates, a community's future hung in the balance.

Curtis Pride came of age precisely during this transformative moment in deaf history. Pride was born deaf, as a result of exposure to rubella, in 1968. There was a pandemic of rubella in the mid–1960s, resulting in an estimated 12.5 million rubella cases, and some 12,500 babies born deaf. A live virus vaccine finally emerged on the market in 1969, quickly followed by the bundled MMR vaccine. Pride was born at the tail end of what became known as the "rubella bulge" of deaf babies. He was raised orally and relied upon speech and lipreading to communicate.

As *The Washington Post* reported, "One of the early and most crucial decisions Sallie and John [Pride] made was to have Curtis not learn sign language." As his father John explained, "When you introduce kids to sign language, they tend to rely on it and it hinders their oral growth. We wanted Curt to rely on oral communication." He was fitted with a hearing aid in his left ear as a baby.[22] He attended mainstream programs from the seventh grade onward. Pride attended his local public high school in Silver Spring, Maryland, where he was the only deaf student.

As a young black deaf man, Pride's access to oral education is as historically significant as his access to his local public school alongside white classmates in Maryland. White deaf children in Maryland acquired access to formal education on 1828. That year, the Maryland state legislature had made arrangements to send such pupils to the Pennsylvania School for the Deaf. When a school for deaf children opened in the District of Columbia in 1860, Maryland started sending its white deaf students there instead. Finally, in 1862, the state opened its own school for white deaf children, the Maryland Institution for the Education of the Deaf, in Frederick, Maryland.[23]

While schools for the deaf in the North were frequently racially integrated, as we have already seen, such schools in the South were always racially segregated. The first school in the country for black deaf children opened in North Carolina in 1869. Maryland opened the second such school in the nation in 1872, the Maryland School for the Colored Deaf, in Baltimore. The black school was perpetually underfunded. While the white school in Frederick received funding from every county, according to how many students attended the school, the black school in Baltimore received a flat rate of support, regardless either of student population numbers or of increasing student enrollment figures as the 19th century wore on.[24]

The Baltimore school hired only white staff members, refusing any hiring practice, including that of hiring its own alumni, which would seem to put white and black teachers on common, equal footing in the classroom. The staff at the Baltimore school was therefore largely made up of white men.

As oralism became more prevalent in deaf education, that pedagogical revolution largely did not touch black deaf education in the segregated South. As historian Douglas C. Baynton explains, in the late 19th century, oralists frequently adopted a kind of linguistic Social Darwinism, with sign language being seen as an inferior form of communication that did not deserve to survive and therefore must make way for its superior, speech. As such, some oralists asserted that, while signs were still used for communication by so-called savages, in places like Africa, in America, the white race should surely reject them. Baynton asks, "If oralists associated sign language with Africans, what did they do then they encountered African-American deaf students?" He answers that in southern black schools, "oral education was clearly not extended to blacks on the same basis as whites."[25] Black students were not deserving of speech.

As many scholars have pointed out, segregation, both in terms of the racial composition of the schools and of their educational methodologies, gave rise to two versions of ASL, a white ASL, seen as simply standard ASL to observers, rather than racially inflected, and Black ASL, which was all too frequently viewed as inferior to the signed language that whites used.[26] In Pride's Maryland, white deaf residents and black deaf residents would likely have signed differently as a direct result of their separate educations.[27] The Frederick and Baltimore schools finally united as the integrated Maryland School for the Deaf in 1956, only 12 years before Pride was born.

Still, even as late as 1940, a survey of black schools for the deaf found that 11 of 16 of them were still entirely manual.[28] Oralism as an educational practice was largely reserved for white deaf children only. Historian Susan Burch notes, "Ironically, oralists' disinterest in African American students may have allowed them greater freedom to use the sign language, the very language

6. Pride, of the Expos

white deaf leaders had to fight to preserve."[29] For Hoy, Taylor, and Sipek, all white deaf men, in the first half of the 20th century, theirs was a fight against oralism, a battle to save their sign language. But for Pride's hearing parents, in the second half of the 20th century, raising a black deaf son, theirs was a quest for access to a method long denied to African Americans, a chance for their deaf son to learn how to speak.

In the end, as a young black man, Pride gained access to the oral education that his hearing parents wanted for him because he was born at the right time. There was no question that he would be able to attend his local public school. By the time he attended high school in 1982, an education supported by speech training and hearing aids in the mainstream setting of a local public school was similarly within the reach of both white and black deaf students.

Graduating from high school in 1986, Pride went on to attend the College of William and Mary, on a basketball scholarship. Still, baseball was his first love and his favorite sport to play.[30] He was selected by the New York Mets in the draft in 1986, while he was on his way to college. He balanced baseball and college, as he played in the Mets minor league system and worked towards his degree. He graduated in 1990 with a degree in finance. In 1993, Pride broke into the majors, by then with the Montreal Expos, and on September 23, 1993, recorded his first hit in a major league game.

All the media coverage that I have seen to date of his first major league hit focused on how he was the first deaf player in over four decades to record a hit in major league baseball. None noted that he was the first black deaf player ever to record a hit in major league baseball. In fact, Pride was not the first black deaf player to record a hit as a professional baseball player. There had been one earlier player, whose existence was lost in the annals of the 19th-century minor leagues until his rediscovery in the 21st century. Monroe Ingram (1867?–1944) was a black deaf baseball player from Kansas. The son of slaves from Georgia, Ingram was the only deaf children among the family's 12 children. The family moved in freedom first to Oklahoma in 1879, before settling in Coffeyville, Kansas, in 1880.[31] Author Karen Christie and illustrator Nancy Rourke, in their book *ABC Portraits of Deaf Ancestors*, rightly point to Monroe Ingram as a "Deaf ancestor," as one of those "brave and bold Deaf people from the past" who can inspire today, among deaf people, a "sense of kinship" and "a sense of pride."[32]

In Kansas, Ingram would become one of six students of color, three girls and three boys, who integrated the Kansas School for the Deaf together. These African American students, including Monroe Ingram, arrived at the school for the 1884–85 academic year.[33] So did a young Luther Taylor. Ingram

153

was described as "a mulatto boy" and "a model student."[34] His local paper, *The Coffeyville Daily Journal,* would call Ingram a "well known colored scholar and ball player."[35] (Incidentally, Coffeyville's most famous ball player resident, was Walter "The Big Train" Johnson, who lived outside the town on a working farm with his wife until her death in 1930.)

The Kansas School for the Deaf's baseball team was organized the same year that Ingram arrived at the school, in 1884. By 1886, the school was supporting two baseball teams, the Clippers and the Crescents. Ingram served as captain of the Clippers in 1887. Luther Taylor, meanwhile, would play for the Crescents in 1890. Following in Ingram's footsteps, Taylor would become captain of the Clippers in 1894.[36]

Ingram also served as the vice president of the school's Olympic Athletic Club. He was a very good student and served as vice president of the school's Gallaudet Literary Society. Ingram graduated at the top of his class in 1889,

The 1894 baseball teams of the Kansas School for the Deaf. The school had two teams, the Crescents and the Clippers. In 1894, Luther Taylor was captain of the Clippers. He is seated in the second row from the bottom, the fifth from the left, beside the man in the suit, the school's superintendent, A.A. Stewart. Monroe Ingram had served as captain of the Clippers in 1887.

becoming the first black graduate of the Kansas School for the Deaf. His success as a student athlete that year was noted in one of the most prominent papers of deaf press of the 19th century, *The Deaf-Mutes' Journal*. The *Journal*, published from 1874 to 1938, effectively stood as the paper of record for the deaf community. Here, in 1889, it let readers know that "Monroe Ingram won the Institution athletic championship badge again this year. He has won it two years in succession."[37] The paper also offered coverage of Kansas's graduation ceremonies and noted that "Ingram's salutatory received encomiums of praise from all.... He is a bright colored boy, and a credit to the mute pupils and his race."[38]

In the 1890s, Ingram was a part of the minor league baseball scene in Kansas, a state with the most integrated baseball teams in the country. Ingram was remembered as "the man who as a base ball pitcher used to have all the ball teams in Southern Kansas scared to death ... [because he] used to throw a ball like a cannon shot."[39] As Gregory Bond reports, between 1895 and 1899, there were seven integrated professional baseball leagues in the country and four of those were in Kansas. As a result, more than a dozen teams boasted racially integrated rosters.[40] Ingram appeared as a pitcher on teams in Independence, Emporia, and Topeka in those very years. He was thought to be perhaps "the best baseball pitcher in Kansas" as his minor league career began. And yet, Bond argues, white support for integrated baseball in Kansas, as elsewhere, "proved to be illusory and surprisingly shallow."[41]

Many white owners were eager to hire the best talent, white or black, and many white fans seemed comfortable with racially integrated play. However, a small but vocal group of white players resisted. In 1899, the Emporia team signed two black players, Monroe Ingram and Gaitha Page. Other new recruits to Emporia, white players, were soon working to sabotage their own team in order to undermine their black teammates. Led by Tom Drummy, the white players focused their efforts on Ingram. It is not clear why they targeted him first; perhaps it was on account of his dual minority status.[42]

In any case, as Gregory Bond ably outlines, in June 1899, whenever Ingram was on the mound, the team, led by Drummy in the outfield, began to commit deliberate errors to sabotage him. Team management, to their credit, rallied around Ingram. Drummy was benched. But that did not stop him. Drummy simply directed his white supporters in the field from the bench. By July, he had also recruited community help. A local cigar maker and businessman, Claude Aney, signaled his support for Drummy's efforts. When Aney agreed to serve as umpire for a game in July, he made questionable calls against Ingram while Drummy did his part, directing his teammates to a total of eight errors on the field. Ingram lost the contest, 13–5. The local press reacted by calling out Aney for his "punk" and "rotten" calls. But the major complaint of some in the local press was not with the white player's obvious goal of scuttling integrated play but rather with these particular tactics. The *Daily Gazette* advised, "If the team doesn't want to play with colored men, let them kick to the directors."[43]

Faced with this impossible situation, Monroe Ingram quit baseball in 1899. It was only a part-time endeavor, after all. Ingram had a full-time job, as a teacher of what was then called "the colored department" at the Missouri School for the Deaf. The Missouri School for the Deaf opened in 1851 in Fulton, Missouri. After the Civil War, the school integrated and opened its doors to black deaf pupils. The first black student to enroll was Sarah Nelson. She arrived in 1867 and went to class alongside her white peers. The state government, however, became increasingly hostile to racial integration as the 19th

The School bowed to state demands to segregate the students into separate educational units, but it resisted segregation in other ways. Their baseball team, for instance, remained integrated, welcoming Ingram to its ranks in 1889. The team included students, alumni, and staff. The school's superintendent James Tate played on the team; he can be found in the middle row, with the beard. Ingram is in the back row, to the far right. The team was known as the Fulton Silents. Image used with permission from the Missouri School for the Deaf Museum.

century wore on. The first calls to separate the races at the Missouri School for the Deaf came in 1882, but the state legislature did not begin passing laws to mandate segregation in schools until 1889.

Initially, state leaders proposed erecting a new building in another city and sending the black deaf students away to study there. The Missouri School greatly opposed this idea. The solution that was at last reached was to separate the races into a white department and a black department, while keeping all of the students on the same campus together. Each unit had its own classrooms, dormitories, and dining hall. But, significantly, the teaching ratio was the same in both departments; the school administrators mandated one teacher for every 20 pupils, regardless of race. At the time, the new black department had 12 students, and so the school hired one black teacher, Monroe Ingram.

Ingram joined the staff of the Missouri School for the Deaf in August 1889. Reports from the school indicate that he "was liked by members of both races, both pupils and staff." It turns out that his "skill as a baseball player served him well. He was quickly welcomed as a member of the School's integrated team which included staff, older pupils, and former pupils." The state may have mandated racial separation in the classroom, but it seems that the School tried to continue to allow social contact and interaction across racial lines otherwise, at least in the years that Ingram worked there.[44]

Ingram served not only as a teacher but also as the head of this new black department at the Missouri School until 1908. In September 1909, the state of Oklahoma opened the Oklahoma Industrial Institute for Deaf, Blind, and Orphans of the Colored Race. Ingram was then hired as a teacher there, presumably to put an experienced teacher in the classroom at the fledgling school.[45] Ingram's career success in deaf education offers an important example of how educated black deaf men did sometimes make it into classrooms as teachers and role models for black deaf students in the years around the turn of the century.

Meanwhile, back in Kansas, it turns out that the white players had succeeded only too well. They not only eliminated integrated baseball, but the Emporia team itself played its last season in 1899. As Gregory Bond observes, white Kansans proved far less committed to racial justice than to social peace. "With talented integrated teams falling apart, many local whites, who had previously tolerated the status quo," Bond concludes, "quickly turned against integration and opted for Jim Crow to restore peace and harmony. Once black athletes had become a divisive factor, their white supporters proved powerless to resist the onset of segregation, and the color line quickly descended."[46] When minor league baseball continued on in Kansas in the 20th century, it would do so with all-white teams. All too soon, people would forget that it had ever been otherwise.

In the accounts of this history, Monroe Ingram has mostly been portrayed as a black baseball player pioneer in Kansas, and his story has been told as a part of the larger history of how racial segregation steadily overtook and replaced integrated baseball in the late 19th century. But Monroe Ingram was also deaf. He had been a part of a supportive, racially integrated community at the Kansas School for the Deaf. Being black at a predominantly white school had not prevented him from being captain of the baseball team or vice president of a school club, nor from winning mention and praise from a national level deaf newspaper. Ingram had come of age in a social world where his deafness had made him part of larger community.

Ingram's experience of being both black and deaf seems to demonstrate researcher Anja Werner's argument that "at times…. Black deaf individuals [gain] more favorable chances of upward social mobility than their black hearing peers."[47] When the Kansas School for the Deaf made the decision to integrate, Ingram's horizons suddenly expanded. There, he received an education, while gaining a language, a community, and a profession. He continued to work within that larger deaf community. As a teacher at the Minnesota School, he worked with white deaf teachers, even as he taught, and, perhaps just as crucially, served as an adult role model for, black deaf youth. Within deaf social circles, Ingram was a valued member of his community.

But in the hearing town of Emporia, it seems likely that his deafness had marked him as even more of an outsider, just as much so as his racial identity. As McCay Vernon suggested in his forward to Ernest Hairston and Linwood Smith's 1983 landmark study *Black and Deaf in America: Are We That Different?*, "Being both Black and deaf is in many ways a 'double whammy' because of society's abrogation of each of these two minorities. When the conditions of Blackness and deafness are combined in one person, the individual effects of prejudice, discrimination, and negative self-image are compounded exponentially."[48] In deaf society, he belonged; he was just like his deaf peers. But, in hearing society, Ingram was different. He was not like his fellow ballplayers. To them, he was doubly an outsider. He was black on a white team and deaf on a hearing team.

The example of Monroe Ingram's minor league career had long been forgotten by the time Curtis Pride came to the majors. He went unmentioned in newspaper accounts of previous deaf players in baseball. Still, Ingram's career makes the difficulties of playing professional baseball as a black deaf man in a majority white and hearing society quite clear.

6. *Pride, of the Expos*

When it came to covering Pride, on the one hand, the sporting press did correctly place his arrival within the larger history of deaf players who had played in major league baseball. On the other hand, Pride was consistently portrayed as a deaf player, not as a black player, and never as the major's first black deaf player. His deafness seems to have pushed his race aside altogether in the public imagination.[49]

Curiously, in the deaf press, too, his race was barely mentioned. But in the deaf press, Pride's communication choices attracted far greater attention than they did in the mainstream hearing press. Pride came into the majors in 1993 not knowing any sign language at all. It was the beginning of a journeyman career in professional baseball that spanned 13 years, including 11 seasons at the major-league level. Beyond the Expos, over the years, he made appearances with the Detroit Tigers, the Boston Red Sox, the Atlanta Braves, the New York Yankees, and, lastly, the Los Angeles Angels of Anaheim, where he made his last major league appearance in 2006 at the age of 37.

Pride got to bat most frequently as a pinch hitter, rather like Sipek. In all, he made 989 plate appearances with 199 base hits and a career batting average of .250, a career on-base percentage of .327, and a career slugging percentage of .405. David Laurila, writing for the SABR Biography Project, has wondered why Pride did not get more opportunities at the major league level and why he moved between organizations so frequently. "Asked if his deafness played a role, Pride wouldn't speculate as to whether he was discriminated against. All he'd say was 'Teams appreciated my ability on the field, and more importantly, I was a very good team player.'"[50]

Pride was not a deaf baseball player, in quite the same that Hoy, Taylor, and Sipek were. Pride was not seen as deaf, in terms of being a member of a larger deaf community. Rather, he was seen as an individual with a hearing impairment. This was not to say that deaf baseball fans were not excited about Pride's appearance in the majors; they were happy and excited to see another deaf player in major league baseball. The deaf press of the 1990s covered his arrival in major league baseball as the history making event that it was, but they were also fairly muted in their interest. Pride's inability to communicate using sign language drew negative attention within the deaf press. *Deaf Life*, for instance, noted, "During his well-publicized career, Pride was upheld as an oral deaf exemplar."[51]

The deaf press, in other words, did not see Curtis Pride as a representative of the larger signing deaf community, mostly because he wasn't. He was "an oral deaf exemplar." As such, Pride was also not seen as a member of the deaf community by the larger hearing public. By not signing, by communicating exclusively with speech, Pride was literally not seen by hearing fans as a representative of the larger deaf community, as Hoy, Taylor, and Sipek had been. Rather, Pride was most frequently portrayed as an individual with a hearing impairment, and as someone who had overcome a disability.

While Pride was very much aware of his presence as the only deaf player in the majors in nearly 50 years, he frequently spoke about his place in the game very differently than his predecessors had. He commented in an interview in 1993, when he broke in, "I try to send a message that people with disabilities can get what they want as long as they set their minds to it, set goals, and not be discouraged by what some people might think of their capabilities."[52] He made a similar statement the following year. "I'm not doing this for myself," Pride was quoted as saying in *The Washington Post* in 1994. "I'm doing it so other people can do whatever they want and not let their disabilities get in their way. There's nothing you can't do if you want it bad enough."[53]

In his interviews with the press, this was the most common way that Pride framed his deafness. Disability was an individual matter that could be overcome with determination and grit. Disabled people could simply not allow their disabilities to get in their way. This was a very different statement about deafness and a departure from earlier deaf major leaguers who largely embraced both their physical deafness as well as the deaf community. They were unafraid to call out hearing prejudice and hoped to see society overcome its prejudice against disabled people. (Dick Sipek, for instance, surely would have affirmed that Pride's deafness was almost certainly a reason why clubs seemed uninterested in investing in him for the long run. He was the one who bluntly stated to a hearing reporter that people want to keep the deaf down, after all.)

However, it is important to understand that Pride's more individualistic view of deafness was shaped just as much by his historical times as the older generation's collective view of deafness had been by theirs. It is not that their view is somehow right and his is wrong. Pride's view of his deafness was a reflection of the deaf world in which he came of age. During the 1980s and 1990s, with the rise of mainstreaming, deaf children were increasingly unlikely to go to school with deaf peers. Pride himself experienced his deafness as a lone individual and not as a member of a community. He had no deaf peers in school with him and he used an oral interpreter, and not sign language, in his mainstream classrooms. It is not that surprising that he would discuss his own deafness in such individualistic terms, given the very different historical context in which he experienced being deaf. As Pride himself said in 1994, "I never let my deafness hold me back. I never feel sorry for myself. Never. I know I have a disability. I've accepted it. I can't worry about it. I want to make the most of my life. And I am."[54]

By framing his deafness as a disability that he had to overcome, Pride reinforced a narrative line that the hearing press very much expected to hear, for this was the way that most hearing people thought about deafness, as a deficiency and an obstacle. But, at other times, much like Hoy, Taylor, and Sipek had done, Pride too challenged the very idea that deafness would ever hold a player back. As Pride told *New York Times* reporter Claire Smith in 1996, "To me, I've never looked at my deafness as a handicap. I've always thought of myself as one of the guys. The only difference is I can't hear. But I know that people see it as a great accomplishment, a person with disabilities who became a baseball player."

Having set up the usual social expectations, Pride proceeded to reverse them. He let Smith in on the truth: his appearance as a deaf man on a major league roster was no "great accomplishment" because no one needs to hear to play baseball. "People need their hearing for lots of things," he said, "but what do you need hearing for to play baseball—to hear the crowd cheering you?" When she replied by countering that baseball lore has it that outfielders like Pride need to be able to hear the crack of the bat to get a jump on the ball, Pride diplomatically "stopped short of calling it a myth" and instead "credited a sixth sense for his ability to track the ball as well as other outfielders."[55]

He also relied on Hoy's old system to patrol centerfield, though it was not identified as such in the press of the 1990s. He explained, "We have one simple rule. Any time I call for the ball, it's automatically mine. If someone else calls for it, he'll wave me off with a glove."[56] Finally, like Hoy had done, Pride called his deafness an advantage, especially at bat. "The crowd noise won't get to me. I'm able to maintain my full concentration."[57] And he called himself "probably more visually astute than most ballplayers," as a result of his deafness.[58] Like both Taylor and Sipek had done, Pride used his deafness as competitive fuel on the ball field. "Being deaf definitely makes me more motivated," he said. "I don't want people to look at me differently because of my disability. People tend to look at deaf people differently and feel sorry for us. That motivates me. Even though I am disabled, I am able to accomplish a lot."[59]

Pride exhibited here what scholar Christopher Krentz characterized as a "deaf double self." Drawing on W.E.B. DuBois' conception of double consciousness. Deaf Americans too, Krentz argued, "expressed ... that sense of internal division and 'two-ness' that seems to characterize so many groups that live in a society that views them as inferior."[60] Pride was a speaking deaf player who also asserted that his deafness offered him advantages as a player, in spite of hearing observers' tendency to view his deafness only as a condition to pity.

Pride's emergence as a new kind of deaf player in major league baseball, a speaking, hearing-impaired player, occurred during the same decade that witnessed the spread of cochlear implant technology. This technology was meant to provide deaf people better access to sound and to speech. Cochlear implants were approved by the FDA for implantation in children as young as two in 1990. By 2000, more than 35,000 people around the world had received implants and about half of those people were under the age of 18. It was hoped that technologies such as cochlear implants would finally do what speech lessons of oral education alone could not and make deaf people over in a hearing image. The whole point of the technology was to allow the deaf person to overcome the deafness of their body and become, as much as technologically possible, a hearing person.[61]

Pride was already an important public example of how deaf people could fit into hearing society. Even with his positive statements about his deafness, his frequent promotion of the overcoming disability narrative converged powerfully with the largely positive mainstream press coverage of the development of cochlear implant technology. Pride was overcoming deafness and, increasingly, others could too, especially with the help of this new technology.

Much of the press coverage of Pride's career in the years since he retired continues to be aimed at remembering him as an example of how physical disability may be overcome by sheer force of will, with his story serving as a narrative of individual achievement. "Luckily for him, he was strong enough to overcome his disability with hard work, perseverance, and the gift of athletic ability," wrote Ron Pasceri in the *Bleacher Report* 2012.[62] "We are all inspired by the resiliency of the human spirit," wrote Norm King for SABR about Pride's first major league game. "Everyone loves to see people succeed after overcoming a physical or mental disability, especially in professional sports."[63] The Kenwood Hearing Center, an audiology practice in Ohio, reported excitedly in 2012 that Pride would be giving a public lecture in Ohio and would share his "overcoming hearing loss story" with his audience.[64]

While Pride did not have implants himself, he was supportive of the spread of this auditory technology. The work of Pride's private foundation, Together with Pride, combined a quest to overcome disability with the technological quest to hear. The Foundation counted as a key element of its mission a hearing aid donation program. Providing hearing aids to needy children is not an unworthy goal. The foundation's reasons for doing so are striking, however. As the foundation's website puts it,

> The Hearing Aid Donation program is an important element of the Together With Pride Foundation, Inc. Hearing aids are integral tools for deaf and hard of hearing students. Quality aids help these students in the classroom, at home, and with their social activities. Hearing impaired students rely on their aids to be their 'ears' and to open the door to the world for them. Without aids—a child can become isolated from his/her family and friends and the hearing world. A child's self-esteem can suffer. The learning can stop. The Foundation works to improve a child's self-esteem and educational level. A quality hearing aid is the first step. The Foundation wants to be there to help a child have the opportunity with this first step.

Pride's foundation suggests that without aids, that is, without ears, a deaf child can become isolated from the hearing world. Hearing opens the door to the world for deaf children.

This viewpoint breaks sharply with that of Hoy, Taylor, and Sipek, none of whom believed hearing was a requirement for entry to life, either on the field or off. They did not want to overcome their deafness; they wanted to overcome hearing prejudice. They did not view their deafness as an individual problem to solve; they viewed the prejudice against deaf people as a social problem that society, deaf and hearing alike, would need to solve together. Finally, they did not view deaf people as in any way isolated from the so-called hearing world; they lived in it and worked in it every day. They wanted to be able to work in it as deaf people, on equal terms with hearing people.

This emphasis on technologies that encouraged hearing and speech for deaf children posed a new threat to the sign language. Since cochlear implants first emerged into the medical marketplace in the 1990s, the signing deaf community has worried about its future. When *Deaf Life* asked its readers whether or not they thought that medical professionals care about what the signing deaf community thinks about cochlear implants, the response was overwhelming. Ninety-seven percent of responders said no. Comments were filled with real anger. "We are guinea pigs," one reader wrote. Doctors all think "we are wannabe hearing people," commented another; in any conversations about these technologies, "hearing people come first." No, one person wrote simply, "they don't give a damn."[65] The deaf community was largely opposed to implant technology in the early 21st century. *Deaf Life* published several articles in 2002 that took a very critical view of implants, as representing a kind of war between supporters of biomedical technology and the deaf community.[66]

If it was a war, by 2009, one could argue that it had already been lost.

That year, it was reported that approximately 40 percent of American deaf children younger than the age of three received at least one implant.[67] Implant surgical centers routinely discourage parents from using any sign language with their children after surgery. A 2017 study concluded, "In a new, multisite study of deaf children with cochlear implants, University of Texas at Dallas researchers have found that children with either no exposure or limited exposure to sign language end up with better auditory, speaking, and reading skills later."[68]

Lead investigator Ann Geers remarked, "This study provides the most compelling support yet available for the benefits of listening and spoken language input for promoting verbal development in children implanted by 3 years of age. Contrary to earlier published assertions, there was no advantage to parents' use of sign language. This result affirms the decision of many hearing parents who choose not to use sign language when their child receives a cochlear implant." Her co-researcher Andrea Warner-Czyz went further. She said, "If you want your deaf child to be an oral communicator and have reading and language measures on par with their hearing peers, then signing to them may not provide the easiest route to that outcome."[69]

Michael Chorost recounted his own experience with a cochlear implant in his memoir *Rebuilt*. He argued that the rising number of implantations heralds the slow death of the deaf community. "The prospect of conquering deafness with binary logic tears my heart with joy and grief in bewilderingly equal measure," he wrote. "Nineteenth-century Americans celebrated the dismembering of Indian tribes with thoughtless cheer. Manifest destiny, they called it. Today we see it as a tragedy. When twenty-second century historians write the history of cochlear implants and the end of ASL, they may come to the same conclusion. However, they will not find malice. Not deliberate genocide. Only thousands of separately made rational decisions gradually accumulating into a computational tidal wave so overwhelming that even the clearest-eyed observers could only stand by in helpless wonder and sorrow."[70]

It may be that Chorost is overestimating the social impact of the technology. There can be no doubt, however, that the rising use of medical technologies will continue to remake the deaf community in fundamental ways.[71] It will not be the same deaf community, its culture, its language, and its values, as the one that shaped the lives of Hoy, Taylor, and Sipek. That version of the deaf community proved remarkably stable from the middle of the 19th century to the middle of the 20th century. Already, the changing historical circumstances of the deaf community have produced a different kind of deaf player in the late 20th century, in Curtis Pride, a player who both reflects and represents the deaf experience of his time. All cultures change over time and that of the deaf community is no different.

Despite Chorost's predictions, however, a kind of technological optimism seems to be growing within the deaf community. Despite the continuing advice of medical professionals, a new belief has begun to emerge from deaf people: we can embrace both technology and sign language. As deaf author Sara Novic commented in 2018, "A cochlear implant isn't inherently bad, but it isn't inherently good, either; it is a neutral piece of technology, a tool, like a hammer. Expecting an implant to cure deafness or magically generate speech is to await the moment the hammer will fly out of one's hand and build a house on its own. The value of the tool lies only in the skill of its user, and for the cochlear implant user, that skill is learned with much effort."[72] A majority of deaf people now believe that cochlear implant users can be welcomed into the deaf community, with one critically important caveat. Cochlear implant users must also respect, know, and use sign language.[73]

This raises the obvious question. Where will these deaf people learn the sign language? And from whom? To which sign language users will they be exposed? As sociologist and implant user John B. Christiansen reports, young implant users who do use any sign language are more likely to sign and voice simultaneously, that is, to sign English, and not ASL, a language with its own grammar and syntax. This is especially the case, Christiansen reports, "if their parents and others subsequently focus on the development of spoken language at the expense of learning how to sign."[74]

But even here, deaf institutions are trying to provide the answers. The only two universities founded specifically to serve deaf people in the United States, Gallaudet University in Washington, D.C., and the National Technical Institute for the Deaf (NTID) in Rochester, New York, have both reported increasing enrollments in the number of students with implants. In 2011, Gallaudet reported 102 implanted students, about 10 percent of the student body, double the number of implanted students who were there in 2005. At NTID, the trend has been more dramatic. In 1999, there were 29 students with implants. In 2017, there were 416, roughly 38 percent of all deaf students.

And yet, in 2017, Gallaudet adopted bilingualism in ASL and English as its top educational priority for its graduates. NTID now offers a two-week ASL immersion program to all new entering students who arrive on campus with minimal or no ASL skills called the New Signers Program.[75] If there was a war, deaf people were increasingly trying to call a truce based on sign language. The deaf community is signaling that any individual deaf people can choose to use these new technologies, but to become a part of the larger deaf community, they must respect sign language.

This truce was particularly hard-fought at Gallaudet University. In 2006, the campus erupted in protest when the university's provost, Jane Fernandes, was elevated to president. Fernandes said that she "represented those who grew up in largely hearing communities, who would crave involvement in the outside world." Additionally, she sought to persuade the campus to look more favorably on modern medical technology and welcome more warmly the growing number of cochlear implant users, on their own terms. As she put it, "More and more deaf babies now are getting cochlear implants, so that means more deaf children are hearing better and speaking better. That's the change that I represent, and it's scary for a lot of deaf people."[76]

The protest was covered in the mass media as a battle over whether Fernandes was "deaf enough," culturally speaking, to lead the university, since she grew up speaking and did not learn ASL until she was in her early 20s, but that characterization really misses the mark. The protest was not really about her at all but about the larger direction and mission of Gallaudet University.[77] As Gallaudet associate professor of English Kathleen Wood explained in a letter to the *Washington Post*, "the majority of Gallaudet students ... come to the university longing to be part of Deaf culture and to improve their ASL skills." They want to become more bilingual and more bicultural, in other words.

Wood argued that students come to a university with a unique mission to serve deaf students, precisely because of that mission and not in spite of it. In the 21st century, deaf students can increasingly choose to attend a mainstream, hearing university via notetakers and interpreters, as educational access services are mandated by the Americans with Disabilities Act. They come to Gallaudet, she suggested, precisely because they want to know more, and not less, about deaf community, language, and culture.

Wood charged that, already, under her leadership as provost, Fernandes was leading the campus in a direction that would make it "more welcoming to non-signers." To Wood, as to many other protesters, that was the wrong direction. Wood feared that it would over time result in "second-class citizenship for users and seekers of Deaf culture and ASL skills."[78] Seen from this point of view, the protest was the campus' way of registering a vote of no-confidence, its way of expressing public opposition to this fundamental change in direction. Fernandes, in the end, was forced to step down. Soon thereafter, in 2007, the university adopted a new vision statement, declaring Gallaudet to be a "bilingual, multicultural institution of higher education that ensures the intellectual and professional advancement of deaf and hard of hearing individuals through American Sign Language and English." It calls this approach "inclusive bilingualism."[79]

As it happened, Curtis Pride embarked on the next phase of his professional career by making his own personal journey deeper into the larger deaf community. He joined this newly energized community of Gallaudet University in 2008, when he accepted a job there as head baseball coach. With his acceptance, Pride began to learn sign language. While he had to have an assistant coach interpret for him in his first season, Pride has communicated directly with his team in sign language for himself ever since.[80]

Pride faced enormous challenges as he took over the helm at Gallaudet. The school had only enjoyed two winning seasons since World War II, once in 1966 and again in 1977.[81] He admitted that they had a lot of work ahead of them. "We have a lot of work to do," he said, "but it will get better."[82] His arrival electrified Gallaudet players. As pitcher Danny Gabel explained, "Curtis Pride is a hero in the deaf community. He's exciting and gives hope. It's amazing to be playing for the guy I loved watching as a kid. He's inspirational, someone that I look up to."[83]

Pride's impact on the Gallaudet Bison was transformational. In 2012, the

Pride brought the Bison to one of their best years ever in 2012, when the team won 25 games. As one his players explained, "Curtis Pride is a hero in the deaf community. He's exciting and gives hope." Here, Coach works with his players. Courtesy Gallaudet University.

team had one of its best seasons ever. The Bison played that season on the newly remodeled and newly named Hoy Field, named in honor of William "Dummy" Hoy. They won a university record 25 games, with an overall record of 27–17, and a 10–4 record in conference play, in the North Eastern Athletic Conference (NEAC). Pride was named the NEAC Coach of the Year. In the 2013 season, the Bison did even better in the NEAC, going 11–3. Pride was again named the NEAC Coach of the Year.

In 2014, the Bison posted the most wins in university history, with 27 victories on the season. They went 12–6 in NEAC play and were the regular season NEAC co-champions. That team boasted six All-NEAC players as well as the NEAC Player of the Year, in catcher Casey Hicks. Of his mission as Gallaudet coach, Pride says, "I want to establish a winning tradition for the Gallaudet baseball program that will attract quality scholar-athletes who not only want to be a part of that tradition but also will represent the highest ideals and principles of Gallaudet at all times."[84] In 2016, Pride also made a return to the majors, when he was appointed Major League Baseball's "Ambassador for Inclusion," to provide guidance, training, and assistance to ensure an inclusive environment in major league baseball for both players and fans.[85]

Dick Sipek, for one, would undoubtedly be pleased, and perhaps even relieved, at where Pride's baseball journey has taken him. Sipek admitted that he was pained by Pride's signlessness, when the young man made it into the majors. "It hurts my feelings," Sipek had commented. "What's wrong with sign language?" That response was entirely understandable. For Sipek, sign language was a powerful symbol of deaf community and deaf pride, much as it had been for William Hoy and Luther Taylor. Who would deaf people be if they did not sign? One might argue that all individuals should be free to make their own language choices. But that argument imagines that each deaf person is simply an individual with a medical condition. It fails to see deaf people as many of them see themselves, as members of a distinct community, one with a history, tradition, and culture all its own.

For deaf people who identify as members of the deaf community and who value their community, these linguistic choices matter enormously. How could there continue to be a deaf community if their sign language went extinct? What would be uniquely deaf about a deaf community if all the individual deaf people in it communicated like hearing people? Can there be a truly deaf community if its members increasingly speak and hear, rather than sign? Seen from the vantage point of older deaf people, like Sipek's generation, it becomes even easier to understand why Pride's initial lack of recognizably deaf communication skills would be so disappointing. They had fought so

hard to keep the sign language alive at oralism's peak. Would all that struggle prove to have been for nothing?

While he focused on Pride's language choices, Sipek's concerns clearly went deeper. Pride had grown up in a world of hearing aids, speech lessons, and public schools, so unlike the signing world of the residential school that Sipek had known. Major league baseball has seen so few deaf players. They occupy a rare place in public view, one that has brought only a fortunate few deaf men to the attention of the wider, hearing public. Sipek was not only worried about the sign language. How would Pride be seen by hearing fans and hearing sportswriters? Did Pride think of himself as a member of the deaf community? Would Pride, like the players that came before him, stand up for the deaf community? Could he embrace deaf history and deaf icons?

Indeed, he could. After Pride recorded his first major league hit September 23, 1993, the headline in the *Wilmington Morning Star* the following morning read, "Pride doesn't let being deaf keep him from success."[86] The paper's headline seems like the kind of characterization that Pride frequently offered himself, and here was a story of Pride overcoming his deafness. But, instead, in talking to the hearing reporter, Pride seized the moment to draw attention to the deaf history of baseball. As he entered major league baseball, Pride chose to claim that deaf history as his own, by reminding hearing fans of the importance of baseball's first deaf star, William "Dummy" Hoy, and of his legacy to the sport. Pride said, "He invented umpire's hand signals for balls and strikes because he couldn't hear it when they called the pitches."[87]

Pride become coach of the Gallaudet Bison baseball team in 2008. Courtesy Gallaudet University.

Pride was not the same kind of deaf player that Hoy had been. The many decades of history between the two men had shaped their views of deafness in profoundly different ways. Pride had his own unique baseball journey to make, and he tried to strike a balance between being an individual deaf player pursuing his own baseball dream and honoring the deaf players who had come before him.

When Pride's journey finally led him to become head baseball coach of the Bison, he

was not simply taking a coaching position. Gallaudet University is arguably the most important public symbol of the American deaf community, embodying its history, language, culture, and pride. As H. Dirksen L. Bauman points out, "It is the only plot of land in the entire world where Deaf people may have direct access to higher education through a signed language." As a result, Bauman notes, Gallaudet plays a "near mythic role" within the deaf community.[88]

Gallaudet's roots as an institution go back to the Civil War, when Abraham Lincoln signed the charter that founded the school. Its long institutional history means that it has served as the public face of the deaf community in American culture for more than 150 years.[89] In the early 20th century, its commencement services brought American presidents and other prominent hearing politicians to the campus.[90] It has long seen its larger mission as trying to demonstrate, through the quality of its graduates, the capability and worth of the deaf citizens of the United States. The linguistic research conducted at Gallaudet proved that signed languages were the linguistic equals to spoken languages. Before the strike that toppled Fernandes, the first student strike at Gallaudet in 1988 was hailed as a civil rights break-through when it brought the campus its first ever deaf president, I. King Jordan, who famously told his supporters that "deaf people can do anything except hear."[91]

Like, for instance, deaf people can coach a college baseball team at a competitive level, as Pride forcefully demonstrates. It matters enormously to have a deaf university with a deaf college baseball team be headed by a deaf coach, as all of these things are still so atypical for most deaf Americans. Hoy, Taylor, and Sipek all attended and graduated from a residential school for the deaf. None of them attended college, though that would have been an increasingly common circumstance for hearing people over the course of their respective playing careers. Pride graduated from college, an absolute rarity still, even in the 21st century, within the American deaf community.[92]

In 2017, only 18 percent of deaf adults overall in the United States had completed a bachelor's degree.[93] While 20 percent of white deaf people earned a bachelor's degree (compared to 37 percent of their hearing peers), among black deaf people the completion rate fell to only 11 percent (compared to the 22 percent of their hearing peers).[94] There are only 14 black Deaf Americans who hold doctoral degrees in the United States, as of 2017.[95] As both a former major leaguer and a college educated black deaf man, the importance of Pride's representation at Gallaudet can scarcely be overstated. Pride is a powerful symbol of deaf success, on both levels. Coming to Gallaudet meant that Pride was aligning himself publicly with an institution that has long stood for

6. *Pride, of the Expos*

deaf equality and capability, the very things that he himself had most wanted to exemplify during his major league career. While then he had stood out mostly as a deaf individual within a hearing league, Pride now firmly stands for and within a larger deaf community.

He also advocates for that community. In an interview in the fall of 2014, Pride called out the continuing prejudice against deaf players in major league baseball. Asked by a reporter about how long it would take for another deaf player to enter the majors, Pride replied, "Hopefully not long, but it is tough because there are some good deaf players not getting an opportunity to play pro ball. One of my former players, who graduated last year, definitely had Major League potential. He was a two-time All-American and a five tool prospect. I think his deafness is the only reason he was not signed by a professional organization."[96] (Pride was referring to his outfielder William Bissell, who batted .386 for the Bison in the 2014 season.)

Finally, 10 years after Sipek's death, Pride affirmed once again his own pride in the very same deaf man that Sipek had called his hero, and in doing so revealed that he and Sipek shared the same dream. Pride said in 2015, "I think the Deaf community would be ecstatic about Hoy being inducted into the Hall of Fame and would be proud of him. William 'Dummy' Hoy is to the Deaf community what Jackie Robison is to the African-American community."[97] Spoken truly like a man who stands proudly as a member of both communities.

For as much as the deaf community has changed over time, one thing, at least, has remained the same. William Ellsworth Hoy remains a household name in the deaf community, and a hero for the ages.

Epilogue

As I was bringing this project to a conclusion, a major baseball scandal broke into public view, arguably the worst scandal since the Black Sox scandal of one hundred years ago. The Chicago White Sox had cheated to lose a World Series in 1919. In early 2020, word spread that the Houston Astros had cheated to win one in 2017, using cameras and video feeds to analyze and steal the signs of opposing catchers. Astros manager A.J. Hinch and G.M. Jeff Luhnow were first suspended from major league baseball for a year and then fired. The team was fined a $5 million, a record, though admittedly walking around money for a professional baseball franchise. Of course, as Emma Baccellieri points out in *Sports Illustrated*, "$5 million is also the maximum that a team can be fined under the Major League Constitution. It would be nothing, if it were not constitutionally everything."[1]

The scandal shakes the faith of all fans in the integrity of the game and the fairness of its outcomes. But it also demonstrates forcefully, once again, how visual a game baseball is and has always been. Stealing signs, in the end, is about seeing signs and interpreting signs. Hearing players proved quite adept at this illicit activity.

But the visuality of the scandal offers a moment to remember that deaf players in major league baseball have always been exemplary visual players. By 1900, William Hoy was regarded as an outfielder who "probably has the best eye for a fly ball of any player now on the field." The *New York Clipper* commented of Luther Taylor that his deafness "is really an asset on the baseball diamond. He is never confused, as others are, by the mass of sounds that comes up when a play starts. Under such a condition, he simply gets accurate information with utmost speed through use of his extremely alert and well-trained eyes." Curtis Pride thought of himself as "probably more visually astute than most ballplayers," on account of his deafness.

Finally, Dick Sipek was seen by some observers as playing the outfield by "using his eyes to compensate for his poor hearing." Others took a closer look. As one sportswriter noted in 1944, Sipek's real talent was in the mental side of the sport, as "he is brilliant in sizing up opposing pitchers, stealing signals, and accomplishing the headwork tasks of the diamond that some players never learn."

Stealing them, that is, the old-fashioned way. With his well-trained deaf eyes.

Chapter Notes

Preface

1. See Brian McKenna's entry "Dummy Stephenson," for the SABR Biography Project. Available at https://sabr.org/bioproj/person/a036ff64.

2. For more on Stephenson, see Brian McKenna's biographical entry, written for the SABR Biography Project and available at SABR.org.

3. Murphy's baseball stats are available at baseball-reference.com.

4. For more on Murphy and the Empire League, see William F. Ross III, "The Empire State League: South Georgia Baseball in 1913," *The National Pastime: Baseball in the Peach State* (2010), 42–51. *The National Pastime* journal is a publication of the Society for American Baseball Research and can be accessed through their website, SABR.org.

Chapter 1

1. Deegan appeared in the majors only in August 1901. Leitner survived for one additional year, playing his last game in August 1902. Taylor had the longest career of any deaf pitcher, hurling in the majors from 1900 to 1908, and in the minors from 1909 to 1915.

2. For more, see Susan M. Schweik, *The Ugly Laws: Disability in Public* (New York: New York University Press, 2009).

3. See Susan Burch, *Signs of Resistance: American Deaf Cultural History, 1900–1942* (New York: New York University Press, 2002), 76.

4. "The Alumni," *A Historical and Biographical Souvenir of the Ohio School for the Deaf. Seventy Years' History of a Notable Seat of Learning, with Personal Recollections of Its Founders and Early Officials. The Institution of the Present Day. Official, Educational, and Industrial Departments, Domestic and Social Life. Portraits and Biographical Sketches of representative Alumni* (Columbus: The Berlin Printing Co., 1898), 72.

5. *A Historical and Biographical Souvenir of the Ohio School for the Deaf,* 72.

6. "Athletics," *A Historical and Biographical Souvenir of the Ohio School for the Deaf,* 137.

7. *A Historical and Biographical Souvenir of the Ohio School for the Deaf,* 72.

8. "Athletics," *A Historical and Biographical Souvenir of the Ohio School for the Deaf,* 137.

9. All information on the Ohio Independents from Ralph LinWeber, "The Ohio Independents of 1879," *The Silent Worker* (July 1959), 17–18. There is also a good team picture on page 20.

10. For more on professional baseball in Rochester, see http://www.milb.com/content/page.jsp?sid=t534&ymd=20120216&content_id=26712722&vkey=team4.

11. "Base Ball Notes," *Rochester Times-Union* (July 10, 1879). My thanks to baseball historian and fellow Rochesterian Priscilla Astifan for tracking down this article.

12. "Muscle and Speed," *Rochester Democrat and Chronicle* (July 10, 1879), 4. My thanks to baseball historian and fellow Rochesterian Priscilla Astifan for tracking down this article.

13. See Brock Helander, "The Western Baseball Tours of 1879," *The National Pastime, expanded e-edition* (SABR, 2015).

14. "Athletics," *A Historical and Biographical Souvenir of the Ohio School for the Deaf,* 137.

15. "Athletics," *A Historical and Biographical Souvenir of the Ohio School for the Deaf*, 137.

16. *Sunday Mercury Telegraph* (May 13, 1877), 5.

17. *Sunday Mercury Telegraph* (May 13, 1877), 5.

18. Ralph Lin Weber, "The Ohio Independents of 1879," *The Silent Worker* (July 1959), 18.

19. Howe as quoted in Mary Klages, *Woeful Afflictions: Disability and Sentimentality in Victorian America* (Philadelphia: University of Pennsylvania, 1999), 47.

20. See Klages for more on Howe's views of blind people. See Ernest Freeberg, *The Education of Laura Bridgman, First Deaf and Blind Person to Learn Language* (Cambridge: Harvard University Press, 2001). See also R.A.R. Edwards, *Words Made Flesh: Nineteenth-Century Deaf Education and the Growth of Deaf Culture* (New York: New York University Press, 2012), especially 150–153.

21. For more on 19th-century deaf history, see Douglas C. Baynton, Jack R. Gannon, and Jean Lindquist Bergey, *Through Deaf Eyes: A Photographic History of an American Community* (Washington, D.C.: Gallaudet University Press, 2007); see John Vickrey Van Cleve and Barry A. Crouch, *A Place of Their Own: Creating the Deaf Community in America* (Washington, D.C.: Gallaudet University Press, 1989); see R.A.R. Edwards, *Words Made Flesh: Nineteenth-Century Deaf Education and the Growth of Deaf Culture* (New York: New York University Press, 2012); see John Vickrey Van Cleve, editor, *The Deaf History Reader* (Washington, D.C.: Gallaudet University Press, 2007).

22. Christopher Krentz, *Writing Deafness: The Hearing Line in Nineteenth-Century American Literature* (Chapel Hill: University of North Carolina Press, 2007), 14.

23. See Lawrence Baldassaro's introduction in Lawrence Baldassaro and Richard A. Johnson, eds., *The American Game: Baseball and Ethnicity* (Carbondale: Southern Illinois University Press, 2002), 5.

24. "The Manual Work and the Sign Language," *A Historical and Biographical Souvenir of the Ohio School for the Deaf*, 37.

25. "The Manual Work and the Sign Language," *A Historical and Biographical Souvenir of the Ohio School for the Deaf*, 38.

26. "The Manual Work and the Sign Language," *A Historical and Biographical Souvenir of the Ohio School for the Deaf*, 38.

27. "Superintendent Jones on Systems," *A Historical and Biographical Souvenir of the Ohio School for the Deaf*, 46.

28. The system had changed by 1898, at the time the 70th anniversary bulletin was printed. Beginning in 1896, "regular oral classes extending to all grades now form an integral part of the school work. A new pupil on arriving at the Institution undergoes a series of tests to see whether he gives promise of learning to talk. If he responds to the tests, he is placed in an oral primary class, and he is taught by this method up through the various grades until his school life closes. Should he wholly lack the power of speech he is assigned to the manual department. A new pupil is also tested for hearing by means of bells and whistles, and if the results are satisfactory he is placed in the aural department." However, all oral students were encouraged to interact with the manual students, and all were expected, and indeed encouraged, to learn the sign language. See "Superintendent Jones on Systems," *A Historical and Biographical Souvenir of the Ohio School for the Deaf*, 46. And this curricular change occurred well after all of the men under discussion here had graduated from the Ohio School.

29. "Sporting Record," *New Hampshire Patriot* (November 27, 1879), 4.

30. "Silent Ball Players," *Biloxi Herald* (November 10, 1888), 2.

31. *Indianapolis Journal* (July 14, 1889), 5.

32. Data taken from an ongoing research project. Please contact the author for more information.

33. Brian McKenna, "Ed Dundon," SABR Biography Project, available on-line at sabr.org.

34. Article in *Macon Telegraph* (March 25, 1886), 5. Dundon's umpiring also covered in *Washington Critic-Record* (November 10, 1886), 1.

35. McKenna, "Ed Dundon" entry.

36. *The Sporting News* (November 6, 1886), 5.

37. Brian Malzkuhn, "Dummy Hoy: Re-Debating His Credentials for Nomina-

tion to the Hall of Fame," *Deaf Studies Digital Journal* 2 (2010).

38. David W. Zang, *Fleet Walker's Divided Heart: The Life of Baseball's First Black Major Leaguer* (Lincoln: University of Nebraska Press, 1995), 33.

39. Zang 41.

40. See Zang 41

41. Zang 43.

42. Zang 54.

43. Story recounted in Susan Jacoby, *Why Baseball Matters* (New Haven: Yale University Press, 2018), 154.

44. As reported in Howard Rosenberg, "One Hundred Years Ago, Chicago's City Clerk Was Future Baseball Hall of Famer Cap Anson," at the website *Cap Chronicled* available at capanson.com, accessed 10 August 2019.

45. See Peter Mancuso, "May 2, 1887: First African American Battery," Society for American Baseball Research, 2013, available at sabr.org.

46. For more on Higgins stats, see baseball-reference.com.

47. For more on Grant's career and life, see Brian McKenna's entry on Grant for the SABR Biography Project, available on-line at sabr.org.

48. Zang 54–55.

49. Zang 58.

50. Zang 58.

51. Zang 59–60.

52. "The Alumni," *A Historical and Biographical Souvenir of the Ohio School for the Deaf,* 100.

53. "The Alumni," *A Historical and Biographical Souvenir of the Ohio School for the Deaf,* 100.

54. David F. Armstrong, *The History of Gallaudet University: 150 Years of a Deaf American Institution* (Washington, D.C.: Gallaudet University Press, 2014), 30.

55. Armstrong 30.

56. Edward Miner Gallaudet, *The History of the College of the Deaf, 1857-1907,* ed. Lance J. Fischer and David C. DeLorenzo (Washington, D.C.: Gallaudet University Press, 1983), 202.

57. Armstrong 30.

58. Armstrong 30.

59. Armstrong 31.

60. McKenna, "Ed Dundon."

61. McKenna, "Ed Dundon."

62. See John R. Husman's entry on Walker for the SABR Biography Project, available on-line at sabr.org.

63. M.F. Walker, *Our Home Colony: A Treatise on the Past, Present, and Future of the Negro Race in America* (Steubenville, OH: The Herald Printing Company, 1908), 5, 19.

64. All information on Dundon from Ralph LinWeber, "The Dundon Story," *The Silent Worker* (July 1959), 19–21. An image of Dundon graces the cover of the issue.

65. "The Alumni," *A Historical and Biographical Souvenir of the Ohio School for the Deaf,* 100.

66. Zang 65.

67. "Ex-Pupils in Active Life," *A Historical and Biographical Souvenir of the Ohio School for the Deaf,* 139.

68. Figure as reported in Douglas C. Baynton, Jack R. Gannon, and Jean Lindquist Bergey, *Through Deaf Eyes: A Photographic History of an American Community* (Washington, D.C.: Gallaudet University Press, 2007), 41. Given the School's focus on the trade, many male alumni were found in the shoe industry, with 31 shoemakers, 14 shoe shop owners, and 27 shoe factory hands. There were 11 carpenters, 17 bookbinders, and 6 tailors. Female alumni reported work, too: 14 dressmakers, 10 domestics, and 9 tailoresses. Additionally, 25 alumni were working as teachers of the deaf. This source does not list the names of the baseball players. However, from other historical records, we know that there were others. Arthur Hinch played as an outfielder in the Western League, Harry Dix as a pitcher in the Cotton States League, and William Fankhauser as a third baseman in the Indiana State League. See Ralph E. LinWeber, "The Ohio Independents of 1879," *The Silent Worker* (July 1959), 18.

69. "Industrial Department," *A Historical and Biographical Souvenir of the Ohio School for the Deaf,* 48.

70. Peter Morris, *A Game of Inches: A Story Behind the Innovations That Shaped Baseball* (Chicago: Ivan R. Dee, 2010), 523.

71. "Athletics," *A Historical and Biographical Souvenir of the Ohio School for the Deaf,* 137.

72. "The Alumni," *A Historical and Biographical Souvenir of the Ohio School for*

the Deaf, 82. His parents were William and Amelia Sawhill, who both attended the Ohio School.

73. "The Alumni," *A Historical and Biographical Souvenir of the Ohio School for the Deaf*, 94.

74. "The Alumni," *A Historical and Biographical Souvenir of the Ohio School for the Deaf*, 94.

75. "The Alumni," *A Historical and Biographical Souvenir of the Ohio School for the Deaf*, 94.

76. "Athletics," *A Historical and Biographical Souvenir of the Ohio School for the Deaf*, 137.

77. All information on Ryn from Brian McKenna, "John Ryn," SABR Biography Project, available on-line at sabr.org.

78. Peter Morris, *A Game of Inches: A Story Behind the Innovations that Shaped Baseball* (Chicago: Ivan R. Dee, 2010), 523.

79. As quoted by Brian McKenna in his biography of Ryn.

80. McKenna, "John Ryn."

81. "Minneapolis Mems.," *The Sporting Life* 15, 1 (April 5, 1890), 5.

82. McKenna, "John Ryn."

83. "Mixed Briefs," *The Sporting Life* 15, 17 (July 26, 1890), 1.

84. McKenna, "John Ryn."

85. McKenna, "John Ryn."

86. Bob Ebbeskotte, "George Kihm and the Delphos Reds," http://delphoscanalcommission.com/banks-yesteryear, posted April 23, 2014.

87. McKenna, "George Kihm," SABR Biography Project, available on-line at sabr.org.

88. McKenna, "George Kihm."

89. *Wilkes-Barre News* (June 28, 1904), 5.

90. McKenna, "George Kihm."

91. Bill Weiss and Marshall Wright, "27: 1902 Indianapolis Indians," http://www.milb.com/milb/history/top100.jsp?idx=27.

92. McKenna, "George Kihm."

93. "Dummy Kihm Is Remarkable Player," *Star Tribune* (May 17, 1908), 44.

94. "Here's How Dummy Kihm Teaches Players the Sign Language," *The Dayton Herald* (July 10, 1909), 6.

95. Bill Weiss and Marshall Wright, "59: 1905 Columbus Senators," http://www.milb.com/milb/history/top100.jsp?idx=59.

96. Bill Weiss and Marshall Wright, "59: 1905 Columbus Senators," http://www.milb.com/milb/history/top100.jsp?idx=59.

97. McKenna, "George Kihm."

98. McKenna, "George Kihm."

99. McKenna, "George Kihm."

100. "Dummy Kihm Wears His Mustache Every Other Year and This Is an Off Year; Looks Five Years Younger Without It," *The Dayton Herald* (June 11, 1910), 8.

101. "Dummy Kihm Wears His Mustache Every Other Season," *The Fort Wayne Journal-Gazette* (June 13, 1910), 2.

102. McKenna, "George Kihm."

103. "Nothing to Say But There with the Goods," *The Seattle Star* (December 17, 1908), 2.

104. "Three Deaf Mutes Made Good Record In Major League," *The Silent Worker* 32, 2 (November 1918), 28.

105. McKenna, "George Kihm."

106. "Ball Player Dies," *The Cincinnati Enquirer* (October 12, 1936), 14.

107. "Alumni," *A Historical and Biographical Souvenir of the Ohio School for the Deaf*, 94.

108. *A Historical and Biographical Souvenir of the Ohio School for the Deaf*, 38.

109. "Alumni," *A Historical and Biographical Souvenir of the Ohio School for the Deaf*, 74.

110. Krentz, *Writing Deafness*, 47.

111. For more on the emergence of the 19th-century deaf community, see R.A.R. Edwards, *Words Made Flesh: Nineteenth-Century Deaf Education and the Growth of Deaf Culture* (New York: New York University Press, 2012).

112. "Alumni," *A Historical and Biographical Souvenir of the Ohio School for the Deaf*, 74.

113. "The Ohio Deaf Mute Alumni Association," *A Historical and Biographical Souvenir of the Ohio School for the Deaf*, 121.

114. "The Ohio Deaf Mute Alumni Association," *A Historical and Biographical Souvenir of the Ohio School for the Deaf*, 125.

115. Details from Stone's life in Ralph E. LinWeber, Graduation Classes of the Ohio School for the Deaf, 1869-1949, including *Gallaudet College Entrants from Ohio Since 1864, an 80 Year Record* (Toledo: Ralph E. LinWeber, 1949), 31, 112.

116. Gilbert Otis Fay, "Reminiscences of Ex-Superintendent Gilbert Otis Fay," *A His-*

torical and Biographical Souvenir of the Ohio
School for the Deaf, 17.

117. "Athletics," *A Historical and
Biographical Souvenir of the Ohio School for
the Deaf*, 139.

Chapter 2

1. Hoy as quoted in Art Kruger, "AAAD
Hall of Fame Created," *The Silent Worker*
(July 1952), 26.

2. Career summary in Stephen Jay Gould,
Triumph and Tragedy in Mudville (New
York: W.W. Norton, 2003), 116–7.

3. See http://www.milb.com/milb/
history/top100.jsp?idx=29. Bill Weiss and
Marshall Wright place the team at number
29 out of their list of the top 100 minor
leagues teams.

4. For more on the remarkable career
of Bud Fowler, see Brian McKenna, "Bud
Fowler," SABR Biography Project, available
on-line at sabr.org.

5. For the history of the team, see Mitch
Lutzke, *The Page Fence Giants: A History
of Black Baseball's Pioneering Champions*
(McFarland, 2018).

6. All coverage and quotes of the game
from Mitch Lutzke, *The Page Fence Giants: A
History of Black Baseball's Pioneering Champions* (McFarland, 2018), 56–57.

7. Coverage in Lutzke 57–58.

8. Brian McKenna, "Bud Fowler," SABR
Biography Project. All information on
Fowler here from this SABR biography.

9. Susan Burch, *Signs of Inclusion*, 80.

10. *Sporting Life* (May 9, 1891), 2.
The reference here is to third baseman
Arlie Latham, who played in the American Association for the St. Louis Browns
from 1883–1889, and then in the National
League for the Cincinnati Reds from 1890–
1895.

11. "Hoy Signs a Chicago Contract," *The
Chicago Daily Tribune* (April 15, 1900), 18.
The other players mentioned here are most
likely centerfielder Curt Welch and outfielder Jim Fogarty.

12. "Joe Corbett, Lost LooLoo," *Los Angeles Times* (January 14, 1904), 11.

13. Honus Wagner, "Coaching Good
and Bad," *Boston Daily Globe* (February 13,
1916), 36.

14. Warren Miller, artist statement found
at www.warrenmillerart.com.

15. For more on the use of the term
speaking people, see R.A.R. Edwards, *Words
Made Flesh*, especially 92, 93–97, and 227.

16. "Died. William Ellsworth Hoy," *Time*
(December 22, 1961), 50.

17. Alexander Pach, "With the Silent
Workers," *The Silent Worker* (May 1905),
124.

18. Alexander Pach, "With the Silent
Workers," *The Silent Worker* (December
1914), 54.

19. For more on Pach, see James E. Gallaher, ed., *Representative Deaf Persons of the
United States of America, Containing Portraits and Character Sketches of Prominent
Deaf Persons (Commonly called Deaf-Mutes),
Who are Engaged in the Higher Pursuits of
Life* (Chicago: James E. Gallaher, 1898),
"Alexander L. Pach," 171–4. For more on
the newspaper he contributed to, see Robert Buchanan, "The Silent Worker Newspaper and the Building of a Deaf Community,
1890–1929," *Deaf History Unveiled*, ed. John
Vickrey van Cleve (Washington, D.C.: Gallaudet University Press, 1993), 172–197.

20. H-Dirksen Bauman and Joseph J.
Murray, "Deaf Gain: An Introduction," *Deaf
Gain: Raising the Stakes for Human Diver-
sity* (Minneapolis: University of Minnesota
Press, 2014), xv.

21. See Bauman and Murray, "Deaf Gain:
An Introduction," xxiv–xxxiii.

22. Douglas C. Baynton, *Forbidden Signs*
(Chicago: University of Chicago Press,
1996), 5.

23. See Bernard Bragg's story as recounted
in Jack Gannon, *Deaf Heritage: A Narrative
History of Deaf America*, eds. Jane Butler
and Laura-Jean Gilbert (Silver Spring, MD:
National Association of the Deaf, 1981), 355.

24. The rise of oralism at the turn of the
century as summarized in Susan Burch,
*Signs of Resistance: American Deaf Cultural
History, 1900 to 1942* (New York: New York
University Press, 2002), 13, 14.

25. For more on Bell and eugenics, see
Brian Greenwald, "Taking Stock: Alexander
Graham Bell and Eugenics, 1883–1922," in
The Deaf History Reader, ed. John Vickrey
Van Cleve (Washington, D.C.: Gallaudet
University Press, 2007), 136–152, and his
"The Real 'Toll' of A.G.Bell: Lessons about

Eugenics," in *Genetics, Disability, and Deafess*, ed. John Vickrey Van Cleve (Washington, D.C.: Gallaudet University Press, 2004), 35–41. See also Joseph J. Murray, "'True Love and Sympathy': The Deaf-Deaf Marriage Debate in Transatlantic Perspective," also in *Genetics, Disability, and Deafness*, 42–71.

26. Baynon 31.

27. In fact, the death of *The Silent Worker* was tied directly to the manual-oral conflict. A new oralist superintendent was hired at the New Jersey School. He tired of the manulist leanings of *The Silent Worker*, and its corresponding attacks on the oralist method, and responded by censoring the paper and firing its Deaf editor and, finally, killing the paper altogether. See Robert Buchanan, "The Silent Worker Newspaper and the Building of a Deaf Community: 1890–1929," in *Deaf History Unveiled*, ed. John Vickrey Van Cleve (Washington, D.C.: Gallaudet University Press, 1993), 172–197.

28. Susan Burch, *Signs of Resistance: American Deaf Cultural History, 1900 to World War II* (New York University Press, 2002), 105.

29. Sarah Abrevaya Stein, "Deaf American Jewish Culture in Historical Perspective," *American Jewish History* 95, 3 (September 2009), 277.

30. Burch 81.

31. Burch 31. For more on the practice of labeling students "oral failures," see Burch 137.

32. "Comiskey's Great Joke," *The Silent Hoosier* 6, 31 (May 18, 1893), 3.

33. "Comiskey's Great Joke," *The Silent Hoosier* 6, 31 (May 18, 1893), 3.

34. Reported by Michael Zitz, "Local Man wants deaf player added to Baseball Hall of Fame," for fredericksburg.com, the on-line edition of *The Free Lance Star*, on 30 July 2006.

35. Griffith as quoted in Ira Smith, *Baseball's Famous Outfielders*, 24.

36. "Editorial Views, News, Comment," *The Sporting Life* (May 27, 1893), 2.

37. For more on these terms, see Edwards, *Words Made Flesh*, 90–94.

38. Information on Ohio's pedagogical history from the school's entry in Edward Allen Fay, ed., *Histories of American Schools for the Deaf, 1817–1893* (Washington, D.C.: Volta Bureau, 1893).

39. As quoted in Ralph Berger, "Dummy Hoy," SABR Baseball Biography Project.

40. Tommy Leach as quoted in Lawrence S. Ritter, *The Glory of Their Times*, 23.

41. William E. Hoy, "Isn't Hoy Right?" *The Silent Worker* (January 1924), 151.

42. Dummy Hoy as quoted in "How A Mute Plays Ball," *Rochester Democrat and Chronicle* (January 5, 1902), 22.

43. "Hoy as a Ball Player," *The Silent Hoosier* vol. XIX, no. 12 (March 15, 1906), 1.

44. All statistics from baseball-reference.com.

45. Ed Koszarek, *The Players League: History, Clubs, Ballplayers, and Statistics* (Jefferson, NC: McFarland, 2006), 152.

46. Win a bar bet. You're welcome.

47. See Bill Weiss and Marshall Wright, "Top 100 Teams: Number 29: 1903 Los Angeles Angels," www.milb.com, accessed 14 November 2012.

48. His top ten seasons were 1888, 1889, 1890, 1891, 1892, 1894, 1896, 1897, 1898, and 1901.

49. All numbers and ranks accurate as of January 2018.

50. Bill James, *The New Bill James Historical Baseball Abstract* (New York: Free Press, 2001), 735, 739.

51. See Bill James, *The New Bill James Historical Baseball Abstract*, rev. ed. (New York: Free Press, 2001), 85, 735, 739, 781.

52. Frederick Taylor, *The Runmakers* (Baltimore: Johns Hopkins University Press, 2011), 185.

53. See Joseph Overfield, "William Ellsworth Hoy (Dummy)," *Nineteenth-Century Stars*, ed. Robert Tiemann and Mark Rucker (Kansas City, MO: Society for American Baseball Research, 1989), 64; Mac Davis, *100 Greatest Baseball Heroes* (New York: Grosset & Dunlop, 1974), see the chapter "Bill Hoy: The Amazing Dummy"; Ira Smith, *Baseball's Famous Outfielders* (New York: A.S. Barnes, 1954), 22–26. W.W. Aulick's comments as reproduced in *Lewiston Evening Journal* (July 27, 1911), 10.

54. Panara as quoted in Scott Pitoniak, "He fans the flame for deaf ballplayer," *Rochester (New York) Democrat & Chronicle* (1997), 1A. Exact date not recorded on this clipping, in the Hoy file, at the National Baseball Hall of Fame library and archive.

55. Shirley Povich, "This Morning," *The Washington Post* (January 11, 1953), C1.

56. Flaherty's *L.A. Examiner* column of 21 May 1952, as reprinted in *The Silent Worker* (July 1952), 25.

57. Stephen V. Rice, "Rube Bressler," SABR Biography Project.

58. Letter of May 7, 1958. National Baseball Hall of Fame Archive files.

59. Memorandum of May 9, 1958. National Baseball Hall of Fame Archive files.

60. Letter as it appears in *Language, Culture, Communities: 200 Years of Impact by the American School for the Deaf* (West Hartford, CT: American School for the Deaf, 2017), 92.

61. Dwight Eisenhower's remarks to the President's Committee on the Employment of the Physically Handicapped. Delivered May 23, 1955.

62. Dwight Eisenhower to Ray Bressler. Telegram of May 16, 1958. National Baseball Hall of Fame Archive files.

63. For more on the Bell-NBC dust up, see *Through Deaf Eyes*, 116–117. The quotes from the Association's letter can be found in *Deaf Heritage*, 346. For more on the National Theatre, see *Deaf Heritage*, 346–356.

64. For more on deaf humor, see Susan Rutherford, *A Study of Deaf American Folklore* (Burtonsville, MD: Linstok Press, 1993).

65. Yes, this is quite possibly the most humorless, as well as linguistically misguided, organization in the United States today. The Pepsi commercial is still available for viewing on YouTube; see https://www.youtube.com/watch?v=EAXhpXVWXVI. And if Nyle DiMarco cannot bring us all together, I ask you: who can?

66. Susan Burch, *Signs of Inclusion*, 80.

67. See their website for on Hoy's induction, http://www.baseballreliquary.org/awards/shrine-of-the-eternals/the-shrine-of-the-eternals-2004/.

68. Brian Malzkuhn, "Dummy Hoy: Redebating his Credentials for Nomination to the Hall of Fame," *Deaf Studies Digital Journal*, Issue 2 (2010).

69. Sipek interview recounted in Matthew Moore, "The Colorful Legacy of Dummy Hoy, Part Two," *Deaf Life* (December 1992), 25.

70. See Gould, *Triumph and Tragedy in Mudville*, 112–129, for his discussion of Hoy.

71. Story recounted in Robert Panara, "Why a Short Ohio Farm Boy Belongs in the Hall of Fame," *The Beacon Journal* (July 19, 1991), A15.

72. Stuart Miller, "Umpire's Signs: The Movie," *The New York Times* (25 July 2010), sports section, page 2.

73. Gould, *Triumph and Tragedy in Mudville*, 128.

74. Simi Linton, *Claiming Disability: Knowledge and Identity* (New York: New York University Press, 1998), 17–18.

75. Linton 18.

76. "One reason why," *The Silent Worker* (October 1903).

77. An article from Robert Panara, called "Dummy Hoy," as reprinted in the column of Leon Auerbach, "Looking Back…," *The NAD Broadcaster* (November 1990), 16.

Chapter 3

1. Peter Morris, "Safe and Out Signals," in *A Game of Inches: The Story Behind the Innovations that Shaped Baseball* (Chicago: Ivan R. Dee, 2010), 267.

2. "The Referee: Sporting Comment of the Week: Gesture System for Umpires Not Mandatory," *Chicago Tribune* (February 24, 1907), A1.

3. Peter Morris, "Ball and Strike Signals," in *Game of Inches: The Story Behind the Innovations that Shaped Baseball* (Chicago: Ivan R. Dee, 2010), 264–267. He mentions reports from papers in 1883 and 1886.

4. Peter Morris, "Ball and Strike Signals," in *Game of Inches: The Story Behind the Innovations that Shaped Baseball* (Chicago: Ivan R. Dee, 2010), 265.

5. Stuart Miller, "Umpires' Signs: The Movie," *The New York Times* (25 July 2010), Sports section, p. 2.

6. Letter of Bill Deane to Steven Sandy, July 17, 1990. From the Hoy Files of the National Baseball Library and Archive, Cooperstown, New York.

7. Lawrence Ritter, *The Glory of Their Times: The Story of the Early Days of Baseball Told by the Men who Played It,* enlarged edition (New York: Perennial, 2002), 54.

8. Deane as quoted in Miller, "Umpires' Signs: The Movie," *The New York Times* (25 July 2010), Sports Sections, p. 2.

9. See Jonathan Fraser, *The Cultural Encyclopedia of Baseball*, 2nd edition (McFarland, 2005). He cites both Cy Rigler and Bill Klem as pioneers in using hand gestures for both balls and strikes, and fair and foul balls. See also Peter Morris, "Ball and Strike Signals," in *Game of Inches: The Story Behind the Innovations that Shaped Baseball* (Chicago: Ivan R. Dee, 2010), 264–267. Morris argues that Rigler is cited for introducing the practice in a Central League game in 1905 but admits that it is not clear how the signals got into the National League or the American League. He argues that Klem is "erroneously credited with pioneering umpire signals."

10. Dan Krueckeberg, "Take-Charge Cy," *The National Pastime: A Review of Baseball History* 4, 1 (Spring 1985), 3–4.

11. Bill Deane, *Baseball Myths: Debating, Debunking, and Disproving Tales from the Diamond* (Lanham, MD: Scarecrow Press, 2012), 20.

12. Bill Deane, *Baseball Myths: Debating, Debunking, and Disproving Tales from the Diamond* (Scarecrow Press, 2012), 17, 21. Deane's influence also seen in Ralph Berger, "Dummy Hoy," SABR Baseball Biography Project.

13. William J. Klem with William J. Slocum, "Diamond Rhubarbs," *Collier's* (April 14, 1951), 31.

14. William J. Klem with William J. Slocum, "Diamond Rhubarbs," *Collier's* (April 14, 1951), 31.

15. Klem and Slocum, "Diamond Rhubarbs," 31.

16. For more on baseball in Rochester in the 19th century, see Priscilla Astifan, "Baseball in the 19th Century—Part 1," *Rochester History* vol. LII, No. 3 (Summer 1990), 2–23; "Baseball in the 19th Century—Part 2," *Rochester History* (Spring 2000), 3–23; "Baseball in the 19th Century—Part 3," *Rochester History* vol. LXIII, no. 1 (Winter 2001), 3–23; "Baseball in the 19th Century—Part 4," *Rochester History* vol. LXIII, no. 2 (Spring 2001), 3–23; "Baseball in the Nineteenth Century—Part 5," *Rochester History* vol. LXIV, no. 4 (Fall 2002), 3–24.

17. Timeline of his career in "Silk O'Loughlin King of Umps," *The Sunday Vindicator* (April 29, 1906), 13.

18. William J. Klem and William J. Slocum, "I Never Missed One in My Heart," *Collier's* (March 31, 1951), 59.

19. *Ibid.*

20. *Ibid.*, 65.

21. David Anderson, "Bill Klem," entry in The Baseball Biography Project, SABR.org

22. Timeline of his career in "Silk O'Loughlin King of Umps," *The Sunday Vindicator* (April 29, 1906), 13.

23. For more on this Series, see Bernard A. Weisberger, *When Chicago Ruled Baseball: The Cubs-White Sox World Series of 1906* (New York: Harper, 2006).

24. "Gestures to Tell Umpire's Ruling," *Chicago Tribune* (January 6, 1907), A1.

25. "Nationals Lose Game," *The Washington Post*, Thursday, April 19, 1906, p. 8.

26. "Silk O'Loughlin Unique Umpire," *Meriden Daily Journal* (October 16, 1906), 11.

27. Ren Mulford, Jr., "Red In and Outers," *Sporting Life* (June 9, 1906), 11.

28. "Gestures to Tell Umpire's Ruling," *Chicago Tribune* (January 6, 1907), A1.

29. As reported in Paul Dickinson, *The Hidden Language of Baseball: How Signs and Sign-Stealing Have Influenced the Course of our National Pastime* (New York: Walker & Company, 2003). Peter Morris reports similar early coverage in his *Game of Inches: The Story Behind the Innovations That Shaped Baseball* (Chicago: Ivan Dee, 2010). He writes that the *St. Louis Dispatch* reported the man at third signaling balls and strikes in March 1888 (264).

30. Jonathan Stilwell, "The Chicago White Sox All-Time Starting Rotation," *Bleacher Report*. Accessed online June 6, 2011.

31. *Souvenir of the Cincinnati Base Ball Club: Upon the Occasion of the Dedication of the Grand Stand, May 16th, 1902* (Cincinnati: Manns Engraving & Printing, 1902).

32. For more on the impact of residential schools on the development of deaf athletes, see David A. Stewart, *Deaf Sport: The Impact of Sports Within the Deaf Community* (Washington, D.C.: Gallaudet University Press, 1991), 160–164.

33. "Baseball," *The New York Clipper* (July 19, 1879), 131.

34. "Gestures to Tell Umpire's Ruling" *Chicago Tribune* (January 6, 1907), A1.

35. "Calling Balls and Strikes," *The Sporting News* (January 27, 1900), 5.

36. "Calling Balls and Strikes," *The Sporting News* (January 27, 1900), 5.

37. "Base Ball, the Prize Ring, Foot Ball, and Games of All Sorts," *Bangor Daily Whig and Courier* (February 3, 1900), 6.

38. "Gestures to Tell Umpire's Ruling," A1.

39. "The Referee: Sporting Comments of the Week," *Chicago Tribune* (January 6, 1907), A1.

40. "The Referee: Sporting Comment of the Week," *Chicago Tribune* (January 20, 1907), A1.

41. "American League Notes," *The Sporting Life* (January 12, 1907), 5.

42. "Easy to Execute," *The Sporting Life* (February 23, 1907), 4.

43. "Johnson's Idea," *The Sporting Life* (February 23, 1907), 10.

44. "Electrical Score Boards for the American League," *Chicago Tribune* (February 13, 1907), 12. The Yankees are usually credited for first using an electronic scoreboard in baseball, in the original Yankee Stadium, when it opened in 1923. See G. Edwards White, *Creating the National Pastime: Baseball Transforms Itself, 1903–1953* (Princeton: Princeton University Press, 1996), 41–2. These 1907 articles, however, repeatedly point to this forerunner apparently in use in St. Louis as the inspiration for Johnson's plan to adopt them throughout the American League. For more on the history of electronic scoreboards in baseball, see Rob Edelman, "Electric Scoreboards, Bulletin Boards, and Mimic Diamonds," *Base Ball* 3, 2 (Fall 2009), 76–87.

45. "The Referee: Sports Comment of the Week: Signaling Balls and Strikes," *Chicago Tribune* (February 17, 1907), A1.

46. In theorizing fans as deaf, I follow the lead of Lennard Davis, who argues that the rise of reading in the 18th century similarly transformed hearing people. "Even if you are not Deaf," he writes, "you are deaf while you are reading. You are in a deafened modality or moment. All readers are deaf because they are defined by a process that does not require hearing or speaking [vocalizing]." See Davis, *Enforcing Normalcy: Disability, Deafness, and the Body* (New York: Verso, 1995), 4, 50–72.

47. "The Referee: Sports Comment of the Week: Signaling Balls and Strikes," *Chicago Tribune* (February 17, 1907), A1.

48. "The Referee: Sports Comment of the Week: Gesture System for Umpires for Mandatory," *Chicago Tribune* (February 24, 1907), A1.

49. "Notes of the Cubs," *Chicago Tribune* (March 24, 1907), A2. O'Day remains the only man to play, manage, and umpire in the history of the National League. He served as an umpire in the first World Series in 1903 and would serve in 10 World Series over the course of his career, second only to Klem's 18. When O'Day died in Chicago on July 2, 1935, former NL president John Heydler called him one of the greatest umpires ever in terms of knowledge of the rules, fairness, and courage to make the right call. Bill Klem, however, referred to him as a "misanthropic Irishman," while Christy Mathewson said that arguing with O'Day was like "using a lit match to see how much gasoline was in a fuel tank" (David Anderson, "Hank O'Day," SABR Baseball Biography Project).

50. O'Day as quoted in "Easy to Execute," *The Sporting Life* (February 23, 1907), 4.

51. *Spalding's Official Base Ball Guide* (1909), 351.

52. "Echoes of the Diamond," *The Washington Post* (March 1, 1907), 8.

53. For more on the belief system of oralists, see Douglas C. Baynton, *Forbidden Signs: American Culture and the Campaign Against Sign Language* (Chicago: University of Chicago Press, 1996).

54. For more on the rise of the oralists, see R.A.R. Edwards, *Words Made Flesh: Nineteenth-Century Deaf Education and the Growth of Deaf Culture* (New York: New York University Press, 2012), 183.

55. Bell's 1883 address was published at the time; see Alexander Graham Bell, *Memoir Upon the Formation of a Deaf Variety of the Human Race* (Washington, D.C., 1884). It was later more widely circulated in deaf education circles as well. See Alexander Graham Bell, *Memoir Upon the Formation of a Deaf Variety of the Human Race* (n.p., Alexander Graham Bell Association of the Deaf, 1969). For more on Bell, see R.A.R Edwards, "Chasing Aleck: The Story of a Dorm," *The Public Historian* 29, 3 (Summer 2007): 87–104.

56. Bell as quoted in Douglas C. Baynton, *Forbidden Signs: American Culture and the Campaign Against Sign Language* (Chicago: University of Chicago Press, 1996), 55. The

quote is from 1884. See Baynton for more on oralist philosophy and beliefs. For more on Bell and eugenics, see Brian Greenwald, "Taking Stock: Alexander Graham Bell and Eugenics, 1883–1922," in *The Deaf History Reader*, ed. John Vickrey Van Cleve (Washington, D.C.: Gallaudet University Press, 2007), 136–152, and his "The Real 'Toll' of A.G.Bell: Lessons about Eugenics," in *Genetics, Disability, and Deafness*, ed. John Vickrey Van Cleve (Washington, D.C.: Gallaudet University Press, 2004), 35–41. See also Joseph J. Murray, "'True Love and Sympathy': The Deaf-Deaf Marriage Debate in Transatlantic Perspective," also in *Genetics, Disability, and Deafness*, 42–71.

57. John Vickrey Van Cleve and Barry Crouch, *A Place of Their Own: Creating the Deaf Community in America* (Washington, D.C.: Gallaudet University Press, 1989), 122.

58. See Douglas Baynton, "'The Undesirability of Admitting Deaf Mutes': U.S. Immigration Policy and Deaf Immigrants, 1882–1924," *Sign Language Studies* 6, 4 (Summer 2006), 391–415. See also Douglas C. Baynton, *Defectives in the Land: Disability and Immigration in the Age of Eugenics* (Chicago: University of Chicago Press, 2016).

59. For more on forced sterilization laws, see Kim E. Nielsen, *A Disability History of the United States* (Boston: Beacon Press, 2012), 110–124. A list of states with eugenic laws can be found on page 114.

60. Oralist teacher as quoted in Baynton, *Forbidden Signs*,146.

61. For more on passing, see Baynton, *Forbidden Signs*, 146–148. See also Susan Burch, *Signs of Resistance: American Deaf Cultural History, 1900 to 1942* (New York: New York University Press, 2002), especially 146–149, and *Words Made Flesh*, especially 158–159, 200.

62. Burch 27.

63. Burch 81.

64. Burch 83.

65. Story as found in Michael Zitz, "Local Man wants deaf player added to Baseball Hall of Fame," for fredericksburg.com, the on-line edition of *The Free Lance Star*, 30 July 2006.

66. "The Referee: Sporting Comment of the Week: Too Much Consideration for the Umpire," *Chicago Tribune* (April 14, 1907), A1.

67. "Easy to Execute," *The Sporting Life* (February 23, 1907), 4.

68. Bill Deane, *Baseball Myths: Debating, Debunking, and Disproving Tales from the Diamond* (Lanham, MD: Scarecrow Press, 2012), 20.

69. "Arm Signal System Endorsed," *The Sporting Life* (February 9, 1907), 4.

70. "Timely Topics," *The Sporting Life* (May 18, 1907), 7.

71. *Sporting Life* (October 19, 1907), 8.

72. "The Signal System," *Sporting Life* (March 23, 1907), 4.

73. John Brush as quoted in "Meeting of the Board of Directors of the National League of Professional Base Ball Clubs," for the annual meeting of December 10–13, 1907. The quote is on page 194 of the meeting minutes. Records held at the Archive and Collection at the National Baseball Hall of Fame.

74. Vote results on page 197 of the minutes.

75. Rob Edelman, "Electric Scoreboards, Bulletin Boards, and Mimic Diamonds," *Base Ball* 3, 2 (Fall 2009), 78.

76. *Spalding's Official Base Ball Guide* (1909), 351.

77. "Baseball Loses a Picturesque Figure in Death of Umpire Silk O'Loughlin," *The Washington Post* (December 21,1918), 14.

78. "Chief Umpire Calls Silk O'Loughlin Out in Combat with Flu," *Chicago Tribune* (December 21, 1918), 11.

79. Bob Ray, "The Sports X-Ray," *Los Angeles Times* (June 4, 1939), A10.

80. Guy Butler, "Topics of the Tropics: Seconding the Bill Klem Motion," *Miami News* (September 15, 1943), 2-B. He may have ranked only a maybe to Butler, but Billy Evans was inducted to the Hall in 1973. His other two choices have not been.

81. "Immortal Umpires," *Lewiston Morning Tribune* (June 22, 1943), 4.

82. John Kieran, "Sports of the Times: Sixteen Years Behind the Plate," *The New York Times* (May 15, 1941), 32.

83. For coverage of Klem's throat injury, see "Bill Klem May Not Be Ready at Start," *The Pittsburgh Press* (April 11, 1914), 16. The quote is from this article. See also "Bill Klem Undergoes Successful Operation," *Hartford Courant* (March 20, 1914), 18. For more on the baseball tour during which he was

injured, see "Bill Klem, Able Umpire, Is on Tour with the Sox-Giants," *Newburgh Journal* (December 19, 1913), 9.

84. Frederick G. Lieb, "Great Umpire Calls Out Old Arbitrator Klem," *The Sporting News* (September 26, 1951), 13–14. *The New York Times* also recalled his famous line; see "Bill Klem, 77, Dies; Dean of Umpires," September 17, 1951, p.21.

85. Matthew Moore, "The Colorful Legacy of Dummy Hoy," *Deaf Life* (November 1992), 16.

86. "The Colorful Legacy of Dummy Hoy," 16–7.

87. "The Colorful Legacy of Dummy Hoy," 18.

88. Matthew Moore, "The Colorful Legacy of Dummy Hoy—Part 2," *Deaf Life* (December 1992), 22–3.

89. Letter of Bill Deane to Steven Sandy, July 17, 1990. From the Hoy Files of the National Baseball Library and Archive, Cooperstown, New York.

90. Letter of Bill Deane to Steven Sandy, October 16, 1990. Emphasis in original. From the Hoy Files of the National Baseball Library and Archive, Cooperstown, New York.

91. Deane as quoted in Miller, "Umpire Signs: The Movie," SP2.

92. Tom Humphries, *Communicating across cultures (deaf-hearing) and language learning*, doctoral dissertation (Cincinnati: Union Institute and University, 1977), p.12.

93. Harlan Lane, *The Mask of Benevolence: Disabling the Deaf Community* (New York: Knopf, 1992), 43.

94. Deane, *Baseball Myths: Debating, Debunking, and Disproving Tales from the Diamond* (Scarecrow Press, 2012), 17.

95. Stewart, *Deaf Sport*, 123.

96. Stephen Jay Gould, *Triumph and Tragedy in Mudville: A Lifelong Passion for Baseball* (New York: Norton, 2004), 129.

97. Gould, *Triumph and Tragedy in Mudville*, 128.

98. Gould 128.

99. Gould 129.

100. Deane, *Baseball Myths*, 17, 21. Deane's influence also seen in Ralph Berger, "Dummy Hoy," SABR Baseball Biography Project.

Chapter 4

1. Randy Fisher and James Goodwin, "The 100th Anniversary of 'Dummy' vs. 'Dummy,'" *The National Pastime: A Review of Baseball History* 23 (2003), 77.

2. "Dummy Taylor: Rediscovering an Original," *Deaf Life* (December 2007), 30.

3. Phrase from Christopher Krentz, ed., *A Mighty Change: An Anthology of Deaf American Writing, 1816–1864* (Washington, D.C.: Gallaudet University Press, 2000), 141. For more on the Deaf community of the 19th century, see John Vickrey Van Cleve and Barry Crouch, *A Place of Their Own: Creating the Deaf Community in America* (Washington, D.C.: Gallaudet University Press, 1989).

4. For more on the rise of oralism, see Douglas C. Baynton, *Forbidden Signs: American Culture and the Campaign Against Sign Language* (Chicago: University of Chicago Press, 1996).

5. *History of the Kansas Institution for the Education of the Deaf and Dumb to 1893* (Printed by the Pupils in the Printing Department of the Institution in Olathe, Kansas, 1893), 10–11. For more on the history of the Kansas School, see *ALBUM*, vol. 16, no. 1 (winter 2003).

6. See *History of the Kansas Institution for the Education of the Deaf and Dumb to 1893* (Printed by the Pupils in the Printing Department of the Institution in Olathe, Kansas, 1893), 25.

7. See *History of the Kansas Institution for the Education of the Deaf and Dumb to 1893* (Printed by the Pupils in the Printing Department of the Institution in Olathe, Kansas, 1893), 25.

8. As noted on Taylor's student intake papers at the Kansas School for the Deaf.

9. *History of the Kansas Institution for the Education of the Deaf and Dumb to 1893* (Printed by the Pupils in the Printing Department of the Institution in Olathe, Kansas, 1893), 15.

10. Sean Lahman, "Dummy Taylor," SABR Biography Project.

11. Taylor's note on the back of a photograph of the Kansas School for the Deaf. Courtesy of Steve Gietschier from the archives of the *Sporting News*.

12. "United States Census, 1900," data-

base with images, *FamilySearch* (https://
familysearch.org/ark:/61903/1:1:MSDB-
X5G : accessed 9 May 2018), Luther Taylor
in household of Alvin Haynes, Albany city
Ward 4, Albany, New York, United States;
citing enumeration district (ED) 14, sheet
1A, family 7, NARA microfilm publication
T623 (Washington, D.C.: National Archives
and Records Administration, 1972.); FHL
microfilm 1,241,004.

13. *The Silent Worker* 15, 10 (June 1903), 149.

14. "Quakerisms," *Deaf-Mutes Journal* vol. XXXIII, no. 13 (March 31, 1904), 2.

15. *The Silent Worker* 17, 8 (May 1905), 124.

16. Both comments in *The Silent Worker* 20, 9 (June 1908), 177.

17. Alexander Pach, "New York," *The Silent Worker* 22, 9 (June 1910), 168.

18. As reported in Arthur Mann, "Mute Testimony," *Baseball Magazine* (September 1945), 343.

19. As quoted in Arthur Mann, "Mute Testimony," *Baseball Magazine* (September 1945), 344.

20. "Devore Delights in Story," *Chicago Eagle* (June 3, 1916), 11.

21. Employment at St. Joseph's recorded in *American Annals of the Deaf* (1919), 34.

22. See his minor league stats at https://www.baseball-reference.com/register/player.fcgi?id=deegan001wil

23. "Deegan and Nelson," *The Central New Jersey Home News* (March 28, 1908), 3.

24. For more on Deegan see https://www.findagrave.com/memorial/49845983/william-joseph-deegan. See "United States Census, 1900," database with images, *FamilySearch* (https://familysearch.org/ark:/61903/1:1:MS28-Y1G: accessed 9 May 2018), William Deegan in household of Mary Gallagher, St. Joseph's Institute for the Imp. Instruction of Deaf Mutes New York City Ward Annexed Dist., Westchester, New York, United States; citing enumeration district (ED) 1100, sheet 1B, family 1, NARA microfilm publication T623 (Washington, D.C.: National Archives and Records Administration, 1972.); FHL microfilm 1,241,127. Deegan died in the Bronx in 1957.

25. Kathleen Brockway, *Baltimore's Deaf Heritage* (Charleston, S.C.: Arcadia Press, 2014), 12.

26. See https://www.baseball-reference.com/register/player.fcgi?id=leitne001geo. He died in Baltimore in 1960 at the age of 87.

27. For more on the Wells and Leitner families, see Kathleen Brockway, *Baltimore's Deaf Heritage*, especially 2, 7, 9, 11–14, 56–57, and 81.

28. "George Leitner, Ex-Athlete, Dies," *The Baltimore Sun* (February 21, 1960), 36.

29. "McGraw's Worst Panning Given by Dummy Taylor," *The Silent Worker* (October 1916), 9.

30. "McGraw's Worst Panning Given by Dummy Taylor," *The Silent Worker* (October 1916), 9.

31. Fred Snodgrass as quoted in Lawrence S. Ritter, *The Glory of Their Times: The Story of the Early Days of Baseball Told by the Men Who Played It*, rev. ed. (New York: Perennial, 2002), 101.

32. Tol Broome, "Dummy Taylor was part of the best rotation in history," *Sports Collectors Digest* (November 11, 1994), 161.

33. As recounted by Gordon H. Fleming in *The Unforgettable Season* (New York: Holt, Rinehart and Winston, 1981), 205.

34. Snodgrass in *The Glory of Their Times*, 101.

35. Recalled in Harold Lonigan, "Dummy Taylor, Who Let Fast Ball and Curve Speak for Him, When with Giants, Puts His Story on Paper," *The Sporting News* (December 24, 1942), 5.

36. Arthur Mann, "Mute Testimony," *Baseball Magazine* (September 1945), 343–4.

37. "Deaf and Dumb Athlete Most Remarkable Known," *The Atlanta Constitution* (August 27, 1907), 9.

38. As reported in R.E. Lloyd, "With Our Exchanges," *The Silent Worker* (June 1905), 148.

39. Sean Lahman, "New York: Luther Haden 'Dummy' Taylor," *Deadball Stars of the National League* (SABR 2004), 38.

40. Figures from Douglas C. Baynton, *Forbidden Signs: American Culture and the Campaign Against Sign Language* (Chicago: University of Chicago Press, 1996), 4–5.

41. "Taylor and John M'Graw Were Like Two Brothers," *The Buffalo Commercial* (April, 12, 1909), 6. According to the account, some players noticed a couple of deaf men trying to shield their conversation. When they asked Taylor if he could tell what

they were talking about, he replied, "Why, he's telling a naughty story."

42. Sean Lahman, "New York: Luther Haden 'Dummy' Taylor," *Deadball Stars of the National League* (SABR 2004), 37.

43. Tol Broome, "Dummy Taylor Was Part of the Best Rotation in History," *Sports Collectors Digest* (November 11, 1994), 160.

44. Sean Lehman, "Dummy Taylor," SABR Biography Project.

45. Recalled in Harold Lonigan, "Dummy Taylor, Who Let Fast Ball and Curve Speak for Him, When with Giants, Puts His Story on Paper," *The Sporting News* (December 24, 1942), 5.

46. "Cunning of Dummy Taylor," *The Silent Worker* 19, 1 (October 1903), 7.

47. As quoted in "Mute Pitcher a Star," *The Washington Post* (February 13, 1910), M7.

48. David W. Anderson, "Dummy Taylor," SABR Biography Project.

49. Recalled in Harold Lonigan, "Dummy Taylor, Who Let Fast Ball and Curve Speak for Him, When with Giants, Puts His Story on Paper," *The Sporting News* (December 24, 1942), 5.

50. Story recounted in Ira Smith, "Luther Hayden (Dummy) Taylor," *Baseball's Famous Pitchers* (New York: A.S. Barnes, 1954), 56–7.

51. "Deaf and Dumb Athlete Most Remarkable Known," *The Atlanta Constitution* (August 27, 1907), 9.

52. As quoted in Ira Smith, "Luther Hayden (Dummy) Taylor," *Baseball's Famous Pitchers* (New York: A.S. Barnes, 1954), 57.

53. Sean Lahman, "New York: Luther Haden 'Dummy' Taylor," *Deadball Stars of the National League* (SABR 2004), 37–8.

54. "New York," *Deaf-Mutes' Journal* vol. XXX, no. 26 (June 27, 1901), 3.

55. All stats on the trio from Tol Broome, "Dummy Taylor was part of the best rotation in history," *Sports Collectors Digest* (November 11, 1994), 160.

56. Tol Broome, "Dummy Taylor was part of the best rotation in history," *Sports Collectors Digest* (November 11, 1994), 160.

57. Tol Broome, "Dummy Taylor was part of the best rotation in history," *Sports Collectors Digest* (November 11, 1994), 160.

58. For more on the Series, see Lloyd Graybar, "World Series Rarities: The Three Game Winners," *SABR Baseball Research Journal*, 1982. And where was this major league pitcher living in New York in 1905? As a boarder in a house in Manhattan on 124th Street. His occupation was listed in the city census as "ball player." See "New York State Census, 1905," database with images, *FamilySearch* (https://familysearch.org/ark:/61903/1:1:SPN4–8DQ: 21 December 2017), Luther Taylor in household of Lemuel H Russell, Manhattan, A.D. 31, E.D. 25, New York, New York; citing p. 24, line 8, various county clerk offices, New York; FHL microfilm 1,433,113.

59. As described in Tol Broome, "Dummy Taylor was part of the best rotation in history," *Sports Collectors Digest* (November 11, 1994), 160.

60. Taylor letter. Thanks again to Steve Gietschier.

61. Joan M. Thomas, "Roger Bresnahan," SABR Biography Project.

62. John Kieran, "Sports of the Times," *New York Times* (August 13, 1936), 15.

63. Harry A. Williams, "Broken Finger Made Munsell A Pitcher," *Los Angeles Times* (June 6, 1913), III2.

64. "One on Bres," *The Dayton Herald* (April 9, 1913), 6.

65. Tol Broome, "Dummy Taylor was part of the best rotation in history," *Sports Collectors Digest* (November 11, 1994), 160.

66. The history of pitcher and catcher signs reported in Peter Morris, *A Game of Inches*, 33–34.

67. "Luther Taylor, 82, Dies," *New York Times* (August 24, 1958), 86.

68. The first account is from an undated newspaper clipping, "Hank O'Day's Death Recalls Stirring Baseball Chapters" in the files at the Hall of Fame Library and Archive. The second is from "Mute Pitcher Was A Star," *The Washington Post* (February 13, 1910), M7. Many versions of this story of Taylor and O'Day claim that O'Day could fingerspell back to Taylor because O'Day's parents were deaf. However, having tracked down O'Day's parents in multiple census records, there is no indication in any of these records that either of them were deaf. The U.S. Census would ask if the person was deaf and O'Day's parents were never identified as deaf. It seems that these two versions had it right; O'Day learned to fingerspell just to call Taylor out.

69. "Taylor and John M'Graw Were Like Two Brothers," *The Buffalo Commercial* (April 12, 1909), 6.

70. Recalled in Harold Lonigan, "Dummy Taylor, Who Let Fast Ball and Curve Speak for Him, When with Giants, Puts His Story on Paper," *The Sporting News* (December 24, 1942), 5.

71. As quoted in Sean Lahman, SABR Baseball Biography Project.

72. Frank Deford, *The Old Ball Game: How John McGraw, Christy Mathewson, and the New York Giants Created Modern Baseball* (New York: Grove Press, 2005), 70.

73. David W. Anderson, "Dummy Taylor," SABR Biography Project

74. Tol Broome, "Dummy Taylor was part of the best rotation in history," *Sports Collectors Digest* (November 11, 1994), 161.

75. It is hard to overstate how culturally subversive this practice was. Laura Bridgman was one of the first deaf-blind people to be educated in American history. She arrived at the Perkins School for the Blind in 1837. As her education progressed, her hearing-sighted teachers were appalled at Laura's continued willingness to use her voice, calling her sounds uncouth, unladylike, disagreeable, and bad. They urged her to remain silent. Laura resisted this effort to silence her. "Some of my noises are not bad, some are pretty noises," she countered. "I must make noises to call someone. God gave me much voice." To break the impasse, her teachers agreed, by 1845, that Laura would agree to stay silent most of the time and they in return would allow her to shut herself in a closet now and again to make as much noise as she wanted. See Elisabeth Gitter, *The Imprisoned Guest: Samuel Howe and Laura Bridgman, The Original Deaf-Blind Girl* (New York: Farrar, Straus, and Giroux, 2001), 116.

76. "West Virginia," *Deaf-Mutes' Friend* vol. XXXIV, no. 15 (April 13, 1905), 3.

77. "Taylor and John M'Graw Were Like Two Brothers," *The Buffalo Commercial* (April 12, 1909), 6.

78. "West Virginia," *Deaf-Mutes' Journal* vol. XXXIV, no. 15 (April 13, 1905), 3.

79. "New York," *Deaf-Mutes' Journal* vol. XXXVIII, no. 39 (September 30, 1909), 3.

80. Information on dues from Bob Buchanan, editor, *Gaillard in Deaf America: A Portrait of the Deaf Community, 1917* (Washington, D.C.: Gallaudet University Press, 2002), 56.

81. Coverage of the Union League from John Vickrey Van Cleve and Barry Crouch, *A Place of Their Own: Creating the Deaf Community in America* (Washington, D.C.: Gallaudet University Press, 1989), 94–97.

82. John Vickrey Van Cleve and Barry Crouch, *A Place of Their Own: Creating the Deaf Community in America* (Washington, D.C.: Gallaudet University Press, 1989), 97.

83. For more on these homes for elderly deaf people, see Susan Burch, *Signs of Resistance: American Deaf Cultural History, 1900–1942* (New York: New York University Press, 2002), 83–88. See also Jack R. Gannon, *Deaf Heritage: A Narrative History of Deaf America*, eds. Jane Butler and Laura-Jean Gilbert (Silver Spring: National Association of the Deaf, 1981), 165–66.

84. From Bob Buchanan, editor, *Gaillard in Deaf America: A Portrait of the Deaf Community, 1917* (Washington, D.C.: Gallaudet University Press, 2002), 89–90.

85. See the League's entry in *The American Almanac, Year Book, Cyclopedia, and Atlas*, second edition (1904), 224.

86. From Bob Buchanan, editor, *Gaillard in Deaf America: A Portrait of the Deaf Community, 1917* (Washington, D.C.: Gallaudet University Press, 2002), 44.

87. Burch 104–5.

88. You can see one of these outings for yourself. Gallaudet University has a video of a picnic of the Baltimore Frat from 1938, available on-line at http://videocatalog.gallaudet.edu/?search=Baltimore+Frat.

89. Burch 109.

90. Burch 111.

91. Burch 31.

92. For more on the Deaf community's response to the challenges of these years, see Susan Burch's *Signs of Resistance*. She includes a brief discussion of Hoy and Taylor on pages 80–81.

93. Burch 80.

94. Douglas C. Baynton, *Defectives in the Land: Disability and Immigration in the Age of Eugenics* (Chicago: University of Chicago Press, 2016), 80. As Baynton points out, immigration authorities were still authorized to refuse entry to those with a physical defect or disability that "may affect"

their ability to earn a living as late as 1990. The disability language was removed but the public charge standard was retained. As a result, disabled people could still find themselves denied entry, given that many able-bodied people assume that disabled people cannot work to support themselves. Baynton draws attention to an immigration case from 1995, where several family members applied for entry; six were granted visas but two were denied on the grounds that, because they were deaf, they were likely to become public charges (137).

95. "Luther Taylor," *The Silent Worker* (November 1904), 22.

96. J.F. Meagher, "Nadfratities," *The Silent Worker* (July 1919), 204.

97. See Jack R. Gannon, *Deaf Heritage: A Narrative History of Deaf America*, eds. Jane Butler and Laura-Jean Gilbert (Silver Spring: National Association of the Deaf, 1981), 299.

98. James Brady, "The Deaf in Athletics," *The Silent Worker* (January 1924), 147. Brady was an alumni of the Pennsylvania School for the Deaf and an oralist. He was a good lipreader. However, he also knew the sign language and he and his deaf wife signed with each other to communicate clearly. He wanted more deaf children to be exposed to sign language, arguing against the oralists of his day that "the greatest good for the greatest number should be the aim of the schools and the greatest good can be accomplished with and by properly supervised signs."

99. James F. Brady, "Pros and Cons," *The Silent Worker* 35, 8 (May 1923). As reproduced in Jennifer L. Nelson and Kristen C. Harmon, eds. *Deaf American Prose, 1830–1930* (Washington, D.C.: Gallaudet University Press, 2013), 231. They include the details about Brady's life history on page 228.

100. Burch, *Signs of Resistance*, 76. The question of displaying the masculinity of deaf bodies in sports, especially baseball, is further explored in Robert E. Bionaz, "Unmanly Professional Athletes: Disability and Masculinity in the Unites States, 1888–1908, *Disability Studies Quarterly* 25, 2 (Spring 2005).

101. Robert E. Bionaz, "Unmanly Professional Athletes: Disability and Masculinity in the Unites States, 1888–1908, *Disability Studies Quarterly* 25, 2 (Spring 2005). http://dx.doi.org/10.18061/dsq.v25i2.546.

102. Burch, *Signs of Resistance*, 83.

103. "Taylor Is All Right," *Deaf-Mutes' Journal* vol. XXXIII, no. 24 (June 16, 1904), 3.

104. "Taylor and John M'Graw Were Like Two Brothers," *The Buffalo Commercial* (April 12, 1909), 6.

105. David Waldstein, "A Pioneer Pitcher's Trail of Wins and Wit," *The New York Times* (October 23, 2014), B14.

106. Umpire career covered in "Dummy Taylor: Rediscovering an Original," *DeafLife* (December 2007), 37. His New York City appearance recounted in "Poor Old 'Dummy,' T'Was a Tough Job," *Deseret Evening News* (July 4, 1908), 12.

107. Douglas C. Baynton, Jack R. Gannon, and Jean Lindquist Bergey, *Through Deaf Eyes: A Photographic History of an American Community* (Washington, D.C.: Gallaudet University Press, 2007), 92.

108. Robert M. Buchanan, *Illusions of Equality: Deaf Americans in School and Factory, 1850–1950* (Washington, D.C.: Gallaudet University Press, 1999), 78.

109. "Room for Silent Machinists," *The Wingfoot Clan* 7, 43 (May 11, 1918), 3. These newspaper clippings from local Akron sources, including *The Wingfoot Clan*, are found in a remarkable compilation of a deaf Ohio native. See Clyde Wilson's *Akron History of the Deaf* (1993).

110. Newspaper clipping of October 29, 1918, "Akron First to Give Equality to Deaf Mutes." From *Akron History of the Deaf*, 58.

111. *Illusions of Equality*, 67.

112. *The Wingfoot Clan* 7, 43 (May 11, 1918), 2.

113. *Illusions of Equality*, 78.

114. 1918 newspaper clipping from Clyde Wilson, *Akron History of the Deaf*, 16.

115. *Akron History of the Deaf*, 56.

116. "Akron Silents Organize Grocery," *Akron Evening Times* (22 February 1920), 3.

117. *Through Deaf Eyes*, 92–93.

118. See Clyde Wilson's *Akron History of the Deaf* for coverage.

119. *Akron History of the Deaf*, 20.

120. "Goodyear's Mutes," *The Wingfoot Clan* 7, 43 (May 11, 2018), 6.

121. "Attention Mutes," newspaper clipping dated January 26, 1918, Clyde Wilson, *Akron History of the Deaf*, 15.

122. Susan Burch, *Signs of Resistance*, 78.

For more on the football team, including some great pictures, see *Through Deaf Eyes*, 93–96. See also *Illusions of Equality*, 79. See Jack R. Gannon, *Deaf Heritage: A Narrative History of Deaf America*, eds. Jane Butler and Laura-Jean Gilbert (Silver Spring: National Association of the Deaf, 1981), 280–281.

123. *Through Deaf Eyes*, 94.

124. "Coaching Mute Athletes," *The Silent Worker* 30, 10 (July 1918), 182.

125. "One of Goodyear's Diamond Trios," newspaper clipping from July 24, 1918. *Akron History of the Deaf*, 34.

126. *Signs of Resistance*, 79.

127. *Through Deaf Eyes*, 93.

128. *Illusions of Equality*, 81.

129. "46 Akronites Blind, 276 Are Deaf Mutes," newspaper clipping from July 20, 1931. *Akron History of the Deaf*, 60.

130. Robert Buchanan, "Building a Silent Colony: Life and Work in the Deaf Community of Akron, Ohio, from 1910 through 1950," *The Deaf Way* (Washington, D.C.: Gallaudet University Press, 1994), 254.

131. "New York City," *Deaf-Mutes' Journal* vol. LXIV, no. 16 (April 18, 1935), 5.

132. The AAAD was founded in Akron, Ohio, in 1945. The father of the AAAD is widely considered to be Art Kruger, a graduate of Gallaudet, Class of 1933. For more on Kruger's athletic legacy in the deaf community, see *Deaf Sport*, 181–183.

133. Cody Howard, "New monument to be dedicated for player," *Lawrence Journal World* (May 24, 2008). Accessed online at http://www2.ljworld.com/news/2008/may/24/new_monument_be_dedicated_player/ on May 7, 2018.

Chapter 5

1. Sipek personal history as recounted in "Sipek, one of the majors' few deaf players, dies at 82," *Herald-Whig*, Tuesday, July 19, 2005.

2. Charles F. Faber, "Dick Sipek," SABR Biography Project.

3. As reported in Arthur Mann, "Mute Testimony," *Baseball Magazine* (September 1945), 344.

4. Letter from the archives of *The Sporting News*. My thanks to Steve Gietschier for bringing it to my attention.

5. Arthur Mann, "Mute Testimony," 344.

6. John Neal, "Sipek Is Given Contract," in "The Acoustic Reporter" (written and edited by students), published in *The Illinois Advance* vol. 3, no. 6 (March 1943), 4.

7. Mann, "Mute Testimony," 343.

8. John Neal, "Sipek Is Hitting Well in Training With Birmingham," "The Acoustic Reporter" (written and edited by students), published in *The Illinois Advance* vol. 3, no. 5 (April 1943), 2.

9. For more on the school's educational methods, see Minnie Wait Cleary, "History of the Illinois School for the Deaf," *Journal of the Illinois State Historical Society* 35, 4 (December 1942), 387.

10. "Sipek Crack Grid Player, Baron Outfielder All-Around Star," *Birmingham Post* (August 6, 1943).

11. "Perrin to Face Crax in Opener," *The Birmingham Post* (June 17, 1943)

12. John Neal, "Sipek Bats Well for Birmingham in First Year," in "The Acoustic Reporter" (written and edited by students), published in *The Illinois Advance* vol. 4, no. 1 (November 1943), 4.

13. *The Birmingham Post*, August 31, 1944

14. Al Kuettner, "Barons' Dick Sipek… The 'Personality Kid'…A Crack Outfielder," *The Birmingham Post* (21 June 1944).

15. "Barons' Dick Sipek…The 'Personality Kid'…A Crack Outfielder."

16. From William Mead's interview with Sipek, included in *Baseball Goes to War* (Washington, D.C.: Farragut Publishing, 1985), 211–214.

17. "Deaf Mute May Play in Majors," *Spartanburg Herald Journal*, June 18, 1944, p. 18.

18. Hoyt Harwell, "Rickwood Field Full of Nostalgia," *Gadsden Times*, March 11, 1987, p. 5.

19. Mead 211–214.

20. "Mute Most Popular," *Tuscaloosa News*, August 30, 1944, p. 7.

21. Newman, "Sipek Conquers Nature's Handicap," 20.

22. "Barons' Dick Sipek…The Personality Kid…A Crack Outfielder"

23. Unknown source, press clipping file, Cooperstown.

24. Greason as quoted in Roger Wallenstein, "The Ghosts of Birmingham,"

posted on June 4, 2012, on The Beachwood Reporter.

25. All information on Weaver from Marene Clark-Mattern of the Illinois School for the Deaf Museum. She found the coverage of the Texas football story in the *Illinois Advance* (December 1941). My thanks to her. My thanks as well to Bob Dramin and to Ralph Reese, Sipek's classmate, for their help in sharing stories about Sipek's school days.

26. For more on Meagher, see *Deaf Heritage*, 299.

27. All information on the tournament and the teams from "National Deaf Basketball Tournament," *Illinois Advance* 74, 5 (March 1941), 10–13. Descriptions of Durham and Sipek can be found in "Retrospect of the 1940–41 Basketball Season," 13.

28. Again, my thanks to Marene Clark-Mattern.

29. "Retrospect of the 1940–41 Basketball Season," *Illinois Advance* 74, 5 (March 1941), 13.

30. See R.A.R. Edwards, *Words Made Flesh* (New York: New York University Press, 2012), 65–69.

31. *Deaf Heritage*, 26–27.

32. Florence quote and throwing stats from Zipp Newman, "Sipek Conquers Nature's Handicaps to Gain Trial with Reds," *Baseball Digest* (September 1945), 19.

33. Alfred Kuettner, "Deaf Mute Seems Headed for Trial in Big Leagues," *St Petersburg Times*, June 18, 1944, p. 19.

34. "Barons' Dick Sipek…The Personality Kid…A Crack Outfielder"

35. Newman, 'Sipek Conquers Nature's Handicaps," 20.

36. Mann, "Mute Testimony," 343.

37. Billy Barrett, "Dick Sipek Begins With Cincinnati Reds This Season," in "The Acoustic Reporter" (written and edited by students), published in *The Illinois Advance* vol. 5, no. 5 (March 1945), 4.

38. 'What Other Editors Think," *The Evening Independent*, February 13, 1945, p. 4.

39. Clyde W. Johnson, "Deaf and Not So Dumb," *Saturday Evening Post* (October 2, 1943) as reprinted in *The Buff and Blue* (Gallaudet University's student newspaper, showing how the deaf community was following Sipek's progress) vol. LII, no. II (April 10, 1944), p. 1.

40. Frank McGowan, "Dick Sipek," *Rick-wood Field, Birmingham, Alabama, Official Score Card and Program—1944*, 5.

41. "He Was Dumb," *The Buckingham Post*, May 6, 1955, vol. 59, no. 49.

42. "Barons' Dick Sipek…The Personality Kid…A Crack Outfielder"

43. Mead, *Baseball Goes to War*.

44. Mead, *Baseball Goes to War*.

45. Zipp Newman, "Sipek Conquers Nature's Handicaps," *Baseball Digest* (September 1945), 20.

46. In fact, both Sipek and Wahl would be sent down to AAA Syracuse together in for the 1946 season.

47. Sipek in William Mead, *Baseball Goes to War*.

48. Barry Strassler, "Sipek's Solo Major League Session Recalled on 50th Anniversary," *Silent News* (May 1995).

49. "Sipek Crack Grid Player," *Birmingham Post* (August 6, 1943).

50. Richard Goldstein, *Spartan Seasons: How Baseball Survived the Second World War* (New York: Macmillan, 1980), 213.

51. "Illinois School Alumnus Is Baseball Star," *The Pelican* vol. LXV, no. 4 (January 1945), 3.

52. "Sipek, One of Majors' Few Deaf Players, Dies at 82," *Herald-Whig* (Tuesday, 19 July 2005).

53. Jack R. Gannon, *Deaf Heritage: A Narrative History of Deaf America*, ed. Jane Butler and Laura-Jean Gilbert (Silver Spring, MD: National Association of the Deaf, 1981), 219.

54. See Susan Burch's *Signs of Resistance*, especially chapters one and two, for more on the deaf community's efforts to combat oralism in this time period.

55. Steven Selden, *Inheriting Shame: The Story of Eugenics and Racism in America* (New York: Teachers College press, 1999), 64.

56. Selden 68.

57. Selden 69.

58. Hunter's text as quoted in Selden 75. For more on eugenics in mid-century, see Wendy Kline, *Building a Better Race: Gender, Sexuality, and Eugenics from the Turn of the Century to the Baby Boom* (Berkeley: University of California Press, 2001).

59. Susan Burch, *Signs of Resistance: American Deaf Cultural History, 1900 to World War II* (New York: NYU Press, 2002), 165.

60. Burch 166.

61. All information on deaf drivers from Susan Burch, *Signs of Resistance: American Deaf Cultural History, 1900 to World War II* (New York: NYU Press, 2002), 155–165. Quote on page 164.

62. Burch, *Signs of Resistance,* 164.

63. Henry Best, *Deafness and the Deaf in the United States* (New York: The Macmillan Company, 1943), 334.

64. Best, 332.

65. Best, 530–531.

66. In fact, even in the coverage of his minor league career, I have so far only seen one article that called him "Dummy Sipek," in the *Herald,* on August 14, 1943.

67. Christopher Krentz, *Writing Deafness: The Hearing Line in Nineteenth-Century American Literature* (Chapel Hill: University of North Carolina Press, 2007), 76.

68. "Want a Steady Job? Read This Advice," *The Pelican* vol. LXV, no. 4 (January 1945), 3.

69. For more on attacks on the rights of the Deaf community in this time, see Susan Burch's *Signs of Resistance.*

70. See results of the poll on residential schools from 2007. Asked "have residential schools outlived their usefulness," 58% said no." "Deaf View: Readers' Viewpoint," *DeafLife* (December 2007), 46–7.

71. Mann, "Mute Testimony," 344.

72. "Illinois School Alumnus Is Baseball Star," *The Pelican* vol. LXV, no. 4 (January 1945), 3.

73. Lawrence Baldassaro, "Introduction," *The American Game: Baseball and Ethnicity,* ed. Lawrence Baldassaro and Richard Johnson (Carbondale: Southern Illinois University Press, 2002), 5.

74. As quoted in Matt Schuckman, "Sipek, One of Majors Few Deaf Players, Dies at 82," *The Herald Whig* (July 19, 2005).

75. Story as told in video interview with Sipek. Found on YouTube as "Dick Sipek of the Cincinnati Reds," (www.youtube.com/watch?v=7EFFHjn7zs8) accessed 19 October 2016.

76. To see when they might have met, go to www.milb.com for the feature "Remembering Jackie Robinson in 1946: 1946–2006, the 60th Anniversary of His Only Minor League Season." The entire schedule for the

1946 International League season, regular and postseason, is there.

77. Robinson never mentioned a meeting with Sipek. However, if the two men crossed paths, as Sipek said, Sipek's interest in and support of Robinson would surely have been welcome. The Syracuse Chiefs were considered one of the most prejudiced teams that Robinson would face in the IL. "The late Garton DelSavio, a New Yorker on the 1946 Syracuse team, told *The Post Standard* that many of his teammates hated the idea of a black man in 'white' baseball. DelSavio recalled how those players would call Robinson the 'worst things' you could call another human being." As reported on April 10, 2013, by Sean Kirst, "Jackie Robinson in Syracuse: For Opening Day, Honoring Deep Ties and One Essential Moment," www.syracuse.com, accessed 10/19/2016.

78. Myron Uhlberg, *Hands of My Father: A Hearing Boy, His Deaf Parents, and the Language of Love* (New York: Bantam Books, 2008), 201.

79. Myron Uhlberg, *Hands of My Father: A Hearing Boy, His Deaf Parents, and the Language of Love* (New York: Bantam Books, 2008), 203.

80. Pete Gray as quoted in William C. Kashatus, *One-Armed Wonder: Pete Gray, Wartime Baseball, and the American Dream* (Jefferson: McFarland and Company, 1995), 71.

81. Kashatus 71.

82. Henry Vance, "On the Level," *Birmingham Herald* (May 4, 1944)

83. Kashatus 76.

84. John Klima, *The Game Must Go On: Hank Greenberg, Pete Gray, and the Great Days of Baseball on the Homefront in World War II* (New York: St. Martin's Press, 2015), 251.

85. "Majors Put Out Boycott Against Gray," *Birmingham Post* (September 21, 1944)

86. As related in Kashatus 76.

87. SABR, *The Baseball Research Journal,* vol. 12 (1983).

88. As quoted in Klima 253.

89. As quoted in Klima 253.

90. Zipp Newman, "Sipek Conquers Nature's handicaps to Gain Trial with Reds," *Baseball Digest* (September 1945), 19.

91. Barry Strassler, "Sipek's Solo Major-

League Season Recalled on 50th Anniversary," *Silent News* (May 1995).

92. All from Klima 265.

93. Willam Mead, *Baseball Goes to War*, 214.

94. Notarized letter of April 11, 2002, of Dick Sipek to Steve Sandy. In Archives of the National Baseball Hall of Fame.

95. Kashatus 105.

96. Kashatus 105.

97. See Kashatus 105.

98. Kashatus 111.

99. Barry Strassler, "Sipek's Solo Major-League Season Recalled on 50th Anniversary," *Silent News* (May 1995).

100. As noted on-line at i711.com by Deaf blogger Trudy Suggs, in her entry "Another Era Goes By," dated 27 July 2005.

101. "Sipek, one of majors' few deaf players, dies at 82," *Herald-Whig* (posted 19 July 2005).

102. Charles F. Faber, "Dick Sipek," SABR Biography Project entry.

103. Matt Schuckman, "Sipek, One of Majors' Few Deaf Players, Dies at 82," *Herald-Whig* (posted July 19, 2005).

104. Story recounted in Rick Swaine, *Beating the Break: Major League Ballplayers Who Overcame Disabilities*, 118.

105. Charles F. Faber, "Dick Sipek," SABR Biography Project entry.

106. Barry Strassler, "Sipek's Solo Major-League Season Recalled on 50th Anniversary," *Silent News* (May 1995).

Chapter 6

1. Sheryl Flatow, "Curtis Pride, an outfielder in the Expos organization says he has never let his deafness stand in his way: 'I Know What I Can Do,'" *Washington Post* (August 7, 1994), R12.

2. Flatow, "'I Know What I Can Do,'" R12.

3. Story recounted in Claire Smith, "Compensating with Feel for Game," *New York Times* (August 11, 1996), S7.

4. See results of the poll on residential schools from 2007. Asked "have residential schools outlived their usefulness," 58% said no." "Deaf View: Readers' Viewpoint," *DeafLife* (December 2007), 46-7.

5. Helmer R. Myklebust, *Your Deaf Child:*

A Guide for Parents (Springfield, Illinois: Charles C. Thomas, 1950), 4.

6. Myklebust, *The Psychology of Deafness* (New York: Grune and Stratton), 241-42.

7. "Education of the Deaf: A Report to the Secretary of Health, Education, and Welfare by his Advisory Committee on the Education of the Deaf," (Washington, D.C.: U.S. Department of Health, Education, and Welfare, 1965), xv. Hereafter referred to as the Babbidge Report.

8. Babbidge Report, 25.

9. Babbidge Report, 32.

10. Babbidge Report, 33.

11. Babbidge Report, xxx.

12. For more on Stokoe's work and its impact, see *Deaf Heritage* 364-367 and *Through Deaf Eyes* 114-117. See also *Sign Language and the Deaf Community: Essays in Honor of William C. Stokoe*, eds. Charlotte Baker and Robbin Battison (National Association of the Deaf, 1980).

13. For more, see Stephen C. Baldwin, *Pictures in the Air: The Story of the National Theatre of the Deaf* (Washington, D.C.: Gallaudet University Press, 1994).

14. Jack Gannon, *Deaf Heritage*, 328.

15. For more on the development of the TTY and the relay system, see Harry G. Lang, *A Phone of Our Own: The Deaf Insurrection Against Ma Bell* (Washington, D.C.: Gallaudet University Press, 2000).

16. For more on captioning, see Karen Peltz Strauss, *A New Civil Right: Telecommunications Equality for Deaf and Hard of Hearing Americans* (Washington, D.C.: Gallaudet University Press, 2006).

17. *Through Deaf Eyes*, 125.

18. "Readers' Responses," *DeafLife* (February 1992), 29. Interpreter Leah Hager Cohen wrote against mainstreaming in an op-ed in 1994. She explained how deaf students can fall behind educationally in such a setting. "Sometimes the teacher uses a roll down map or an overhead projector and all the students train their eyes on the visual information while listening to the teacher.... The girl looks at me and then at the visual display the teacher talks on. By the time the student looks at me again, she has lost three sentences. She looks at her notes and loses more sentences. Frustration flickers across her face." But her hearing "parents are proud that she attends a regular public school. They

do not use sign language. On Mondays, she comes to school ravenous for conversation with me." See Cohen, "An Interpreter Isn't Enough," *New York Times* (22 February 1994).

19. Garrett and Bell as quoted in *Forbidden Signs*, 152.

20. *Forbidden Signs*, 152–3.

21. Babbidge Report, C9.

22. All childhood details from Sheryl Flatow, "'I Know What I Can Do,'" *The Washington Post* (August 7, 1994), R12.

23. See Jannelle Legg, "The Congregation Divided: A History of Deaf Religious Segregation, 1895–1955," available on-line at jannelllegg.com/portfolio/final/index.html. For more on the history of the Maryland School for the Deaf, see Charles W. Ely, *The History of the Maryland School for the Deaf and Dumb* (Frederick City: Maryland School for the Deaf, 1893). See also Hannah Dellinger and Cameron Dodd, "Maryland School for the Deaf—'a sanctuary for language'—celebrates 150 years of progressive education," posted on fredericknewspost.com on 16 June 2018.

24. See Jannelle Legg, "The Congregation Divided."

25. See Baynton, *Forbidden Signs*, especially 44–49. The quote is from 45.

26. For more on Black ASL, see Carolyn McCaskill, Ceil Lucas, Robert Bayley, and Joseph Hill, *The Hidden Treasure of Black ASL: Its History and Structure* (Washington, D.C.: Gallaudet University Press, 2011).

27. For more on the linguistic impact of racial segregation in the deaf community, see Carolyn McCaskill, Ceil Lucas, Robert Bayley, and Joseph Hill, "Citizenship and Education: The Case of the Black Deaf Community," in *In Our Own Hands: Essays in Deaf History 1780–1970*, eds. Brian H. Greenwald and Joseph J. Murray (Washington, D.C.: Gallaudet University Press, 2016), 40–60.

28. Baynton 46.

29. Burch, *Signs of Resistance*, 184–5. She also notes that black deaf children were largely spared the label of 'oral failure' as well, though their lack of communication skills with hearing white authority figures left them vulnerable to charges of being mentally disabled (137). For more on the historical impact of lives lived at the inter-

section of race and deafness, see Susan Burch and Hannah Joyner, *Unspeakable: The Story of Junius Wilson* (Chapel Hill: University of North Carolina Press, 2007).

30. Pride biography from David Laurila, "Curtis Pride," SABR Biography Project.

31. See Mark E. Eberle, "Bert Wakefield and the End of Integrated Minor League Baseball in Kansas." *Monographs*, 4 (2018), 2–3. Accessed at https://scholars.fhsu.edu/all_monographs/4. With thanks to the Fort Hays State University.

32. See Karen Christie and Nancy Rourke, *ABC Portraits of Deaf Ancestors* (Surdists United, 2019). The quotes are all from the Introduction. Rourke's portrait of Ingram is found under "I Is for Ingram."

33. Mark E. Eberle. "Deaf Baseball Players in Kansas and Kansas City, 1878–1911." Fort Hays State University, Kansas. 25 pages. Page 2. Available at https//scholars.fhsu.edu/all_monographs.

34. "What a Colored Boy Can Do," *The Olathe Mirror* (15 August 1889), 3.

35. *The Coffeyville Daily Journal* (11 September 1896), 1.

36. Eberle, "Deaf Baseball Players in Kansas and Kansas City," 3–5.

37. "Kansas Notes," *The Deaf-Mutes' Journal* vol. XVIII, no. 26 (4 July 1889), 1.

38. "Kansas Notes," *The Deaf-Mutes' Journal* vol. XVIII, no. 26 (4 July 1889), 4.

39. "Monroe Ingram Teacher at Missouri," *The Evening Star* (Independence, KS) (30 August 1905), 5.

40. Gregory Bond, "The Segregation of Professional Baseball in Kansas, 1895–1899: A Case Study in the Rise of Jim Crow During the Gilded Age," in *The Cooperstown Symposium on Baseball and American Culture, 2002*, ed. William M. Simons (McFarland, 2003), 61.

41. Bond 65, 61.

42. Bond 69–70.

43. Bond 70–71.

44. All information on the history of the school from Richard D. Reed, *Historic MSD: The Story of the Missouri School for the Deaf* (Fulton: Ovid Bell Press, 2000), 59–61. The school remained a racially segregated facility until 1954. The information about Ingram can be found on page 61. My thanks to my colleague Karen Christie for bringing this source to my attention.

45. See *Deaf Heritage*, 70. See also note on teachers in *American Annals of the Deaf*, vol. 50, no. 1 (January 1910), 203.
46. Bond 61–62.
47. Anja Werner, "'Double Whammy': Historical Glimpse of Black Deaf Americans," *COPAS* 18.2 (2017), 3.
48. From McCay Vernon's forward to Ernest Hairston and Linwood Smith, *Black and Deaf in America: Are We That Different?* (Silver Spring, MD: TJ Publishing, 1983), 1.
49. In her *Claiming Disability: Knowledge and Identity* (New York: New York University Press, 1998), pioneering disability studies scholar Simi Linton would suggest that this is because disability is too often seen as a totalizing identity. As she explains, in considering the words that are used to refer to some disabled people, such as 'invalid,' one notices that "the totalizing noun, invalid, does not confine the weakness to the specific bodily functions; it is more encompassing" (29). From an able-bodied perspective, disability is understood as a totalizing identity, and, frequently, a stigmatized one at that.
50. Pride biography from David Laurila, "Curtis Pride," SABR Biography Project.
51. "Curtis Pride: As Gallaudet's Head Baseball Coach, He's Making Headlines Again," *Deaf Life* (June 2010), 15.
52. William Gildea, "Seeing Pride in His Accomplishments," *The Washington Post* (August 29, 1993), D9.
53. Saul Wisnia, "For Pride, Dream Is Interrupted by Reality," *The Washington Post* (April 5, 1994), AC6.
54. Pride quoted in *Parade Magazine* as reported by http://deafnewstoday.blogspot.com/2018/12/happy-birthday-curtis-pride.html.
55. All from Claire Smith, "Compensating with Feel for Game," *New York Times* (August 11, 1996), S7.
56. Flatow, "'I Know What I Can Do,'" R12.
57. Flatow, R12.
58. Flatow, R12.
59. As quoted in Bill Finley, "For Pride, 'It Was Like A Dream,'" *New York Times* (July 7, 2003), D3.
60. Christopher Krentz, *Writing Deafness: The Hearing Line in Nineteenth-Century American Literature* (Chapel Hill: University of North Carolina Press, 2007), 35.

61. For more on implants, see R.A.R. Edwards, "Sound and Fury; Or, Much Ado About Nothing? Cochlear Implants in Historical Perspective," *The Journal of American History* 92, 3 (December 2005), 892–920.
62. Ron Pasceri, "Deafness Didn't Hinder Curtis Pride's Drive Toward a Remarkable MLB Career," Bleacher Report (May 17, 2012).
63. Norm King, SABR Games Project.
64. www.kenwoodhearing.blogspot.com/2012/09/curtis-pride-deaf-major-league-baseball-html
65. "Readers' Response," *Deaf Life* (October 1998), 30.
66. See *Deaf Life*: "Implants for Deaf Kids: What's Best for the Child?" (February 2002), 12–27 and "The Quiet War Between Biomedical Technology and Deaf Culture," (March 2002), 14–19.
67. Reported in an article in the *Los Angeles Times* and discussed in John B. Christiansen, *Reflections: My Life in the Deaf and Hearing Worlds* (Washington, D.C.: Gallaudet University Press, 2010), 162.
68. A.E. Geers, C.M. Mitchell, A. Warner-Czyz, N.-Y. Wang, L.S. Eisenberg, CDaCI Investigative Team, Early Sign Language Exposures And Cochlear Implantation Benefits," *Pediatrics*. June 2017. DOI: 10.1542/peds.2016-3489.
69. Ann Geers and Andrea Warner-Czyz as quoted in "For Children with Cochlear Implants, Oral Communication May Provide Better Outcomes," *UTD News Center* (June 15, 2017).
70. Michael Chorost, *Rebuilt: How Becoming Part Computer Made Me More Human* (New York: Houghton Mifflin, 2005), 143–44.
71. The deaf community has a long, complicated history with technologies. Silent movies were a favorite of the deaf but were replaced with less accessible talkies. The invention of the telephone made deaf people seem less employable in white collar positions; the TTY gave them access to long distance personal communication. Closed captioning made television accessible to deaf viewers. Assistive listening devices have a long history, going back to ear trumpets. Early 20th-century oralists adopted the first generation of hearing aids to their classrooms. The deaf community

proved an eager, early adopter of pagers and of texting. Every generation of deaf people was influenced by the technological environment of their time, in other words. For more on the deaf community and technology, see Harry G. Lang, *A Phone of Our Own: The Deaf Insurrection Against Ma Bell* (Washington, D.C.: Gallaudet University Press, 2000), John S. Schuchman, *Hollywood Speaks: Deafness and the Film Entertainment Industry* (Chicago: University of Illinois Press, 1988), Gregory J. Downey, *Closed Captioning: Subtitling, Stenography, and the Digital Convergence of Text with Television* (Baltimore: Johns Hopkins University Press, 2008), and Karen Peltz Strauss, *A New Civil Right: Telecommunications Equality for Deaf and Hard of Hearing Americans* (Washington, D.C.: Gallaudet University Press, 2006).

72. Sara Novic, "A Clearer Message on Cochlear Implants," *The New York Times* (November 21, 2018).

73. For more on deaf identity in the early twenty-first century, see Irene Leigh, *A Lens on Deaf Identities* (New York: Oxford University Press, 2009).

74. For more on the deaf community's view of implants, see Christiansen, *Reflections*, 168–170.

75. See *2017 NTID Annual Report* and the *2017 Gallaudet Annual Report* for more on the student bodies and the educational philosophies of the schools. See also "Gallaudet University adjusts to a culture that includes more hearing students," *Washington Post* (September 24, 2011), for Gallaudet rates of CI usage.

76. Suzanne Goldenberg, "'Not Deaf Enough' university head is forced out," *The Guardian* (October 31, 2006).

77. One of the most insightful takes on the protest comes from H. Dirksen L. Bauman, in his "Postscript: Gallaudet Protests of 2006 and the Myths of In/Exclusion," in *Open Your Eyes: Deaf Studies Talking*, ed. H. Dirksen Bauman (Minneapolis: University of Minnesota Press, 2008), 327–336.

78. Kathleen Wood, "The Right Future for Gallaudet," *Washington Post* (November 2, 2006), A16.

79. Mission statement as quoted in H. Dirksen L. Bauman, "Postscript: Gallaudet Protests of 2006 and the Myths of In/Exclusion," in *Open Your Eyes: Deaf Studies*

Talking, ed. H. Dirksen Bauman (Minneapolis: University of Minnesota Press, 2008), 333.

80. "Curtis Pride: As Gallaudet's Head Baseball Coach, He's Making Headlines Again," *Deaf Life* (June 2010), 16.

81. Mel Antonen, "Gallaudet has faith in Pride," USA Today (April 27, 2010), 1C.

82. Pride as quoted in Antonen, 2C.

83. Gabel as quoted in Antonen, 1C.

84. https://www.gallaudetathletics.com/sports/bsb/coaches/pride_curtis?view=bio.

85. https://www.mlb.com/news/curtis-pride-is-mlbs-ambassador-for-inclusion/c-161261386.

86. Chuck Carree, "Pride doesn't let being deaf keep him from success," *Wilmington Morning Star* (September 24, 1993), 5C.

87. Pride as quoted in Chuck Carree, "Pride doesn't let being deaf keep him from success," *Wilmington Morning Star* (September 24, 1993), 5C.

88. H. Dirksen L. Bauman, "Postscript: Gallaudet Protests of 2006 and the Myths of In/Exclusion," in *Open Your Eyes: Deaf Studies Talking*, ed. H. Dirksen Bauman (Minneapolis: University of Minnesota Press, 2008), 329.

89. For more on the importance of Gallaudet in the life of the deaf community, see Brian H. Greenwald and John Vickrey Van Cleve, eds., *A Fair Chance in the Race of Life: The Role of Gallaudet University in Deaf History* (Washington, D.C.: Gallaudet University Press, 2008).

90. For more, see Joseph Murray, " 'Enlightened Selfishness': Gallaudet College and Deaf Citizenship in the United States, 1864–1904," in *In Our Own Hands: Essays in Deaf History 1780–1970*, eds. Brian H. Greenwald and Joseph J. Murray (Washington, D.C.: Gallaudet University Press, 2016), 18–39.

91. For more on the Deaf President Now Strike of 1988, see John B. Christiansen and Sharon N. Barnartt, *Deaf President Now!: The 1988 Revolution at Gallaudet University* (Washington, D.C.: Gallaudet University Press, 1995).

92. For more on the challenges that face black deaf Americans in college, see Lissa Denielle Stapleton, "The unexpected talented tenth: Black d/Deaf students thriving

within the margins," (Iowa State University, 2014). Graduate theses and dissertations. Paper 13891.

93. Carrie Lou Garberoglio, Stephanie Cawthon, and Adam Sales, *Deaf People and Educational Attainment in the United States: 2017* (National Deaf Center on Postsecondary Outcomes, 2017), 4.

94. *Deaf People and Educational Attainment*, 7–9.

95. B.R.J. O'Donnell, "'We Have 14 Black Deaf Americans with Ph.D.s—14,'" *The Atlantic*, posted on-line 16 August 2017.

96. See Graham Neysmith, "Interview: Curtis Pride Talks About the Montreal Expos," in https://lametropolesports.

com/2014/09/19/curtis-pride-interview/. Accessed 15 August 2019.

97. Pride as quoted in Daniel J. Vance, "Ex-Major Leaguer Takes Pride in Career," *Atlanta Highlands Herald* (May 30, 2015) in http://www.ahherald.com/columns-list/262-disabilities-week/20151-ex-major-leaguer-takes-pride-in-career. Accessed 15 May 2018.

Epilogue

1. Emma Baccellieri, "The Meaning Behind MLB's Unprecedented Astros Punishment," *Sports Illustrated*, posted on-line on 14 January 2020.

Bibliography

The heart of the research for these chapters rests in newspaper and journal articles, from both the hearing press and the deaf press. Citations of these late–19th and 20th century articles can be found in the notes to each chapter. The resources of the Society for American Baseball Research (SABR) were invaluable, especially their short player biographies, available on the SABR website. These citations are cited also in the notes.

Achorn, Edward. *The Summer of Beer and Whiskey: How Brewers, Barkeeps, Rowdies, Immigrants, and A Wild Pennant Fight Made Baseball America's Game.* New York: Public Affairs, 2014.

Alexander, Charles C. *Turbulent Seasons: Baseball in 1890–1891.* Dallas: Southern Methodist University Press, 2011.

Aramburo, Anthony J. "Sociolinguistic Aspects of the Black Deaf Community." In *The Sociolinguistics of the Deaf Community,* ed. Ceil Lucas. 103–119. New York: Academic Press, 1989.

Astifan, Priscilla. "Baseball in the 19th Century—Part 1." *Rochester History* vol. 52, No. 3 (Summer 1990): 1–24.

Astifan, Priscilla. "Baseball in the 19th Century—Part 2." *Rochester History* vol.62, no. 2 (Spring 2000): 1–24.

Astifan, Priscilla. "Baseball in the 19th Century—Part 3." *Rochester History* vol. 63, no. 1 (Winter 2001): 1–24.

Astifan, Priscilla. "Baseball in the 19th Century—Part 4." *Rochester History* vol. 63, no. 2 (Spring 2001): 1–24.

Astifan, Priscilla. "Baseball in the Nineteenth Century—Part 5." *Rochester History* vol. 64, no. 4 (Fall 2002): 1–24.

Baker, Charlotte, and Robbin Battison, eds. *Sign Language and the Deaf Community: Essays in Honor of William C. Stokoe.* Silver Spring: National Association of the Deaf, 1980.

Baldassaro, Lawrence, and Richard A. Johnson, eds. *The American Game: Baseball and Ethnicity.* Carbondale: Southern Illinois University Press, 2002.

Baldwin, Stephen C. *Pictures in the Air: The Story of the National Theatre of the Deaf.* Washington, D.C.: Gallaudet University Press, 1994.

Bauman, H-Dirksen L. "Postscript: Gallaudet Protests of 2006 and the Myths of In/Exclusion." In *Open Your Eyes: Deaf Studies Talking,* ed. H-Dirksen Bauman, 327–336. Minneapolis: University of Minnesota Press, 2008.

Bauman, H-Dirksen, and Joseph J. Murray. *Deaf Gain: Raising the Stakes for Human Diversity.* Minneapolis: University of Minnesota Press, 2014.

Baynton, Douglas C. *Defectives in the Land: Disability and Immigration in the Age of Eugenics.* Chicago: University of Chicago Press, 2016.

Baynton, Douglas C. *Forbidden Signs: American Culture and the Campaign Against Sign Language.* Chicago: University of Chicago Press, 1996.

Baynton, Douglas C. "'The Undesirability of Admitting Deaf Mutes': U.S. Immigration Policy and Deaf Immigrants, 1882–1924." *Sign Language Studies* vol. 6, no. 4 (Summer 2006): 391–415.

Baynton, Douglas C., Jack R. Gannon, and Jean Lindquist Bergey. *Through Deaf Eyes:*

Bibliography

A Photographic History of an American Community. Washington, D.C.: Gallaudet University Press, 2007.

Bell, Alexander Graham Bell. *Memoir Upon the Formation of a Deaf Variety of the Human Race.* Washington, D.C.: National Academy of Sciences, 1884.

Best, Henry. *Deafness and the Deaf in the United States.* New York: The Macmillan Company, 1943.

Bionaz, Robert E. "Unmanly Professional Athletes: Disability and Masculinity in the Unites States, 1888–1908." *Disability Studies Quarterly* vol. 25, no. 2 (Spring 2005).

Bond, Gregory. "The Segregation of Professional Baseball in Kansas, 1895–1899: A Case Study in the Rise of Jim Crow During the Gilded Age." In *The Cooperstown Symposium on Baseball and American Culture, 2002,* ed. William M. Simons. Jefferson: McFarland, 2003.

Brockway, Kathleen. *Baltimore's Deaf Heritage.* Charleston, S.C.: Arcadia Press, 2014.

Brueggemann, Brenda Jo. *Deaf Subjects: Between Identities and Places.* New York: New York University Press, 2009.

Buchanan, Robert. "The Silent Worker Newspaper and the Building of a Deaf Community, 1890–1929." In *Deaf History Unveiled,* ed. John Vickrey Van Cleve, 172–197. Washington, D.C.: Gallaudet University Press, 1993.

Buchanan, Robert M. "Building a Silent Colony: Life and Work in the Deaf Community of Akron, Ohio, from 1910 through 1950." In *The Deaf Way: Perspectives from the International Conference on Deaf Culture,* ed. Carol J. Erting et al., 250–259. Washington, D.C.: Gallaudet University Press, 1994.

Buchanan, Robert M. *Illusions of Equality: Deaf Americans in School and Factory, 1850–1950.* Washington, D.C.: Gallaudet University Press, 1999.

Buchanan, Robert M., ed. *Gaillard in Deaf America: A Portrait of the Deaf Community, 1917.* Washington, D.C.: Gallaudet University Press, 2002.

Burch, Susan. *Signs of Resistance: American Deaf Cultural History, 1900–1942.* New York: New York University Press, 2002.

Burch, Susan, and Hannah Joyner. *Unspeakable: The Story of Junius Wilson.* Chapel Hill: University of North Carolina Press, 2007.

Burk, Robert F. *Never Just a Game: Players, Owners, and American Baseball to 1920.* Chapel Hill: University of North Carolina Press, 1994.

Chase, Dennis T. "William Ellsworth 'Dummy' Hoy." In *The Biographical Dictionary of American Sports,* ed. David Porter, 705. Westport: Greenwood Press, 2000.

Chorost, Michael. *Rebuilt: How Becoming Part Computer Made Me More Human.* New York: Houghton Mifflin, 2005.

Christiansen, John B., and Sharon N. Barnartt. *Deaf President Now!: The 1988 Revolution at Gallaudet University.* Washington, D.C.: Gallaudet University Press, 1995.

Christie, Karen, and Nancy Rourke. *ABC Portraits of Deaf Ancestors.* Surdists United, 2019.

Cleary, Minnie Wait. "History of the Illinois School for the Deaf." *Journal of the Illinois State Historical Society* vol. 35, no. 4 (December 1942): 368–389.

Davis, Lennard. *Enforcing Normalcy: Disability, Deafness, and the Body.* New York: Verso, 1995.

Davis, Mac. *100 Greatest Baseball Heroes.* New York: Grosset & Dunlop, 1974.

Deane, Bill. *Baseball Myths: Debating, Debunking, and Disproving Tales from the Diamond.* Lanham, MD: Scarecrow Press, 2012.

Deford, Frank. *The Old Ball Game: How John McGraw, Christy Mathewson, and the New York Giants Created Modern Baseball.* New York: Grove Press, 2005.

Dickinson, Paul. *The Hidden Language of Baseball: How Signs and Sign-Stealing Have Influenced the Course of Our National Pastime.* New York: Walker & Company, 2003.

Downey, Gregory J. *Closed Captioning: Subtitling, Stenography, and the Digital Convergence of Text with Television.* Baltimore: Johns Hopkins University Press, 2008.

"Education of the Deaf: A Report to the Secretary of Health, Education, and Welfare by his Advisory Committee on the Education of the Deaf." Washington, D.C.: U.S.

Bibliography

Department of Health, Education, and Welfare, 1965.

Edwards, R.A.R. "Sound and Fury; Or, Much Ado About Nothing? Cochlear Implants in Historical Perspective." *The Journal of American History* vol. 92, no.3 (December 2005): 892–920.

Edwards, R.A.R. *Words Made Flesh: Nineteenth-Century Deaf Education and the Growth of Deaf Culture.* New York: New York University Press, 2012.

Ely, Charles W. *The History of the Maryland School for the Deaf and Dumb.* Frederick City: Maryland School for the Deaf, 1893.

Fay, Edward Allen, ed. *Histories of American Schools for the Deaf, 1817–1893.* Washington. D.C.: Volta Bureau, 1893.

Fisher, Randy, and James Goodwin. "The 100th Anniversary of Dummy vs. Dummy." *The National Pastime: A Review of Baseball History* 23 (2003): 77–78.

Fraser, Jonathan. *The Cultural Encyclopedia of Baseball.* 2nd edition. Jefferson, N.C.: McFarland, 2005.

Gallaher, James E., ed. *Representative Deaf Persons of the United States of America, Containing Portraits and Character Sketches of Prominent Deaf Persons (Commonly called Deaf-Mutes), Who are Engaged in the Higher Pursuits of Life.* Chicago: James E. Gallaher, 1898.

Gannon, Jack. *Deaf Heritage: A Narrative History of Deaf America,* eds. Jane Butler and Laura-Jean Gilbert. Silver Spring, MD: National Association of the Deaf, 1981.

Goldstein, Richard. *Spartan Seasons: How Baseball Survived the Second World War.* New York: Macmillan, 1980.

Gould, Stephen Jay. *Triumph and Tragedy in Mudville.* New York: W.W. Norton, 2003.

Greenwald, Brian. "The Real 'Toll' of A.G. Bell: Lessons About Eugenics." In *Genetics, Disability, and Deafess,* ed. John Vickrey Van Cleve, 35–41. Washington, D.C.: Gallaudet University Press, 2004.

Greenwald, Brian. "Taking Stock: Alexander Graham Bell and Eugenics, 1883–1922." In *The Deaf History Reader,* ed. John Vickrey Van Cleve, 136–152. Washington, D.C.: Gallaudet University Press, 2007.

Hairston, Ernest, and Linwood Smith. *Black and Deaf in America: Are We That Different?* Silver Spring, MD: TJ Publishing, 1983.

A Historical and Biographical Souvenir of the Ohio School for the Deaf. Seventy Years' History of a Notable Seat of Learning, with Personal Recollections of Its Founders and Early Officials. The Institution of the Present Day. Official, Education, and Industrial Departments, Domestic and Social Life. Portraits and Biographical Sketches of Representative Alumni. Columbus, Ohio: The Berlin Printing Co., 1898.

History of the Kansas Institution for the Education of the Deaf and Dumb to 1893. Olathe, KS: Printed by the Pupils in the Printing Department of the Institution in Olathe, Kansas, 1893.

Jacoby, Susan. *Why Baseball Matters.* New Haven: Yale University Press, 2018.

James, Bill. *The New Bill James Historical Baseball Abstract.* New York: Free Press, 2001.

Kashatus, William C. *One-Armed Wonder: Pete Gray, Wartime Baseball, and the American Dream.* Jefferson: McFarland, 1995.

Klages, Mary Klages. *Woeful Afflictions: Disability and Sentimentality in Victorian America.* Philadelphia: University of Pennsylvania, 1999.

Klima, John. *The Game Must Go On: Hank Greenberg, Pete Gray, and the Great Days of Baseball on the Homefront in World War II.* New York: St. Martin's Press, 2015.

Kline, Wendy. *Building a Better Race: Gender, Sexuality, and Eugenics from the Turn of the Century to the Baby Boom.* Berkeley: University of California Press, 2001.

Koszarek, Ed. *The Players League: History, Clubs, Ballplayers, and Statistics.* Jefferson, NC: McFarland, 2006.

Krentz, Christopher. "Historical Parallels between the African American and Deaf American Communities." In *Deafness: Historical Perspectives. A Deaf American Monograph,* vol. 46, ed. Mervin D. Garretson, 69–74. Silver Spring: National Association of the Deaf, 1996.

Krentz, Christopher. *Writing Deafness: The Hearing Line in Nineteenth-Century American Literature.* Chapel Hill: University of North Carolina Press, 2007.

Krentz, Christopher, ed. *A Mighty Change: An Anthology of Deaf American Writing,*

Bibliography

1816–1864. Washington, D.C.: Gallaudet University Press, 2000.

Krueckeberg, Dan. "Take-Charge Cy." In *The National Pastime: A Review of Baseball History* vol. 4, no 1 (Spring 1985), 7–11.

Lane, Harlan L., Richard Pillard, and Ulf Hedberg. *The People of the Eye: Deaf Ethnicity and Ancestry.* New York: Oxford University Press, 2011.

Lang, Harry G. *A Phone of Our Own: The Deaf Insurrection Against Ma Bell.* Washington, D.C.: Gallaudet University Press, 2000.

Language, Culture, Communities: 200 Years of Impact by the American School for the Deaf. West Hartford, CT: American School for the Deaf, 2017.

Legg, Jannelle. "The Maryland School for the Deaf, Baltimore." The Congregation Divided. A History of Deaf Religious Segregation, 1895–1955. 2014. http://jannellelegg.com/portfolio/final/background-baltimore.html. Accessed 25 October 2019.

Linton, Simi. *Claiming Disability: Knowledge and Identity.* New York: New York University Press, 1998.

Lutzke, Mitch. *The Page Fence Giants: A History of Black Baseball's Pioneering Champions.* McFarland, 2018.

Malzkuhn, Brian. "Dummy Hoy: Re-Debating His Credentials for Nomination to the Hall of Fame." *Deaf Studies Digital Journal* 2 (2010).

McCaskill, Carolyn, Ceil Lucas, Robert Bayley, and Joseph Hill. "Citizenship and Education: The Case of the Black Deaf Community." In *In Our Own Hands: Essays in Deaf History 1780–1970,* eds. Brian H. Greenwald and Joseph J. Murray, 40–60. Washington, D.C.: Gallaudet University Press, 2016.

McCaskill, Carolyn, Ceil Lucas, Robert Bayley, and Joseph Hill. *The Hidden Treasure of Black ASL: Its History and Structure.* Washington, D.C.: Gallaudet University Press, 2011.

Mead, William B. *Baseball Goes to War.* Washington, D.C.: Broadcast Interview Source, 1998.

Moore, Matthew, and Robert Panara. *Great Deaf Americans.* 2nd edition. Rochester: MSM Productions, 1996.

Morris, Peter. *A Game of Inches: A Story Behind the Innovations that Shaped Baseball.* Chicago: Ivan R. Dee, 2010.

Murray, Joseph. "'Enlightened Selfishness': Gallaudet College and Deaf Citizenship in the United States, 1864–1904." In *In Our Own Hands: Essays in Deaf History 1780–1970,* eds. Brian H. Greenwald and Joseph J. Murray, 18–39. Washington, D.C.: Gallaudet University Press, 2016.

Murray, Joseph J. "'True Love and Sympathy': The Deaf-Deaf Marriage Debate in Transatlantic Perspective." In *Genetics, Disability, and Deafness,* ed. John Vickrey Van Cleve, 42–71. Washington, D.C.: Gallaudet University Press, 2004.

Myklebust, Helmer R. *Your Deaf Child: A Guide for Parents.* Springfield, IL: Charles C. Thomas, 1950.

Nelson, Jennifer L., and Kristen C. Harmon, eds. *Deaf American Prose, 1830–1930.* Washington, D.C.: Gallaudet University Press, 2013.

Nielsen, Kim E. *A Disability History of the United States.* Boston: Beacon Press, 2012.

Padden, Carol, and Tom Humphries. *Deaf In America: Voices from a Culture.* Cambridge: Harvard University Press, 1988.

Rader, Benjamin G. *Baseball: A History of America's Game.* 2nd edition. Chicago: University of Illinois Press, 2002.

Reisler, Jim. *Voices of the Oral Deaf: Fourteen Role Models Speak Out.* Jefferson: McFarland, 2002.

Rittenhouse, Robert K., Calvin Johnson, Betty Overton, Shirley Freeman, and Kyle Jaussi. "The Black and Deaf Movements in America Since 1960." *American Annals of the Deaf,* vol. 136, no. 5 (1991): 392–400.

Ritter, Lawrence. *The Glory of Their Times: The Story of the Early Days of Baseball Told by the Men Who Played It.* Reprint. New York: Perennial, 2002.

Rutherford, Susan. *A Study of Deaf American Folklore.* Burtonsville, MD: Linstok Press, 1993.

Schuchman, John S. *Hollywood Speaks: Deafness and the Film Entertainment Industry.* Chicago: University of Illinois Press, 1988.

Selden, Steven. *Inheriting Shame: The Story of Eugenics and Racism in America.* New York: Teachers College Press, 1999.

Seymour, Harold, and Dorothy Seymour

Bibliography

Mills. *Baseball: The Early Years.* New York: Oxford University Press, 1960.

Seymour, Harold, and Dorothy Seymour Mills. *Baseball: The Golden Age.* New York: Oxford University Press, 1971.

Smith, Ira. *Baseball's Famous Outfielders.* New York: A.S. Barnes, 1954.

Smith, Ira. *Baseball's Famous Pitchers.* New York: A.S. Barnes, 1954.

Souvenir of the Cincinnati Base Ball Club: Upon the Occasion of the Dedication of the Grand Stand, May 16th, 1902. Cincinnati: Manns Engraving & Printing, 1902.

Stein, Sarah Abrevaya. "Deaf American Jewish Culture in Historical Perspective," *American Jewish History* vol. 95, no. 3 (September 2009): 277–305.

Stewart, David A. *Deaf Sport: The Impact of Sports Within the Deaf Community.* Washington, D.C.: Gallaudet University Press, 1991.

Strauss, Karen Peltz. *A New Civil Right: Telecommunications Equality for Deaf and Hard of Hearing Americans.* Washington, D.C.: Gallaudet University Press, 2006.

Taylor, Frederick. *The Runmakers: A New Way to Rate Baseball Players.* Baltimore: Johns Hopkins University Press, 2011.

Tiemann, Robert, and Mark Rucker, eds. *Nineteenth-Century Stars.* Kansas City, MO: Society for American Baseball Research, 1989.

Uhlberg, Myron. *Hands of My Father: A Hearing Boy, His Deaf Parents, and the Language of Love.* New York: Bantam Books, 2008.

Van Cleve, John Vickrey, and Barry A. Crouch. *A Place of Their Own: Creating the Deaf Community in America.* Washington, D.C.: Gallaudet University Press, 1989.

Van Cleve, John Vickrey, ed. *The Deaf History Reader.* Washington, D.C.: Gallaudet University Press, 2007.

Walker, M.F. *Our Home Colony: A Treatise on the Past, Present, and Future of the Negro Race in America.* Steubenville, OH: The Herald Printing Company, 1908.

Weisberger, Bernard A. *When Chicago Ruled Baseball: The Cubs-White Sox World Series of 1906.* New York: Harper, 2006.

Werner, Anja. "'Double Whammy': Historical Glimpse of Black Deaf Americans," *COPAS* 18.2 (2017): 1–29.

White, G. Edward. *Creating the National Pastime: Baseball Transforms Itself, 1903–1953.* Princeton: Princeton University Press, 1996.

Zang, David W. *Fleet Walker's Divided Heart: The Life of Baseball's First Black Major Leaguer.* Lincoln: University of Nebraska Press, 1995.

Index

Numbers in **bold italics** indicate pages with illustrations

205

Index

Index

New York School for the Deaf 13, 44, 98, 110 (and racial integration 23, 126); North Carolina School for Colored Deaf and Blind 152; Ohio School for the Deaf 4–5, 9, *10*, *12*, 15–16, 26, 27, 28, 29–20, 35, 50, 51 (and baseball 4–5, 9, 11, 16, 17, 25, 26, 34; creation of umpires' signs 18, 75, 176*n*28; racial integration 21–22, 23, *24*); Oklahoma Industrial Institute for Deaf, Blind, and Orphans of the Colored Race 157; Pennsylvania School for the Deaf 113, 125, 151, 189*n*98; Rochester School for the Deaf 113; St. Joseph's Institute for the Improved Instruction of Deaf Mutes 97; Texas School for the Deaf 98, 125; *see also* Gallaudet College; National Technical Institute for the Deaf (NTID)
Self Help for Hard of Hearing People (SHHH) 58
The Signal Season of Dummy Hoy 58, 60
Sipek, Dick 6, 8, 119, *136*, 143; as advocate for deaf baseball players 141–142; ; as Birmingham Baron 122–124, 127, 128, 129; and black fans in Birmingham 124, 137; as Cincinnati Red 129–130, 133, *133*, 137–138, 140–141; and deaf fans in Birmingham 124; and deaf gain 127; as deaf hero 122, 124, 130, 133, 134, 136; and discovery by Luther Taylor 120–121, 128, 141; and discrimination faced by 139–140, 140–141; as first deaf major leaguer not nicknamed "Dummy" 133; and Illinois School for the Deaf 120, 121–122, 124–127, *125*; and Jackie Robinson 6, 136–137; meeting Dummy Hoy 140; and minor league career 137; and reaction to Curtis Pride 141, 168–169; and use of sign language 129, 129–130, 134, 141; and use of voice 129; and visual acuity 123, 173–174
Snodgrass, Fred 99
Soper, Isaac N. 110, 111
Southern Association 28, 121, 124, 127, 128, 138, 139
Stephenson, Reuben "Dummy" 6–7
Stone, Collins 35
Stovey, George 21
Swampoodle Grounds 73–74

Syracuse Chiefs 137
Syracuse Stars 18, *19*, 21, 23, 28

Taylor, Luther Haden "Dummy" 5, 6, 8, 9, *97*, *102*, *105*, 112, 113, *118*, *121*, 127, 129, 168, 186*n*41; and career after leaving major league baseball 114, 115, 117, 118–119, 120; and career statistics 92–93; and catchers' signs 106–107; and criticism of prejudice against deaf ball players 135; and deaf fans 108, 109, 111–112; and deaf gain 103; as deaf hero 108, 114, 130; as Dick Sipek's mentor 119, 120–121, 122, 128, 134–135, 140; and Kansas School for the Deaf 93–95, *94*; and manual alphabet cards 100; and nickname "Dummy" 95–96, 114; and 1905 pennant race 103; and 1905 World Series 104; and pitching against William Hoy 92; and sign language use on the Giants 99, 100, 104, 106–107, 108; as umpire 114–115, 115; and use of voice 107–108, 108; and visual acuity 101, 102–103, 173
technologies for the deaf: closed captions 148; cochlear implants 162, 163, 164, 165, 166; hearing aids 8, 59, 122, 144, 149, 151, 162–163; relay service 148; teletypewriters (TTY) 148, 195*n*71
Thomasville Hornets 7
Tinker, Joe 70, 102, 103
Toledo Blue Stockings 20

umpires' signs 5, 62, 64, 66, 67, 68, 70, 71–72, 75, 76–77, 78, 79, 82, 83, 84–85, *86*, 87, 88

Wagner, Honus: on Hoy 41–42
Wahl, Kermit 129
Walker, Moses Fleetwood 18–21, *19*, 23, 25
Walker, Weldy 19, 20
Weaver, Loveless 124, 124–5, *125*
White, Sol 39–40
Wilson, George 39, 40
Wilson, Jimmie 139–140
World Series: and first use of umpires' gestures 70, 71, 75, 77–78; of 1905 104; of 1906 70, 71, 75, 77, 83; of 1961 60